Gender and the Poetics of Excess

Gender

and the

Poetics

of Excess

Moments of Brocade

Karen Jackson Ford

University Press of Mississippi
Jackson

Library of Congress Cataloging-in-Publication Data

Ford, Karen Jackson.
    Gender and the poetics of excess : moments of brocade / Karen
Jackson Ford.
    p.   cm.
    Includes bibliographical references and index.
    ISBN 1-57806-006-0 (cloth : alk. paper)
    1. American poetry—Women authors—History and criticism.
    2. Women and literature—United States—History—20th century
    3. Experimental poetry, American—History and criticism.
    4. American poetry—20th century—History and criticism.
    5. Authorship—Sex differences.   6. Literary form.   I. Title.
PS151.F67   1997
811.009'9287—dc21   97-18929
                                                                CIP

British Library Cataloging-in-Publication Data available

To
Donald Laird

Contents

Acknowledgments

$\mathscr{P}$roper acknowledgment must go back many years to Barry Lia, for a gift of Dickinson's complete poems, and to Patrick Murphy, for the three-volume set of Dickinson's letters. Since their initial generosity, many friends and colleagues have graciously contributed their time and expertise to this study. I am grateful to Leon Chai, Joanne Cutting-Gray, Claudia Johnson, Christine Krueger, Carol Thomas Neely, William Schroeder, and Paula Treichler for reading early drafts of some of these chapters and to Forest Pyle, George Rowe, and Louise Westling for their comments on more recent chapters. Susan Anderson provided excellent research assistance on the Black Arts chapter. The interest and moral support of others also sustained me in my work; for their encouragement throughout the whole project, I am grateful to my mother, Bernadette Ford, and my friends, Marcia Baron, Melody KirkWagner, Teresa Mangum, Sally McMahan, and Cara Ryan.

I am grateful to the University of Oregon Office of Research and Sponsored Programs for a New Faculty Development Grant that enabled me to spend a summer working on the Black Arts chapter.

I owe special debts of gratitude to Cary Nelson, Kathleen Karlyn, and Donald Laird. Cary Nelson has guided and supported my work from the beginning, read tirelessly and commented rigorously on successive drafts, and provided encouragement and inspiration at every turn. His rare respect for reading poetry carefully heartened me in the task of reading the work of these difficult poets. I am pleased to thank Kathleen Karlyn for her extraordinary intellectual generosity and her loyalty. Finally, Donald Laird read and commented on every aspect of this study. His sensitive and sensible contributions reverberate at every level, from stylistic improvements to conceptual clarity. For that, and for filling our days with poems, I dedicate these moments of brocade to him.

CHAPTER 1

The Poetics of Excess

Fantastic Flourishes of Gold Thread

*T*he mythic weaver Philomela has long fascinated feminist literary critics, who recognize in her predicament the situation of many women writers in a masculinist culture traditionally suspicious of women's words and desirous of their silence. Philomela, the innocent sister of Procne, raped and mutilated by Procne's husband Tereus, communicates with her sister, even though Tereus has cut out her tongue and locked her away, by weaving her story in cloth and sending it to Procne. Procne frees Philomela, and the two take revenge on Tereus by killing his son, Itys, and serving him to his father. When Tereus learns that he has eaten the flesh of his flesh, he attempts to kill his wife and sister-in-law, but the women flee and in their "flight" are transformed into birds, a swallow and a nightingale. Cheryl Walker's important 1982 study of American women poets, *The Nightingale's Burden*, emphasizes Philomela's need to communicate her oppression: "Both as a defiled woman and as an artist urgently desiring to communicate through symbolic forms, Philomela is the type of American women poets in the nineteenth century" (21). Playing on

the double sense of "burden" as a poetic refrain and something oner-
ous, Walker identifies a "nightingale tradition, bound up with themes
of aspiration and frustrated longing" (15): "What is significant about
this myth . . . is the way it records the burden of woe the nightingale
carries and the peculiarly autobiographical emphasis of her art, an
emphasis not lost upon another woman" (22). In 1979, in an earlier
groundbreaking study, *The Madwoman in the Attic,* Sandra Gilbert
and Susan Gubar had also invoked the myth of Philomela and Procne
to figure forth the cultural predicament of women writers: "From
the abused Procne to the reclusive Lady of Shallott [another isolated
weaver from a Tennyson poem of the same name] . . . women have
been told that their art . . . is an art of silence" (43). Philomela's appeal
for feminist critics is, of course, that she overcomes silence through
art; however, her art, as the phrase "nightingale's *burden*" suggests,
inevitably expresses her silencing.

  This Philomela provides an apt metaphor for the marginalized
writer, yet a more complicated Philomela might serve us even better.
One of the surprises of reviewing Ovid's version of the myth is to
discover a verbally aggressive Philomela who loses her tongue not
simply because she's the consummate victim but because she *uses*
her tongue so forcefully. We have hints of the power of her speech
when she persuades her father to let her go with Tereus to visit Procne:
"Philomela herself has the same wish [as Tereus]; winding her arms
about her father's neck, she coaxes him to let her visit her sister; by her
own welfare (yes, and against it, too) she urges her prayer" (1:321).
After her rape, she cries out against her attacker, calling him names
and charging him with crimes against herself, her sister, and her father
(1:325). Finally, she warns him that she will win retribution through
her own speech: " 'I will myself cast shame aside and proclaim what
you have done. If I should have the chance, I would go where people
throng and tell it; if I am kept shut up in these woods, I will fill the
woods with my story and move the very rocks to pity. The air of
heaven shall hear it, and, if there is any god in heaven, he shall hear
it too' " (1:327). In a devastating irony, "the savage tyrant's wrath was
aroused by these words," and Tereus cuts out her tongue to keep her
from announcing his guilt. Though this is, of course, not the desired
effect of her speech, the passage registers the tremendous potency of
Philomela's words. Indeed, even her severed tongue "lies palpitating

on the dark earth, faintly murmuring" and "twitches convulsively, and with its last dying movement seeks its mistress's feet" (1:327). The vitality and autonomy of the dying tongue prefigure Philomela's extraordinary expressiveness:

> A guard prevents her flight; stout walls of solid stone fence in the hut; speechless lips can give no token of her wrongs. But grief has sharp wits, and in trouble cunning comes. She hangs a Thracian web on her loom, and skilfully weaving purple signs on a white background, she thus tells the story of her wrongs. This web, when completed, she gives to her one attendant and begs her with gestures to carry it to the queen. The old woman, as she was bid, takes the web to Procne, not knowing what she bears in it. The savage tyrant's wife unrolls the cloth, reads the pitiable tale of her misfortune, and (a miracle that she could!) says not a word. (1:329)

That Procne "says not a word," indicates that she, too, has learned shrewdness from sister's grief: like Philomela, she is made speechless by the tragedy ("Grief chokes the words that rise to her lips, and her questing tongue can find no words strong enough to express her outraged feelings" [1:329]); however, unlike Philomela's, her silence becomes strategic. What Procne learns from Philomela is to hold her tongue, a feat Ovid considers miraculous, in order to achieve the desired ends.

It is an interesting irony that a myth about communication was significantly miscommunicated. As is well known, the Roman recorders of the myth confused the names of the sisters and the birds they were transformed into. Procne is originally changed into a nightingale, who forever after laments the death of her son in song, and Philomela is changed into a swallow, who, tongueless, can only twitter. The Roman writers mistook Philomela to be the nightingale and thus made possible the figure of the nightingale as poet or singer, weaving her sorrow into song, in later traditions, especially English. (Walker, above, refers to the nightingale as Philomela, while Gilbert and Gubar call her Procne.) Edith Hamilton famously comments on this discrepancy: "The Roman writers who told the story somehow got the sisters confused and said that the tongueless Philomela was the nightingale, which was obviously absurd. But so she is always called in English poetry" (271). Yet it is not so absurd, actually, that the myth of Philomela and Procne generates confusion about silence and speech since both are forms of power here, and even when speech is punished with silencing, silence continues to signify. Philomela reveals that to be without a tongue is not necessarily to be inarticulate, just as Procne demonstrates one must sometimes articulate rage through silence. *This* nightingale, who might be Procne *or* Philomela, who might be using language conventionally or inventively, is the nightingale I am interested in.

When Emily Dickinson alludes to Philomela in an elegy for Charlotte Brontë, her only poem in which the nightingale appears, it is this complicated Philomela, weaver of both speech and silence, whom she invokes:

> All overgrown by cunning moss,
> All interspersed with weed,
> The little cage of "Currer Bell"
> In quiet "Haworth" laid.
>
> This Bird—observing others
> When frosts too sharp became
> Retire to other latitudes—
> Quietly did the same—
>
> But differed in returning—
> Since Yorkshire hills are green—
> Yet not in all the nests I meet
> Can Nightingale be seen—
>
>   Or—
>
> Gathered from many wanderings—
> Gethsemane can tell
> Thro' what transporting anguish
> She reached the Asphodel!
>
> Soft fall the sounds of Eden
> Upon her puzzled ear—
> Oh what an afternoon for Heaven,
> When "Bronte" entered there!
>   *(Poems 148)*[1]

Like many Dickinson poems, though more literally than most, this poem offers an "either" and an "or" but refuses to choose between them.[2] Instead it gives a double view of its subject, Charlotte Brontë, first from the perspective of the world she left behind (the editor speculates that the poem was written on the fourth anniversary of Brontë's death), and then from the perspective of the enduring realm(s) she has entered, the spiritual and the literary. The "Or" midway through the poem is poised to hold the loss of Brontë in relation to the recovery of her rather than to suggest that human loss has been transcended through spiritual resurrection.

Dickinson imagines Brontë's hideaways, both her home in Haworth and her masculine pen name, as a "little cage" that clearly protects rather than restricts her. Much like Dickinson's own small bedroom retreat, which she described to her niece as "freedom,"[3] Brontë's home only appears to be a cage: it is overgrown by "cunning moss," a phrase that suggests artful disguise. Indeed, as we shall see, one of Dickinson's phrases for her poetry is "moments of brocade," and Brontë's "cunning moss" is like brocade in being an artful rendering of the wilderness. Similarly, the designing overgrowth recalls Philomela's crafty weaving of fibers into story. Brontë lived a "quiet" life at Haworth and "quietly" passed away, yet like Philomela and Dickinson the silence of her life produced, perhaps even made possible, the words of her books. "This Bird," this mortal Brontë, departs when winter sets in—a natural enough analogy for mortality—yet "differ[s] in returning," an assertion that seems to take the analogy too literally. This bird must differ from other birds, the speaker argues, since others return with the spring but there is no trace of her: "Yet not in all the nests I meet / Can Nightingale be seen—." The speaker's incredulity at Brontë's disappearance draws attention to the doubleness of the novelist's existence. An elegy might typically recur to such natural cycles, which console the bereaved with a paradigm of physical death and spiritual renewal. However, the speaker in this poem seems to expect Brontë to reappear in physical form when spring returns. Brontë, thus, "differs in returning," in one sense by not returning but in another by returning "differently" from others. The distinction between a physical return and a "different" one is hinted at in the speaker's unusual search to see the nightingale rather than to hear it. Like Philomela, whose "return" from silence must be seen (in her weaving) rather than heard, the departed Brontë has also been translated into another form.

The portion of the poem after the "Or" glosses this second coming, as Brontë, Christlike, passes through the anguish of her "Gethsemane" and ascends into heaven. Yet the either/or of earth or heaven only introduces further dualities when Brontë is astonished by entering paradise ("Soft fall the sounds of Eden / Upon her puzzled ear—"), and paradise is astonished by her entrance ("Oh what an afternoon for Heaven, / When 'Bronte' entered there!"). This reciprocity of wonderment makes it difficult to know who has gained more by Brontë's passing, Brontë herself or the other spirits in heaven; further, it distracts attention from the speaker's loss. Or—it calls attention to the speaker's gain: for the phrasing ("what an afternoon") suggests a pleasant afternoon encounter with Brontë, which the speaker could perhaps achieve—even though she's not in heaven—by reading one of the novelist's books. The quotation marks around Brontë's name may indicate her works rather than her person.

At any rate, the quotation marks around "Currer Bell," "Haworth," and "Bronte" signal their figurative import—again registering ambiguity—and foreground Brontë's cunning projections of herself; moreover, they also indicate the opposite, the reductive literalness of names and places, superficial aspects of identity (which would appear on a death certificate, for instance) that fail to represent someone such as Brontë fully. That is, like Philomela and Procne, both silence and significance are registered in the quotation marks, literal reduction of meaning and metaphorical abundance. The punctuated "Bronte" in the last line calls into question the woman writer's complex identity (as the quotation marks around the more obviously constructed identity "Currer Bell" do in the third line) just as that worldly identity is translated anew in the spiritual realm. The quotation marks function like the "cunning moss" to weave a disguise around the things they encase, and thus the elegy casts Brontë as a nightingale whose song is composed of silences and signs. "Currer Bell" is more than "he" seems; "Bronte" is more than she seems. Brontë's "translation" from flesh into spirit is associated with her translation from writer into writings. The spirit leaves no discernible trace, but the writings do.

Such complexities of identity and representation are also at issue in another Philomela figure, who appeared in print about the time Dickinson was coming into her own as a poet. Hester Prynne in *The Scarlet Letter,* using her embroidery as a means of expression, embodies my notion of the female artist of excess. A representation of female creativity in a novel written by a man, Hester may seem an unlikely figure for feminist poetic excess; yet, her status in the cultural imagination makes her an apt emblem for this study. In fact, a recent essay by Susan Griffin, "Red Shoes," explicitly associates Hester's red letter with a feminist notion of individual empowerment through extravagant personal style: *"It is not the inner place of red I am seeking but the right to wear it outwardly. To wear it brazenly. Like a sequined dress. Or a scarlet letter"* (173). Hawthorne's Hester both epitomizes feminist excess and guards against an essentializing notion of feminine aesthetics—and, for that matter, of gender or genre. Hester's predicament and her response to it make sense to us because we recognize not the truths but the assumptions about femininity that underlie them. As this book will demonstrate, Dickinson, Stein, Plath, and many of the poets of the Black Arts movement found themselves in a similar situation: defined by the culture in an extremely limiting way and suppressed on that account, they resisted silence through a poetics of excess. Excess is certainly not limited to women, as my concluding chapter on the Black Arts movement will show, nor is it limited to poetry, though it is especially suited to artists who are marginalized by the dominant culture—women in particular—and to a genre that foregrounds the workings of language.

The letter she must fashion and wear marks Hester as an adulteress and punishes her by identifying and perpetually publishing her sin. But although the letter represents her difference from others, its meaning is made unstable by her use of an aesthetics of excess. While the "A" ensures that Hester remains publicly branded, the letter itself—because it is a linguistic sign—is constantly open to interpretation.

By the time the townspeople first view the letter, Hester has already altered the meaning of the "A" by the way she represents it. The *style* of the letter she has embroidered expresses a pride and flamboyance that contradict the magistrates' intended meaning: "On the breast of her gown, in fine red cloth, surrounded with an elaborate embroidery and fantastic flourishes of gold thread, appeared the letter A. It was so artistically done, and with so much fertility and gorgeous luxuriance of fancy, that it had all the effect of a last and fitting decoration to the apparel which she wore" (53). Significantly Hester's rendering of the letter does not simply negate its original meaning; indeed, she gains control over that meaning precisely by calling attention to it. The stitches take up the accusations against her with great precision: the terms this passage uses to describe the letter, "fertility," "luxuriance," and "fancy," highlight in turn the fruition, sensuality, and pleasure that certainly composed her crime but that are not expected to be represented in her punishment. Hester has reworked the very terms of her transgression here, and it is clear that her artistry has affected the meaning of the "A" when the scarlet letter, rather than suggesting illegitimacy, "had the effect of a last and fitting decoration." Further, while the letter is supposed to assure her continued ostracization by the community, it separates her from them by *its* power, not theirs: "It had the effect of a spell, taking her out of the ordinary relations with humanity, and inclosing her in a sphere by herself" (54). In a sense, then, Hester chooses isolation even before anyone in the town can impose it on her and preempts their rejection of her in first distinguishing herself from them.

The force of Hester's handiwork, however, is not merely contradiction, despite what two of the townsfolk complain: " 'Why, gossips, what is it but to laugh in the faces of our godly magistrates, and make a pride out of what they, worthy gentlemen, meant for a punishment?' " (54). But it is not quite that Hester refutes her punishment by simply rejecting it or by displacing it with a sense of pride; rather Hester acquiesces to her punishment in a manner that refutes it, surprisingly and ironically, by its excessive acceptance. A third neighbor comprehends the intricately elaborated nature of Hester's response: " 'Not a stitch in that embroidered letter, but she has felt it in her heart' " (54). Hester's problematic and self-conscious acceptance puts her into a dialogue with her accusers. And, in fact, the concerns of the crowd of spectators reveal that the letter has not merely reminded them of her crime but rather has raised questions about the meaning of her punishment and the nature of her response to it.

Hester's flamboyant needlework challenges the cultural significance of the "A"; by embroidering her own version of the letter, she is able to represent both her sin and her punishment. In doing so, she takes symbolic possession of the forces that seek to define her— through her representation of them. If the scarlet letter can be considered a sign that expresses the magistrates' view of Hester, then her embroidery revises the meaning of the sign. Her text opposes theirs without negating it: hers will henceforth mediate her relationship with the townspeople just as the magistrates had hoped to intervene between Hester and her neighbors by branding her a sinner; she will be marked as separate from them by the "A," but they will be transfixed by it; the letter will indict her for her sin, but it will also implicate them in her punishment. The presence of the letter will also foreground the absence of her partner in sin; the shame of having sinned will be elaborately interwoven with the flamboyant, almost eroticized version of the pride of repentance. Most important, their power to name her will be subsumed in her power to represent that name.

Until Hester rewrites it, the "A" appears a monologic text, whose meaning seems incontrovertible: it signifies "adulteress" and nothing more. Were it not for the inherent instability of language, the arbitrary relationship of linguistic sign to referent, Hester might have been narrowly and permanently constricted by the scarlet emblem. Even had the magistrates chosen a pictorial image to affix to her clothes— the image of a devil, a crucifix, or the flames of hell, for instance—they would perhaps have recognized the need to control and specify its representation. Then she would hardly have been able so easily to contest its meaning. They imagine, however, that the letter can only signify in one way. But by choosing to refer to language—making the "A" stand for the word "adulteress"—the magistrates gave Hester an inherently plural text, with a history of interpretation behind it and now available for reinterpretation. The visual embroidery in fact merely invokes the existing instability of verbal signification. Indeed, the townspeople come to think of the "A" as standing for "Able" because Hester is reliable and unswerving in her dedication to helping the needy of the town: "many people refused to interpret the scarlet A by its original signification. They said that it meant Able; so strong was Hester Prynne, with a woman's strength" (161).[4] Despite the strictures of her limited text, therefore, Hester's "A" is riddled with historically varied readings and susceptible to continuing revision. She exploits its susceptibility through what might be called her aesthetics of excess, a style that proliferates meaning in the complexities, ambiguities, and redundancies of its pattern.

Hester Prynne and her embroidered letter are paradigmatic of many women poets and their poetry. First, women's creative expression has usually occurred within boundaries determined by a

predominantly male tradition. That sewing is Hester's means of articulating herself points up the traditionally limited outlets for female
creativity; Hawthorne himself says this of Hester's occupation: "It
was the art—then, as now, almost the only one within a woman's
grasp—of needlework" (81). Like Emily Dickinson's unorthodox use
of the hymn stanza as a medium for her skeptical and often revisionary treatments of the nineteenth-century New England Christian
worldview, Hester Prynne's embroidery makes needlework a "mode
of expressing" her challenging response to the magistrates (84). But
more important, Hester challenges and complicates the meaning of
the "A" in the style of her work. Understanding the productive tension
that exists between style and meaning is crucial to understanding
how women poets engage convention and transgression. Next, Hester's method can be called a poetics of excess because it produces
new meanings through a proliferation or "embroidering" of representation. New meaning is concomitant with excessive signification.
There is a surplus in the medium, which produces an overgrowth, as
it were, of signification. Roland Barthes's description of the "obtuse"
or excessive meaning in a text addresses this crucial notion of the self-
creating aspect of style: "it declares its artifice but without in doing
so abandoning the 'good faith' of its referent . . . [it has] a multilayer
of meanings which always lets the previous meaning continue, as
in a geological formation, saying the opposite without giving up the
contrary" ("The Third Meaning" 58). Finally, this ability to say the
opposite without giving up the contrary is what allows Hester to
determine her own relation to her neighbors. A poetics of excess can
contradict, revise, and affirm existing meanings, but it can also generate new ones. These excesses of style enable crucial and liberating
excesses of meaning.

Indeed, the chief criticisms of the practitioners of excess I discuss here are that they write too much, reveal too much, and push
their poetics too far. As we shall see, readers considered Dickinson's
form hysterical and her figures tortured, Stein's works repetitive and
nonsensical, Plath's tone at once virulent and confessional, Cortez's
poems violent and vulgar, and Shange's work vengeful and self-
righteous. The publishing history of these poets demonstrates both
the opposition to such a poetics and the necessity for it. As is well
known, Dickinson's first editors normalized her unorthodox spelling,

punctuation, meters, and rhymes, frequently changing words and omitting whole stanzas in order to present a more felicitous verse. Many of Stein's manuscripts remained unpublished during her lifetime because publishers were unwilling to print such long, hermetic works. She refused several opportunities to publish her work because she would not make it shorter and more accessible. Plath apprenticed herself to the dominant culture in an early style that she hoped would suit the tastes of mainstream magazines. However, when she began writing her best work, the *Ariel* poems, and publishers declined to print it, she overcame her desire for their acceptance and continued to develop her newly excessive style. In the Black Arts movement, Carolyn Rodgers was criticized for her profanity, and Ntozake Shange was rebuked for deforming the language with her colloquial idiom and excoriated for her critique of gender relations. The fact that the most excessive poetry from this movement remains almost entirely out of print and omitted from anthologies because it is still so volatile testifies to the continuing power of the poetic tradition this book explores.

Rather than merely acquiescing to or rejecting a hostile readership, those who employ a poetics of excess seek to establish a relationship—though perhaps an oppositional one—with those who *would* silence them if they could. To return to *The Scarlet Letter,* while Hester's community defines her in a single word and restricts her self-expression to a single art, she is nevertheless able to challenge the sense of that word (a word so powerful that only a single letter is necessary to invoke it) by rendering it in a style that generates excesses of meaning. Hester loses her place in the community through a grievous breach of social decorum, yet she recovers herself and creates a new social space for herself through another breach of aesthetic decorum: her excessive artistic style.

The tremendous expressive force of style is also demonstrated in a less sensational scarlet letter, not the gorgeous emblem that rivets the action of the novel proper but rather that "worn and faded . . . rag of scarlet cloth" (31) that the narrator discovers hidden away in "The Custom House," the prefatory sketch to the novel: "My eyes fastened themselves upon the old scarlet letter, and would not be turned aside. Certainly, there was some deep meaning in it, most worthy of interpretation . . . I happened to place it on my breast. It seemed to me . . . then that I had experienced a sensation not altogether physical, yet almost so, as of burning heat; and as if the letter were not of red cloth, but red-hot iron" (31–32). Even though Hester is now only vaguely remembered as "a very old, but not decrepit woman" (32), an account that hardly approaches her significance, her embroidered letter retains its force—and through it, the narrator is able imaginatively to reconstruct her story and the letter's meanings. This is possible not because the emblem literally signifies its history; remember, its stitch "gives evidence of a now forgotten art, not to be recovered even by the process of picking out the threads" (31). That is, the sign itself is now largely unreadable. Rather, the *style* of the letter, its excess, offers evidence of those deep meanings most worthy of interpretation. This study pursues the meanings promoted by such a style. In Gertrude Stein's terms, poets of excess "reuse" (engage) their troubled and complex relationship to language and culture in order to "refuse" (reject) it—and, most important, in rejecting standards of literary decorum and femininity, to "re-fuse" (fuse again) their letters of red-hot iron ("Poetry and Grammar" 228).

To use the term "excess" in criticism today is to invoke contemporary theories of writing that describe how processes of signification often, or always, exceed the apparent authority and closure of their utterances. Jacques Derrida's term *"differance,"* suggesting both difference and deferral in meaning, identifies the irresolvable contradiction necessarily produced by any use of language. Derrida's interest in the deferment and disruption of conventional meaning leads him to read the discontinuities and ambiguities in texts. Similarly, the French theorists of *l'écriture féminine,* Hélène Cixous, Luce Irigaray, and Julia Kristeva, look to puns, neologisms, disruptions, and rhythms as evidence of a feminine mode of writing that opposes the traditional authority of masculine discourse.[5] The idea of poetic excess developed in this book, however, is best understood in relation to literary decorum, an idea that has been relatively neglected in recent criticism. I choose decorum and excess as the two points of a theoretical compass because they best describe the circle that divides the poets in this study from the dominant literary culture that attempted to silence them, either by coercing them into an approved mode of writing or by excluding them altogether. In this context, excess is a rhetorical strategy adopted to overcome the prohibitions imposed by the application of a disabling concept of decorum. Rather than capitulate to the demands for a conventional mode of writing, these poets practiced their own unconventional mode, excessively intensifying its indecorous aspects in an act of self-recovery and assertion against social negation. Considering excess in a rhetorical context avoids the necessity of dividing language into two modes—one authoritative, dominant, and patriarchal, the other anarchic, subversive, and feminine—and retains the particularity of each writer's deployment of excess as a rhetorical strategy. This is not to say, of course, that authorial intention is final but only to preserve the political force of writing—even as my readings will frequently confirm the deconstructive nature of interpretation. By taking this approach, however, I hope to help restore a degree of historical attention to a criticism that has too often been shaped by ahistorical or essentializing uses of structuralist and poststructuralist theories of language. My goal is to derive a theory of poetic language grounded in the history of form and uncovered by a careful study *of* form.

Literary decorum is one instrument a culture uses to constrain its writers—and perhaps the most effective instrument because it is the least definable. The criteria for acceptable writing have rarely been formulated with the rigor observable in eighteenth-century British criticism. Generally, principles of decorum have remained vague and somewhat flexible; and it may be that their coercive power is increased rather than diminished by the lack of specific definition.[6] Richard Lanham's remarks on decorum remind us that it is a culturally determined value: "decorum as a stylistic criterion finally locates itself entirely in the beholder . . . No textual pattern *per se* is decorous or not. The final criterion for excess, *in*decorum, is the stylistic self-consciousness induced by the text or social situation. We know decorum is present when we don't notice it, and vice versa. Decorum is a gestalt established in the perceiving intelligence. Thus the need for it, and the criteria for it, can attain universal agreement and allegiance, and yet the concept itself remain without specifiable content" (45).

The poetic excesses under discussion here, like the criteria of decorum against which they are perceived, cannot be itemized as an immutable set of stylistic traits. Decorum and excess together offer an account of style that recognizes historical nuance and cultural distinction. Feminist excess is not a transhistorical phenomenon just as femininity is not. Nineteenth-century conventions for femininity and Dickinson's poetic resistance to them are different from the 1960s prescriptions for African-American femininity and Shange's poetic rejection of them. Though decorum and excess shift over time and in different cultural conditions, their structural relationship to each other remains strikingly stable. Thus nineteenth-century standards for women's writing and late twentieth-century standards bear almost no relation; Dickinson's particular excesses, likewise, do not anticipate Stein's or Plath's or Shange's. Yet the charges of indecorousness leveled at these poets repeat a fairly fixed set of abstract grievances. This study does not offer a systematic account of nineteenth- or twentieth-century literary decorums; rather, it argues that notions of decorum were, and are, typically unstated and that we glean indications of the standards of decorum not from explicit prescriptions for them but from charges against marginalized writers that they have transgressed them.

Moreover, the very vagueness of decorum as a prescribed practice permits the dominant culture both to approve of stylistic transgressions in privileged writers, deeming their work innovative or avant-garde, and to disapprove of them in marginalized writers, dismissing their work as unskilled or irrelevant. Thus Dickinson's transgressions against literary propriety, like Stein's or Plath's, were condemned as unladylike. Similarly, Stein's poetic revolution was ridiculed as nonsense by her contemporaries, often the same writers whose revolt against convention was far less radical and effective than hers.

In his discussion of the history of decorum, Thomas Kranidas, like Lanham, insists on the instability of the term "decorum." Yet he identifies "its general configurations" and offers a working definition: "The major 'shapes' of decorum are two. The first is a concept which demands from the parts of a work of art consistency with established traditional social forms . . . The second shape is vaguer but more important. It is a shape that has been felt rather than identified by modern scholars. This is the concept of the highest organic unity: decorum as at once the tool and ideal for adjusting proportions, relationships, colors to achieve a radiant whole. This is the Platonic and Aristotelian ideal" (48). Kranidas calls the latter a "larger decorum" and the former a "smaller 'rhetorical' one" (48). Lanham similarly observes that decorum is "not only a rhetorical criterion but a general test of basic acculturation" (46). The relation of the smaller, rhetorical decorum to the larger ideal of decorum suggests how much is at stake in deploying an indecorous rhetorical style. A writer who observes the unstated and unformulated principles of literary decorum has internalized the social prohibitions of that culture. If the culture functions to empower the individual, there is nothing self-negating in such an observance, just the opposite. If, however, the culture functions to disempower the individual, as women and African-Americans have been in American culture, the observance of literary decorum results in extremely limited social acceptance at the price of self-negation. Such writers must adopt the appropriate modes of writing allotted to them by the dominant culture or suffer invisibility; but the adoption of an approved mode of writing entails an even more immediate and personal sense of erasure. The writers under study here have eluded the disabling alternatives, of complete acquiescence to the dominant culture or outright rejection of it, by engaging in literary excesses that permit both engagement with and resistance to that culture.

Two definitions of "excess" given in the *Oxford English Dictionary* are relevant to this discussion. The first definition, used mainly in legal contexts (law being a partial codification of a society's princi- ples of decorum), states that excess is the "action of overstepping (a prescribed limit), going beyond (one's authority, rights, etc.)." Here excess is an act of transgression but not necessarily an intentional or subversive one. It may be the consequence of ignorance or innocence or mere indifference. One may have no better reason for a transgres- sion than private indulgence. In writing, an author who indulges in an idiosyncratic style for its own sake may be excessive in this limited sense, but such an author has nothing at stake. The writers treated here, in contrast, have everything at stake. Excess is their tool for gaining voice in a literary environment that constantly threatens to silence them.

The other and more important *OED* entry, though it is labeled obsolete (a point I will return to), characterizes excess as an "extrav- agant violation of law, decency, or morality; outrageous conduct." The idea of purposeful transgression is more consonant with my use of the term. One who violates a law extravagantly or perpetrates an outrageous act is usually doing so in full consciousness and with articulate intent; the excess in this case consequently takes on a rhetorical function and becomes a way of making a meaningful statement without being restricted to a potentially self-negating mode of action, speech, or writing that the dominant members of the culture endorse as decorous.

Though the term "excess" calls to mind contemporary critical modes, the word "style" might suggest an outmoded critical practice. In our interest to recognize the political, social, psychological, and philosophical workings of literary texts, we have tended to ignore style as part of our general suspicion of formalist methods. Yet it is precisely through style that writers such as Dickinson, Stein, Plath, Baraka, Smith, Cortez, and Shange are able to engage and express these important historical and political concerns. Helen Vendler has recently reminded us of the "human import" of style:

> It is distressing, to anyone who cares for and respects the concentrated intellectual and imaginative work that goes into a successful poem, to see how rarely that intense (if instinctive) labor is perceived, remarked on, and appreciated. It is even more distressing—given the human perceptual, aesthetic, and moral signals conveyed . . . by such elements as prosody, grammar, and lineation—that most contemporary interpretations of poetry never mention such things, or, if they do, it is to register them factually rather than to deduce their human import. The forgettable writers of verse do not experiment with style in any coherent or strenuous way; they adopt the generic style of their era and . . . repeat themselves in it. (6–7)

The writers treated here are memorable because their experiments with style enabled them to maneuver within the cultural constraints that engross criticism today. As Vendler indicates, an interest in formal matters demands a special kind of critical attention. Sharon Cameron's recent remark that "Dickinson continues to be read as one of the two central nineteenth-century American poets without being read" (44) suggests that poetry criticism needs to engage more rigorously with *poems*. While scholars, especially feminist scholars, are, of course, "reading" Dickinson, the lack of attention to "formal examination" (44) concerns Cameron, as it clearly does Vendler. In

"Optimism and Critical Excess," poet and theorist Charles Bernstein reminds us that "art is still our greatest teacher of methodologies, and we risk losing our ground when we forget what art teaches, that art teaches" (174). The poetry of excess seems to demand an unusually attentive—perhaps even excessive—critical practice. In claiming that poetic excess enables these poets to exceed the reach of conventional representation, I have not relieved myself of the obligation to pursue the meanings of their excesses in my readings. On the contrary, these poems instruct us to keep reading, and my methodology reflects this.

Vendler argues that "style in its largest sense is best understood as a material body" (1), rather than the more familiar metaphor of style as dress, because she wants "to emphasize the inextricable relation of style to theme" (2). Moreover, the body metaphor captures the violent upheaval poets experience when they alter their styles: "When a poet puts off an old style (to speak for a moment as though this were a deliberate undertaking), he or she perpetrates an act of violence, so to speak, on the self" (1). The notion of a material body of style is certainly relevant to the works of women writers, and especially to writers of excess, since women's relation to language has traditionally been imagined in terms of their bodies. In *Literary Fat Ladies,* Patricia Parker traces the many associations between corpulent women and copious texts, a tradition that figures large women as obstructers of textual closure, who extend or dilate discourse and generate (male anxiety about) endless texts. This figure derives from the "tradition of rhetorical *dilatio*—with its references to the 'swelling' style or its relation to the verbal 'interlarding' produced through an excessive application of the principle of 'increase' " (14). Parker analyzes a host of literary fat ladies (and even a fat man in drag, Falstaff) to outline a misogynist tradition whose motive is controlling women's speech: "One of the chief concerns of the tradition that portrays women as unflappable talkers is how to master or contain such feminine mouthing" (26). Regulating women's words is, of course, one way of regulating women's bodies, and Parker rightly recognizes "the link between garrulity and unbridled sexuality" (26).

As a generator of copious texts, by rhetorical amplification that produces seemingly endless interruptions and deferrals, Parker's literary fat lady embodies Derridean (deferral and difference) and French feminist (disruption and writing the body) theories of textuality.

Vendler's notion of the material *body* of style, phrasing that insists on the inseparability of form and meaning, calls in a quite different way for the association of body and text. Yet I persist in employing metaphors of cloth, clothing, and sewing for style, first, because the poets under discussion here and their critics use those metaphors, and further, because their poems suggest that for some women writers clothing is in fact a kind of body. Here Vendler's phrase "material body" can be expanded by a pun on "material" to include all of these ideas, and Dickinson's quip in a letter to Higginson—"truth like Ancestor's Brocades can stand alone" (*Letters* 368)—provides a figure for a style (of dress) that has come to function like a body.

In heading my chapters with phrases from poets and critics that associate needlework and women's writing, I also want to underscore how frequently sewing is employed by women writers and their critics as a metaphor for female writing. Women writers often employ needlework as a familiar and valued creative production from the domestic sphere, but they also recognize that it has traditionally been used to represent the inferior pole of the male/female creative opposition: men produce masterpieces while women make handiwork. In invoking this history of prejudice against their writing by using the metaphor of sewing, literary women at once call on a tradition of female creativity and confront the trivialization of that tradition by men.[7] Though a distinguished, privileged, and centuries-long tradition of *weaving* song and *unraveling* narratives seems to contradict this dismissive association of women's writing with sewing as mere handiwork, the *processes* of weaving and unweaving tend to be invoked to describe the processes of writing and reading privileged works, while the *products* of weaving tend to be invoked to describe the works of marginalized writers.

In the chapters that follow, I examine how poetic excess has defined its own tradition in American letters beginning with Emily Dickinson and culminating with the controversial and neglected Black Arts movement. Chapter 2, "Moments of Brocade," argues that Emily Dickinson's letters reveal that her writing was condemned by her father, brother, and later her editor, because of its unorthodox style. She responded to their demands to write more conventionally with a promise to do so, but in a manner which proliferates the stylistic features they had forbidden. When her brother admonished her to write more simply, Dickinson replied, "As *simple* as you please, the *simplest* sort of simple" (*Letters* 45). The tone and repetitions of her answer exceed compliance to the point of contradiction. Her letters show her dedication to writing according to her own genius, but they also show the productive relationships she formed with resistant readers: her writing takes its shape from opposing the prescriptions of others.

Dickinson's poems about composition responded to a nineteenth-century model of sexual difference that had low expectations for women's writing. The constraints generated by that model, moreover, provided an analogy for the constraints of language itself, which she experienced even more intensely. Language is the material from which poems are made, but its conventional patterns, reinforced by the customs of society in general, always threaten to destroy a poet's originality. Dickinson often depicts her ideas about poetry in her poems and enacts the development of her style in response to the pressures of convention. In "It would never be Common— more—I said—" (*Poems* 430) she formulates her poetics against the anticipated hostility of readers (represented by a goblin) and the potentially destructive conventions of language. This refusal to be "common" (to write in accordance with inhibiting social and literary conventions) structures many of her most excessive poems.

Among the poets I study, Gertrude Stein most clearly and self-consciously articulated a theory of poetic excess, and I turn to her in chapter 3, "A Crazy Quilt of Style." Her infamous line, "Rose is a rose is a rose is a rose," has become a modernist avant-garde cliché, but I read it as a companion to Dickinson's "As *simple* as you please, the *simplest* sort of simple." Stein's line epitomizes her experiment in excess and served as a motto for her life project: to invigorate Western literature by renewing language. When teased about the line, she explained its significance: "in that line the rose is red for the first time in English for a hundred years" (*Four in America* vi). Excess is what enables the rose to be red again, and therefore "read" again. The connotative effects of the line are complex: the first rose is a noun which no longer evocatively names its object; the second rose is a dead metaphor that fails to figure; the third rose is the "insistence," which is Stein's word for the power of repetition to enable words to keep signifying; and the final rose is the renewed word produced by the proliferations of the first three invocations. Disruptions of reference and metaphor are followed by the continuing signification of "insistence" because excess is, above all, a refusal of silence. The rose line exemplifies Stein's resistance to "patriarchal poetry"; it places the traditional symbol of objectified femininity at the center of that resistance and enacts a poetics of excess that distinguishes her entire literary enterprise.

The principles epitomized in the rose line reveal the workings of "Patriarchal Poetry," one of Stein's most difficult poems. The poem is a treatise on male-dominated Western literature and her problematic relationship to it; it is an exposé of literary history and a critique of literary convention; and it advances her own revisionary poetics. Through a thorough analysis of "Patriarchal Poetry," I demonstrate the complexities and allusions of Stein's most complete statement of her poetics. Indeed, the argument of "Patriarchal Poetry" is that a poetics of excess is the only remedy for an ailing literary tradition: it revitalizes a moribund literature, creates space in an overcrowded literary history, and restores the vitalizing but repressed feminine to language and literature. Further, Stein analyzes the failures, parodies the conventions, and dismantles the forms of the dominant literary culture in order to prepare the way for new literatures.

Though in the last twenty years feminist critics have revised our understanding of Dickinson's and Stein's writing, demonstrating the subversiveness of their literary peculiarities and superseding the traditional assessment of their work, this study offers a more systematic account of their rhetorical strategies by placing them in a tradition of poetic excess. In the postwar period, Sylvia Plath knowingly inserts herself into this tradition when she echoes Stein's famous line: "MY WRITING IS MY WRITING IS MY WRITING" (*Journals* 255). The emphatic sentence records her indignation at people who she believed were appropriating her writing and her desire to reclaim it as her own. Though Plath only sometimes recognized the gender conflicts inherent in her writing problems, her struggle was clearly that of a woman poet in a world of "patriarchal poetry." Chapter 4, "Splitting the Seams of Fancy Terza Rima," argues that in her early poems, Plath created a poetics of excess because she felt her style was too weak and pallid to compare with that of the great male poets. What she called her "machinelike syllabic death-blow[s]" (*Journals* 277) in *Colossus* were poems meant to pound out a place for herself as a woman poet in the male literary world. But later, in *Ariel,* when she no longer fears being a "minor poetess" and "dilettante artist" (*Journal* 71) her style alters and excess becomes rearticulated through theme.

The chapter focuses on the five beekeeping poems that conclude Plath's version of *Ariel.* The poems are concerned with self-assessment and redefinition, both personal and poetic, and scrutinize the relationships between the speaker and her world. The sequence moves from a tortured engagement with community in "The Bee Meeting" to a meditation on solitude in "Wintering," in which the speaker respectively settles her relations to others and then to her own past selves. The movement from external preoccupation to internal absorption has formal reverberations and is accompanied by a movement from stylistic to thematic excess. Plath's stylistic excess diminishes as the speaker retreats from external pressures, especially gender conflicts, to her personal exigencies. *Ariel* as a whole is characterized by thematic rather than stylistic excess, and her decision to conclude that volume with the bee sequence indicates her confidence in such formally unmediated confrontations with excess.

Chapter 5, "We Survive in Patches . . . Scraps," begins with the Black Arts movement of the 1960s, a literary movement that promoted excess as a public, political program and that remains perhaps the most explosive and unstudied of the "moments of brocade" included here. This final chapter is less a conclusion than a culmination of the analyses of poetic excess that precede it. Here I show that the poetics I have associated primarily with white women writers does not arise from an essentializing element in language but is a rhetorical strategy effective for and uniquely available to marginalized writers. Like Dickinson, Stein, and Plath, the poets of the 1960s Black Arts movement employed excess to resist the dominant culture: both white American culture and earlier "Negro writing," which had endorsed Anglo-American literary values. Black aesthetician Adam David Miller's use of Stein's formulation in the phrase "a nigger is a nigger is a nigger" (402) suggests certain philosophical and aesthetic affinities among all the poets in my study.

African-American writers in the Black Arts movement advocated the use of a Black Aesthetic, an artistic program that brought poetic excess to a public forum. Two new features in the use of excess by these poets are significant. First, the Black Arts poets did not write in isolation but identified themselves and practiced their writing as a group. Second, the Black Arts movement included male writers who employed excess in ways that were problematic for female writers. The recovery of what was termed "black manhood"—an urgent and necessary political move—involved misogyny, as well as homophobia and anti-Semitism. In projecting the image of the ideal black revolutionary poet, these male artists tended to exclude black women as revolutionary agents, rendering them primarily symbols of black pride and solidarity.

Many black women poets during the movement began their careers by writing in the hypermasculine style of the Black Arts program. For some, however, that persona created new conflicts of gender even as it solved important conflicts of race. Nikki Giovanni, Sonia Sanchez, and Carolyn Rodgers rejected the poetic excesses of the Black Aesthetic, retreating from it to a poetic vision that reproduced the gender conflict—but now in hyperfeminine terms. Romanticism, the Nation of Islam, and Christianity provided Giovanni, Sanchez, and Rodgers, respectively, with an alternative to Black Arts excesses that did not, however, offer an alternative to limiting conceptions of gender. Jayne Cortez, on the other hand, anticipated the black feminism and black feminist excess of Ntozake Shange, Michele Wallace, and others, by using Black Arts excesses to expose and resist constraining definitions of women.

As the literary environment has become less hostile to women writers, the need for an instrument of resistance has lessened, and poetic excess has begun to function more in terms of convention. The work of the contemporary poet Ai exemplifies the shift from the use of excess as an oppositional strategy to its use as a primarily stylistic one. Ai has been aided rather than hindered by the still predominantly male literary establishment; and though her personal background is multiethnic, her most obvious poetic precursor is Robert Browning. Consequently, she aligns herself with neither feminist nor African-American writers. Poetic excess, for Ai and many other contemporary poets, is less a strategy that makes writing possible in an inhospitable literary culture than one that enables poets to represent speakers whose relationship to language is antagonistic.

The dedications and acknowledgments of Ai's five volumes of poetry tell a story of literary mentorship and access to publication quite different from the careers of the other poets treated in this book. In *Killing Floor,* which was the 1978 Lamont Poetry Selection, Ai acknowledges the support of mainstream institutions, including the John Simon Guggenheim Memorial Foundation, the Radcliffe Institute, and the Massachusetts Arts and Humanities Foundation. Her next book, *Sin* (1986), is dedicated to poet Galway Kinnell and acknowledges support from the National Foundation for the Arts, the Ingram Merrill Foundation, the PEN Emergency Fund for Writers, and others. Her most recent book, *Greed* (1993), seems to flaunt this unprecedented support in a gesture that is both grateful and self-parodic: "This book is dedicated to my loyal fans" (n.p.). Indeed, the good humor Ai reveals about the encouragement she has received and the ease with which she expresses it attest to the increasing receptivity of today's literary environment.

In her foreword to the 1987 volume that combined and reprinted Ai's first two books (*Cruelty/Killing Floor*), Carolyn Forché remarks that Ai speaks "not for the distanced self but the dispossessed" (ix). One cannot overstate the fact that Ai's poetry does indeed *speak,* almost invariably through dramatic monologues, for a range of people who would not otherwise be articulate. That is, Ai's speakers tend to be in the cultural position that marginal writers have typically occupied: silenced by the dominant culture, dismissed, trivialized. For example, "Knockout," a poem from *Greed* (47–49), gives voice to a black prostitute who addresses herself to Desiree Washington and Mike Tyson, the subjects of a sensational rape case. "Knockout" refers both to Washington, the glamorous young black woman, and to Tyson, the boxing champion; however, it also comes to signify the speaker, who is a knockout of a different order (mouthy, vulgar, diseased, and violent), and most especially to her diatribe, which will knock them out with its hard-hitting truths. "Knockout" uses various excesses to achieve its force, most notably its unladylike idiom and unflinching honesty:

> Y'all say she respectable, educated.
> Say Tyson shoulda waited
> 'til he found himself a squeezer like me.
> Y'all say nothing shaking there 'cept her hair,

> *but this where I disagree, see,*
> *'cause it's a fine line*
> *between rape and a good time.*
> *You find that out real fast*
> *when you got an uninvited dick up your ass.*

As this passage indicates, the poem emphasizes speaking, as what "y'all say" comes into conflict with what the hooker says, "I'll tell you what." What she has to say is that being a prostitute (earning her own income) allows her not to have to "prostitute" herself in words (as others in the poem do—Washington, Tyson, and her mother who criticizes her but takes her money: "It's just talk. She take my money, don't she?"). Though she's only one of many "poor black crackwhores," she claims the right to speak:

> *This one bitch know what she talking about.*
> *I ain't gonna shut up.*
> *This is my mouth.*

I ain't gonna shut up. This is my mouth. This Philomela is susceptible to rape, poverty, violence, racism, and homelessness, but she can't be silenced. The words that Ai puts into the mouths of her dispossessed speakers are words, I would argue, that have been given to her by poetic precursors for whom excess was not only a rhetorical but also a political strategy. That excess functions rhetorically in much contemporary poetry, that it has become a literary convention frequently employed to represent subjects the dominant culture ignores, is a measure of the success of those earlier projects.

The poetics of excess must be understood in opposition to a poetics of decorum, which imposes an unformulated standard for correct poetry that writers must either conform to or transgress. The fact that the definition of "excess" as an extravagant violation of law or decency is obsolete suggests how differently the concept would have to be understood in the late-twentieth century from how it was understood in earlier cultural situations. Today, when excess itself has become for some a criterion for poetic decorum (consequently limiting its political force), it is especially important to recover a sense of the difficulties faced by marginal writers whose work was either attacked or neglected by a literary culture that strenuously applied a truly prohibitive standard of decorum.

CHAPTER 2

Emily Dickinson

Moments of Brocade

> *As* simple *as you please, the* simplest *sort of simple—*

*E*mily Dickinson's letters reveal that she tried her voice when she was still a young woman, was chastised by her father and brother (and later by her eventual editor) for her unorthodox style, and responded to their strictures that she write more appropriately by promising to do so but in a manner that proliferates the very stylistic features they had forbidden. In a movement I will discuss at length, Dickinson wrote most naturally in a style she associated with brocade because of its rich, intricate, multilayered pattern and its golden threads; her audience, however, demanded that she write in a simple and unadorned style, which she associated with sackcloth both for its plainness and for its suggestion of mortification; and, in response to their attempts to modulate her unique voice to conform to their notions of proper women's writing, she intensified her style, shifting into the extreme, where the lavish qualities of the brocade are released once again in what she termed the wilderness, an aesthetic that necessarily throws off the more domesticated cloth metaphors. In doing this, Dickinson was neither utterly rejecting her culture's conceptions of women's writing nor acquiescing to its demands; she was rendering the language wild so that it could not tame her.

Though Dickinson's poems record an urgent interest in poetic form, she left no official statement of her aesthetics.[1] As many have noted, however, her letters contain a wealth of suggestive material on her ideas about poetry. Her thirty-year correspondence with Thomas Wentworth Higginson, which began in 1862 when she responded to his "Letter to a Young Contributor," published in the *Atlantic Monthly,* and continued until her death in 1886, has been long identified as an especially rich source of information about Dickinson's poetics.[2] Yet letters written much earlier, even as early as 1848 when Dickinson was only eighteen, anticipate the revelations about her creative processes that she would later convey to Higginson. The common element, I think, between the early letters to her brother Austin, written when her poetic identity must have been just taking shape, and the renowned later correspondence with Higginson, written when she had reached artistic maturity, is the conventionality of her two correspondents. Both Austin and Higginson had customary notions of writing—Austin of women's writing and Higginson of poetry—that conflicted in an extremely productive way with Dickinson's own view of herself as a writer.

Though in most cases, we have only Dickinson's letters to others, her reactions to her correspondents are frequently so strong that we can almost recover their letters to her in her responses to them. Several of the early letters to her brother, for instance, refer to the fact that he considered her writing unladylike in both subject and style. In the following letter to Austin, written from Mount Holyoke where she was attending school, she parodies her brother's concern about proper women's writing by sarcastically suggesting that *his* writing needs to be censored before women can read it:

> Your *welcome* letter, found me all engrossed in the history of Sulphuric Acid!!!!! I deliberated for a few moments after it's reception on the propriety of carrying it to Miss. Whitman, your friend. The result of my deliberation was a conclusion to open it with moderation, peruse it's contents with sobriety becoming my station, & if after a close investigation of it's contents I found nothing which savored of rebellion or an unsubdued will, I would lay it away in my folio & forget I had ever received it. Are you not gratified that I am so rapidly gaining correct ideas of female propriety & sedate deportment?[3] (L 22)

Already here in 1848, Dickinson contests the prevailing definition of woman's place by mockingly accepting it rather than by overtly rejecting it. Her disdain for her brother's view of appropriate women's reading (and by implication, writing) is lodged in her sarcastic and overblown compliance to his censorship, in her caricature of the proper woman (moderate, sober, subdued, sedate, and correct), and in her ironic dismissal of Austin's writing (she finds his letter perfectly acceptable for "ladies" and therefore tucks it away as unsuitable for women, a gesture that obviously dispatches his ideas about female propriety as well). It is no coincidence that the manner of retort Dickinson produces here is itself in many ways a "sulphuric style": corrosive, suffocating, vitriolic. The letter provides early evidence that she recognized the potential power of such brimstone, a nineteenth-century synonym for sulfuric acid.[4]

Her next exchange with Austin on the subject of appropriate women's writing, though still playful, has a more ominous edge. In 1851 she reacts quite violently to Austin's request that she comport herself in future letters to him with "female propriety and sedate deportment":

> I feel quite like retiring in the presence of one so grand, and casting my small lot among small birds, and fishes—you say you dont comprehend me, you want a simpler style. *Gratitude* indeed for all my fine philosophy! I strove to be exalted thinking I might reach *you* and while I pant and struggle and climb the nearest cloud, you walk out very leisurely in your slippers from Empyrean, and without the *slightest* notice request me to get down! As *simple* as you please, the *simplest* sort of simple—I'll be a little ninny—a little pussy catty, a little Red Riding Hood, I'll wear a Bee in my Bonnet, and a Rose bud in my hair, and what remains to do you shall be told hereafter. (L 45)

Austin has apparently urged his sister to alter her writing voice by simplifying her style, restricting her subject matter to domestic concerns, and dwarfing her poetic persona.[5] In response to his attempt to stifle her, however, she develops tactics for maintaining her own voice and form. She claims to make the stylistic changes he requests: "As *simple* as you please, the *simplest* sort of simple," she assures Austin; however, her deferrals proliferate the very elements she is promising to avoid: repetition, alliteration, metaphor, personification, and an inflated, indignant persona. What at first may appear to be a mere taunting invocation of the features he disapproves, turns more subtly aggressive with the phrase "a Bee in my Bonnet," which is clearly a trope of anger. It is most obviously a trivializing colloquialism that turns Austin's irritation with what he views as the unimportant obsessions of her letters into her resentment of his response; and it further suggests confined rage. By complying with Austin's strictures so vehemently, Dickinson manages to regain the ground she claims to be relinquishing—and then some. This becomes apparent when the silly string of self-deprecations is followed unexpectedly by a clause that shifts the tone from parody to gravity: "and what remains to do you shall be told hereafter."

The ominous tonal change is felt so strongly in this final line because it breaks the pattern in the rest of the paragraph of Dickinson responding to Austin's demands: I'll do this and I'll do that to placate you, the rest of the passage promises. Here, however, she finally tells Austin what *he* will do, in the end, to make reparations to her. The accompanying grammatical move from the active voice in the lines that describe what she will do to the passive voice in the clause that refers to Austin further undermines his authority. Even when she is supposedly submitting to his demands, she tells him what *she will do* to comply; he, on the other hand, *shall be told* what to do, a construction that at once inverts their power relations and strips him, grammatically, of his capacity to act. The passage ends on a note of warning that there will be some serious consequence for reducing her to a little ninny—if not an immediate one, then one in the "hereafter." Then, Austin shall be told his responsibilities, whether by divine authority (hinted at in the biblical tone of commandment) that will be revealed in the end or by Dickinson herself, empowered in the afterlife to delineate his responsibilities as he is attempting to define hers now. If the "hereafter" encompasses the "afterlife" of literary fame (as a poem like "[This is my letter to the World]" [P 440][6] depicts), then Dickinson has indeed had the last word on the subject of proper women's writing.

In 1862 Dickinson began a correspondence with Thomas Wentworth Higginson, a professional man of letters who would eventually become one of the editors of her posthumous *Poems.* On April 15 she sent him four poems and asked for his opinion and advice. Again, we can glean his attitude toward her writing from her side of the correspondence. A letter she wrote to Higginson on June 7, after she had received two replies from him, records her reaction to his comments on her poems and is reminiscent of her letters to Austin. Excessive compliance characterizes her response to his advice that she "delay 'to publish' ": "You think I am 'spasmodic'—I am in danger—Sir—You think me 'uncontrolled'—I have no Tribunal. Would you have time to be the 'friend' you should think I need? I have a little shape—it would not crowd your Desk—nor make much Racket as the Mouse—that dents your Galleries" (L 265). Like her earlier letter to Austin, this one to Higginson generates a proliferation of words ostensibly in order to enlist his aid in helping her *control* her language. To his complaint that her writing is spasmodic, she responds in disjointed prose that lurches after each dash. To his suggestion that her lines are uncontrolled, she responds with hyperbole, repetition, and the diminutive persona of the "little shape" (like Austin's little ninny) that is as tiny but also as persistent as a mouse. And again, the potential for harm is present in the apparently innocuous image, for that tiny mouse, like the bee in the bonnet, can "dent your Galleries" (can intrude upon and detract from publicly sanctioned art).

More to the point, that little shape on his desk is also the poem she has sent him, which crowds his desk with its importance (something he may miss), not its physical size. What she formulates to Austin as "now vs. hereafter," she reformulates to Higginson as "desk vs. gallery"; both oppositions imply that she envisions a level to which her writing might aspire—the realm of great art—that is beyond the reach of her immediate audience. Thus, while she cultivates their criticisms, she nevertheless sees beyond them, rendering acquiescence always an occasion for assertion. Where she assures Austin she will be as simple as he pleases, she says to Higginson "I have no Saxon, now—" later in this letter, meaning evidently that she has no words with which to thank him for his advice. Yet this claim is followed by a poem that describes in enormously exaggerated terms how greatly she treasures her new relationship with him:

> As if I asked a common Alms,
> And in my wondering hand
> A Stranger pressed a Kingdom,
> And I, bewildered, stand—
> As if I asked the Orient

> Had it for me a Morn—
> And it should lift it's purple Dikes,
> And shatter me with Dawn!
>   *(P 323, L 265)*

The poem figures Dickinson as a poor beggar who receives much more than what she asks for from Higginson, who is associated first with God (the stranger who offers her the kingdom [of heaven]) and then with the godlike East (who, personified as the Orient, gives her the dawn). His generosity is bewildering and shattering in the poem, as it is in the letter proper, where she says twice she is too overwhelmed with gratitude to thank him in words ("if I tried to thank you, my tears would block my tongue" and "The 'hand you stretch me in the Dark,' I put mine in, and turn away—I have no Saxon, now"). Yet the real extravagance in the poem is not his generosity but her gratitude for it.

That her appreciation for his attention to her poems leaves her feeling speechless—though, of course, she isn't—hints at a crucial aspect of their relationship. What she seems to need from Higginson is his capacity to check her words, or as she says in the letter, his criticisms "'twould be control, to me." In her April 25 letter, she had thanked Higginson for his response to the first four poems and indicated that she included others: "Thank you for the surgery—it was not so painful as I supposed. I bring you others—as you ask— though they might not differ" (L 261). His initial comments appear to have been fairly critical. However, his second response, referred to in Dickinson's letter of June 7, was apparently more complimentary. Dickinson distinguishes between the criticisms in his first letter and the praise in his second, and she is clearly more comfortable with criticism: "Your second letter surprised me, and for a moment, swung—I had not supposed it. Your first—gave no dishonor, because the True—are not ashamed—I thanked you for your justice . . . Perhaps the Balm, seemed better, because you bled me, first" (L 265). What she finds surprising and arresting about his second letter is its "balm"—its words of comfort and encouragement. (The phrase "for a moment, swung" calls up the image of the speaker, momentarily overcome by reading, holding the letter in her dropped hand, where it "swings" from her extended arm as though from a pendulum; "swung" also suggests that the speaker herself wavers when she reads the letter.) Yet she trusts the criticisms of his first letter more than the compliments of his second; to respond to flattery risks dishonor. Criticism is associated with truth and justice, praise with dishonor. Yet, she is able to take the balm of his good opinion because she had first taken the wound of his criticisms. The balm "seem[s] better" than praise would ordinarily seem for two reasons, captured in the phrase "because you bled me, first." His praise is acceptable, first, because he has won authority for his opinions by having initially criticized her and, second, because she has proven herself worthy of praise by accepting his criticism. "Bled" is a contradictory word for her contradictory responses, suggesting both a wound and an archaic (and ineffective) procedure for healing. The latter connotation captures the paradoxical quality of Higginson's advice: she seeks a literary relationship that will steady her, and his advice is sobering; yet she recognizes that his manner of reading is not especially relevant to her manner of writing; nevertheless, it serves. His very orthodoxy seems to provide a productive matrix for her decidedly unorthodox writings, both by compensation, offering a static environment for her volatile material, and by contrast, offering a standard that she rejects even while claiming to aspire toward it. A further aspect of this paradox is that Dickinson's espousals of compliance to Higginson's notion of proper writing are gainsaid by the very profusion of words that nevertheless articulates them.

Many readers of Dickinson's letters and poems have noticed similarities between the two genres. Much attention has been given to Dickinson's tendency to fall into metrical cadences in the letters that echo the measures of her poems. Likewise, every aspect of composition, from punctuation to grammatical compression to figurative language, argues that the letters are of a piece with the poems. This is especially true in what I am calling her poetics of excess.[7] An August 1862 letter to Higginson, which included two more poems, enacts the verbal escalations that typify Dickinson's writing process. I quote it in full to demonstrate the momentum that builds from a fairly well controlled opening toward an extremely chaotic ending, the same trajectory from stability to instability that many of her poems follow:

Dear friend—
Are these more orderly? I thank you for the Truth—
I had no Monarch in my life, and cannot rule myself, and when I try to organize—my little Force explodes—and leaves me bare and charred—

I think you called me "Wayward." Will you help me improve?

I suppose the pride that stops the Breath, in the Core of Woods, is not of Ourself—

You say I confess the little mistake, and omit the large—Because I can see Orthography—but the Ignorance out of sight—is my Preceptor's charge—

Of "shunning Men and Women"—they talk of Hallowed things, aloud—and embarrass my Dog—He and I dont object to them, if they'll exist their side. I think Carl[o] [her dog] would please you—He is dumb, and brave—I think you would like the Chestnut Tree, I met in my walk. It hit my notice suddenly—and I thought the Skies were in Blossom—

Then there's a noiseless noise in the Orchard—that I let persons hear— You told me in one letter, you could not come to see me, "now," and I made no answer, not because I had none, but did not think myself the price that you should come so far—

I do not ask so large a pleasure, lest you might deny me—

You say "Beyond your knowledge." You would not jest with me, because I believe you—but Preceptor—you cannot mean it? All men say "What" to me, but I thought it a fashion—

When much in the Woods as a little Girl, I was told that the Snake would bite me, that I might pick a poisonous flower, or Goblins kidnap me, but I went along and met no one but Angels, who were far shyer of me, than I could be of them, so I hav'nt that confidence in fraud which many exercise.

I shall observe your precept—though I dont understand it, always.

I marked a line in One Verse—because I met it after I made it—and never consciously touch a paint, mixed by another person—

I do not let go it, because it is mine.

Have you the portrait of Mrs. Browning? Persons sent me three—If you had none, will you have mine?

Your Scholar— (L 271)

This letter, like the other to Higginson, begins with simple assent and gratitude but almost immediately upsets this posture. The very gesture of acquiescence, perhaps because it is too extreme ("I thank you for the Truth"), may precipitate the eruptions of self-assertion that follow. Dickinson's response takes shape in the process of writing the letter, beginning at one extreme and escalating in a variety of ways to the other: the letter that begins submissively "Are these more orderly?" ends with a poem ("[I cannot dance upon my Toes]," P 326) that absolutely opposes Higginson's notion of order. This occurs, ironically, without negating his idea of order, but by elaborating it, embroidering his idea until it is lost amid her lavish figures and profuse meanings.

For example, the consenting tone of the opening question suggests that orderliness in poetry is something he can evaluate and she can aspire to. Yet this assumption must be reconsidered in the next paragraph where she says that her creative volatility cannot be controlled: "when I try to organize—my little Force explodes—and leaves me bare and charred." She similarly worries his idea of waywardness, and again raises the issue of order and disorder, when she recounts being a girl wandering in the woods; then, the warnings from others about the dangers of waywardness proved incorrect. By implication, Higginson's advice is fraudulent as well. In fact, she avoids fraud—redefined by the end of the letter to mean poor advice rather than the random evils she had been warned about—by following her own instincts in the woods, a fact that, in retrospect, bears upon her declaration of Higginson's "Truth" in the first paragraph of the letter.

Those woods, which figure forth and substantiate her poetic "location," are continuously elaborated in the letter. Indeed, she wanders in and out of them rhetorically, always returning to their mysterious depths as a haven from the crassness and shallowness of the conventional world. This rhetorical wandering, or in Higginson's terms waywardness, structures the opening paragraphs of the letter, where Dickinson shifts from confident acceptance of Higginson's views ("Are these more orderly? I thank you for the Truth"; "I think you called me 'Wayward.' Will you help me improve?"; "You say I confess the little mistake, and omit the large") to enigmatic proclamations about herself that invariably situate her in the woods ("the Core of the Woods," "the Chestnut Tree I met in my walk," "the Orchard," "the Woods") and back again. Midway through the letter, however, she stops this pacing from order to disorder and remains in the woods, as the letter spirals away from the simple acquiescence that opens it.

The woods here have something of the character of Dante's *selva oscura* or "dark wood" in Canto I of the *Inferno,* a place that embodies the obscurity of vision that the poet must overcome. However, only Higginson and the "Men and Women" Dickinson "shuns" experience the chaos and danger of the woods. In her first reference to the woods, she is breathless, but this seems to be the speechlessness and silence of awe rather than of fear: "I suppose the pride that stops the Breath, in the Core of Woods, is not of Ourself." The compressed syntax puts just the right pressure on this sentence. What takes her breath away in the deep of the woods is not pride of self but pride of forest; I deliberately retain the oddity of her locution in order to emphasize a fact that becomes obvious in the third reference to the woods: that the magical qualities of the woods somehow belong to Dickinson. She takes pride in the woods as she takes pride in herself.

Her second reference to the woods occurs in the paragraph explaining why she avoids others. Other people are crass; "they talk of Hallowed things, aloud." They are so vulgar, in fact, that they embarrass her dog. She and her dog are held in opposition to such people because they are "dumb," a homelier term for speechless or perhaps even breathless, and she welcomes Higginson into their superior, silent company: "I think Carl[o] would please you." Another of her silent companions might please him as well: "I think you would like the Chestnut Tree, I met in my walk. It hit my notice suddenly—and I thought the Skies were in Blossom." "Hit my notice" echoes the subtle violence of "stops the Breath" and suggests that the expressiveness of the woods, though wordless, is potent.

In the third reference to the woods, the breath that was taken away before becomes the voice of the orchard—and Dickinson herself now assumes possession of it: "there's a noiseless noise in the Orchard—that *I let* persons hear." The insistent retreat to the wonder of the woods has been a constant return to her own "core." The oxymoron "noiseless noise" suggests the paradox of Dickinson's voice that is at once heard and unheard, at once, therefore, breathtaking and breathless. Finally, the woods motif erupts once more as an allegory of Dickinson's decision to follow her own course despite the warnings of others—and not just of the common men and women she shuns in Amherst but God (the snake suggests the Garden of Eden), Tennyson (the poisonous flower suggests the lotos-eaters), and even fellow women poets (the goblin suggests Christina Rossetti's famous poem).[8] What Dickinson discovers in the woods is authorization for her own waywardness, solitude, instincts, and impulses. Moreover, nature speaks through her because of her special affinities with it: the noiseless noise of the orchard is made audible by her.

The recurring and developing figure of the woods, then, is just one of several ways the letter responds to Higginson's notion of order and embellishes it. There is a great deal more to say about this letter, her usurpation of Higginson's voice ("I think you called me," "You say," "You told me," and perhaps even her signature "Your Scholar") and her verbal jabs ("I think Carlo would please you—He is dumb"), for example. But one of the most significant passages in the letter concerns writing poetry like others do. She says that she crossed out a line of her own verse because she read it, after she had written it, in someone else's work. Her line is initially disqualified by being like someone else's. Yet, she retains it nevertheless and claims it: "because it is mine." This paradoxical relationship between how she writes and how others write is surely related to her discussion with Higginson about how she *should* write. Further, the question of literary originality and influence introduces "Mrs. Browning"—as though Dickinson is marshaling her own poetic models (we know that she admired and wanted to emulate Barrett Browning).[9] The association between Dickinson and Barrett Browning is reiterated subtly when she asks if he has a portrait of Mrs. Browning. She offers, "If you had none [no picture of Barrett Browning], will you have mine?" Certainly, she is offering him one of her three portraits of the famous poet; yet the structure of the sentence, "will you have *mine*," teases us with another meaning. If you have no picture of Mrs. Browning, will you have one of mine, will you have one of *me*? I am not suggesting that Dickinson is actually offering Higginson her portrait. In fact, he had asked for her photograph, but she claimed not to have one (L 268; Sewall 556). I am suggesting that the ambiguous reference to "mine" momentarily associates the two women writers and hints at the level of artistic company Dickinson expects to keep. Despite clear indications in this letter that Dickinson knows she doesn't need Higginson's technical advice, she is sincere when she says to him, "I shall observe your precept," though for her to "observe" will be not merely to follow but to examine.

The poem enclosed with it is a good bit clearer than the letter and provides just such an examination of Higginson's advice that she be more orderly. Several readers have analyzed its relationship to the letter and its place in Dickinson's correspondence with Higginson. Sewall summarizes the best of this work when he points out that the poem at once asserts that she cannot possibly follow his prescriptions for writing and also registers scorn for the type of poetry he values (559–60):

> I cannot dance upon my Toes—
> No Man instructed me—
> But oftentimes, among my mind
> A Glee possesseth me
> That had I Ballet—Knowledge—
> Would put itself abroad
> In Pirouette to blanch a Troupe—
> Or lay a Prima—mad—
> And though I had no Gown of Gauze—
> No Ringlet, to my Hair,
> Nor hopped to Audiences—like Birds,
> One Claw upon the Air—
> Nor tossed my shape in Eider Balls,
> Nor rolled on Wheels of Snow
> Till I was out of sight in sound
> The House encore me so—
>
> Nor any know I know the Art
> I mention—easy—Here—
> Nor any Placard boast me
> It's full as Opera—
>   (L 271, P 326)[10]

The poem equates the sort of poetry Higginson "instructs" her to write with the ballerina's dance, which is depicted as hopelessly artificial and clownish. The ballerina is no more than her costume, the gauze gown, feather ornaments, and contrived curls, and her movements are mechanical at best ("rolled on Wheels of Snow") and awkward ("One Claw upon the Air").

The poem also looks dimly on the dancer's relationship to her audience, first in the picture of her hopping and tossing herself about the stage for their sakes and second in the curious lines about the ballerina's encore. Imagining herself the ballerina, she says she would dance "Till I was out of sight in sound— / The House encore me so—." These lines reverse the normal order of events: an encore is the demand by an audience, usually through a continuing round of applause, for another performance. It occurs, of course, at the end of the scheduled performance when the dancer has left the stage.

That is, an encore is the sound that brings the artist back into sight. Here, however, Dickinson suggests that the claims of an audience will push her "out of sight," that their very desire to see her will in fact obliterate her. As a response to Higginson, the poem suggests that writing to please an audience will only render her invisible.

This poem is set in motion by what I am calling her poetics of excess because she enters into dialogue with Higginson in order to sustain herself against his criticisms. She does not merely reject his views; indeed, she probes them in order to master them. She personifies his poetics as the ballerina, inhabits them, and then enacts them in the extreme to examine their merits. Like Hester Prynne's fantastic flourishes of red and gold that bring to life the lurid connotations of the "A" only to control and dispel them, Dickinson's speaker takes on the gauze and ringlets of the ballerina and then dances with a vengeance to prevent herself from actually becoming the ballerina. Such an excessive dance does not imitate or perpetuate the norm; rather, it destroys conventional ballet. The speaker's devastating dance would be a "Pirouette to blanch a Troupe— / Or lay a Prima—mad."

Other letters support these in documenting Dickinson's insistence on writing as she pleases. In one to Austin from 1853, she describes Edward Dickinson's response to a letter she had written her brother, "Father was very severe to me; he thought I'd been trifling with you, so he gave me quite a trimming about . . . 'modern Literati' " (L 113). Yet her father's low opinion of her writing style causes her, ironically, to have a high opinion of herself, a response she claims to have learned from her brother: "I'm quite in disgrace at present, but I think of that 'pinnacle' on which you always mount, when anybody insults you, and that's quite a comfort to me" (L 113).[11] Similarly, when she senses that Higginson may think her ridiculous, she says with the confidence that has its sights set on larger matters, "Perhaps you smile at me. I could not stop for that—My Business is Circumference" (L 268).

While these letters reveal her dedication to writing according to her own genius, they also express the importance to her of establishing a relationship with an audience. Oddly, it is in opposing their prescriptions for her writing that her unique style takes its fullest shape. Under the weight of custom and of female propriety, yet still in that context, Dickinson's poetics harden like a diamond under pressure. She clearly recognized the necessity of writing in relation to others—even, or especially, those who opposed her.

Dickinson had several more affirming readers who did not oppose her notions of writing—all of whom were women. Her friend and sister-in-law Susan Gilbert Dickinson recognized Dickinson's talent early on, at least as early as 1861, when she and Dickinson had a lively exchange of letters about "[Safe in their Alabaster Chambers—]" (P 216), and perhaps as early as 1853, when Dickinson sent Sue one of her first poems (L 105); Helen Hunt Jackson and Mabel Loomis Todd both expressed unqualified enthusiasm when they read the poems much later (Sewall 217). Jackson strongly encouraged Dickinson's writing and tried indefatigably to convince her to publish her poems (Sewall 577–92; L 444a, L 573a). She was perhaps the only person who gave Dickinson her unconditional approval, "You are a great poet," and yet Dickinson remained unresponsive to her praise (L 444a). Todd was equally impressed with Dickinson's poems, "They are full of power," she wrote in her diary and certainly conveyed that judgment to Dickinson (Sewall 217). She later proved her dedication to Dickinson's writing by becoming the poet's first transcriber and editor. Sue read and commented on at least some of the poems, and Dickinson revised her work with Sue's criticisms in mind (Sewall 201; L 238). Though the literary relationship with Sue was more complicated than those Dickinson held with Helen Hunt Jackson and Mabel Loomis Todd, since Sue offered criticism as well as praise, all three friends took Dickinson to be an accomplished poet, whose style, though strange, was remarkable and proved its own authority.

Betsy Erkkila has recently argued the importance of Dickinson's literary relationship with Susan: "As the recipient of at least 276 of Dickinson's poems, Sue served over many years as the primary audience for Dickinson's work. She was the subject of several poems and the inspiration for many more, perhaps even some of the marriage poems that appear to be addressed to men" (*Wicked Sisters* 39). If Erkkila is correct in her estimation of Sue's role in Dickinson's writing life, then it is because Sue was what Erkkila terms a "wicked sister," a literary protégé whose friendship constituted "a site of dissension, contingency, and ongoing struggle rather than a separate space of some untroubled and essentially cooperative accord among women" (4)—that is, because Sue offered some form of opposition.

Yet, however much Dickinson's women friends encouraged her writing, the record suggests that Dickinson was not ignited by their positive responses as she was by the far more negative comments of Austin, Higginson, and perhaps Samuel Bowles. My argument is not that Dickinson pandered to men but that her literary relationship with hostile readers reproduced her poetic relationship to language in ways that were powerfully productive for her.[12]

Perhaps the double edge of writing poetry—the fact that the poet is at once invincible ("Exterior—to Time" [P 448]) and vulnerable (she may "stun" herself "With Bolts of Melody!" [P 505])—found its apt reflection in the contradictory relationship to an audience that answered expression with suppression. Having withstood her own poems' threat to annihilate her as she wrote them, it is not surprising that she also survived, even cultivated, a repressive audience. And, moreover, the risks that she ran in both ventures seem to have inspired and vitalized her.

These letters therefore dramatize the development of Dickinson's poetics of excess because they duplicate, in the ambivalent association with her readers, that troubled relation to her own writing. In both the correspondence to Austin and Higginson and in her poetry, Dickinson cultivated those conditions under which her "little Force" would most certainly explode. Thus she writes to Austin in a style that is rich with figurative language, literary allusions, shifting personae, elaborate descriptions, humorous narratives, and complex wordplay. He tells her to write in a simpler style. And she responds in a style that not only repeats her original "errors" but now intensifies, redoubles, italicizes, and extends them—and all this to say of course she will comply. The letters to Higginson illustrate the emergence of Dickinson's poetics of excess even more explicitly since her poetry is the subject of their correspondence. Dickinson responded to Higginson's criticisms of her writing just as she did with Austin: she vows to heed his suggestions but in a manner that recreates and reasserts the original style even more emphatically than before.

There are a number of things about Dickinson's poetics that we can draw out of the recurring rhetorical maneuvers that characterize the letters. First, her poetics respond to the nineteenth-century model of sexual difference, with its low expectation of women's writing. The letters about writing typically exaggerate the manner and degree of her complicity with the received tradition of sexual difference, and in obeying with vehement irony she at once undermines the established codes for femininity and creates a space for her sometimes wildly original projects. Second, the constraints of sexual difference seem to have provided a powerful analogy to her experience of language's doubleness, with its contradictory ability to produce poetry yet threaten to annihilate the poet. Third, perhaps because the poetics crystallize *in response* to these pressures, she often depicts their emergence in the process of the poem, enacting the development of her peculiar style rather than merely employing it as later practitioners of excess will do. Thus, we see her poetic devices intensify and escalate in the course of a poem or letter as they respond to her readers' hostilities and to language's destructive potential. And finally, it is at the surface of the poetry that this struggle for self-assertion is fought, where the stylistic features of her writing marshal to the defense of her voice. These escalations are most readily apparent at the surface, or stylistic, level of the poem since it is at that level that the materiality of language is at least momentarily grasped.

Dickinson's confession to Higginson, "when I try to organize— my little Force explodes," abbreviates, I believe, the whole process of her poetics. For her, poetry is by no means emotion recollected in tranquillity. In fact, quite the contrary, the process of writing the poem itself generates emotion because composition puts her under particular pressures, as we have seen. Since writing poetry engages Dickinson in a contest with language, the poems typically juggle two themes: the ostensible subject of the poem and the difficulties of articulating that subject. David Porter mentions two features of Dickinson's poetry that bear upon what I am calling her poetics of enactment; first, he shows that her poems often open with two strong lines and then slacken or become repetitious, and second, he notes that a state of aftermath recurs in her poems (89–94). Porter's observations suggest a poetics of enactment. That Dickinson's emphatic, succinct first two lines invariably introduce a poem that seems less controlled by comparison illustrates her own sense that when she begins to compose something (when she tries to organize), her poetic language reacts with devastating vigor (her little force explodes). Further, the poem expresses and incorporates its own crisis; thus, it often depicts a state of aftermath as a dwelling place for the speaker who survives this crisis of composition.

Perhaps Dickinson never wrote a poetic treatise because her poetics take shape in the course of her poems and are formulated only as they are enacted. Responding to her position as a woman poet in a male-dominated culture and to her experience of the treacheries of language (indeed, she may have considered these obstacles to be related), she develops a poetics of excess as a spontaneous reaction to the forces that threaten to silence her. This attitude informs her sense of the subversive power of her own poetry, which she figures as "A still—Volcano—Life—" with "A quiet—Earthquake Style—" that will blind and destroy if it is ever heard: "The lips that never lie—/ Whose hissing Corals part—and shut— / And Cities—ooze away—" (P 601). Poetry is repeatedly figured as a devastating natural force:

> To pile like Thunder to it's close
> Then crumble grand away
> While Everything created hid
> This—would be Poetry—
>> (P 1247)

Here again, poetry terrifies and intimidates its listeners, who hide from its thunderous voice. Moreover, in the description of the *process* of the thunder—an initial frightening clap succeeded by a gradual recession of sound—we can recognize the poetic structure identified by Porter: emphatic assertion followed by formal disintegration. Yet terms like "crumble" and "disintegration" can distract us from the potency of this metaphor. For while poetry is compared to thunder, whose might is transitory, thunder, in turn, is compared to stone: it first resounds like stones being violently heaped together (as in the spewings of volcanoes or the glacial formation of mountains), and then it recedes, not weakly but grandly, like the centuries-long crumbling away of the mountains. This poem describes poetry as something that builds throughout the course of its own coming into being and then diminishes. It sketches the shape of a poem that enacts its crisis through a poetics of excess (to pile like thunder) and then incorporates that crisis into its structure in order to contain it (then crumbles grand away).

In the letters to Austin and Higginson I have already discussed and in many of her poems, Dickinson records her poetic process, but by enacting it rather than by describing it. By this I mean, as I have mentioned above, that the poetics of excess become the poem's own volition against the countercurrents that threaten it, as Dickinson's peculiar stylistic features proliferate, carrying the poem forward against the resistances of her readers and of language itself.

"[It would never be Common—more—I said—]" (P 430) enacts the emergence of Dickinson's poetics. It takes up her original decision to be a poet, the ensuing tension between, on one level, her poetry and her audience, and, on another level, herself and language, and the resulting necessity of intensifying her style as a means of preserving it:

It would never be Common—more—I said—
Difference—had begun—
Many a bitterness—had been—
But that old sort—was done—

Or—if it sometime—showed—as 'twill—
Upon the Downiest—Morn—
Such bliss—had I—for all the years—
'Twould give an Easier—pain

I'd so much joy—I told it—Red—
Upon my simple Cheek—
I felt it publish—in my Eye—
'Twas needless—any speak—

I walked—as wings—my body bore—
The feet—I former used—
Unnecessary—now to me—
As boots—would be—to Birds—

I put my pleasure all abroad—
I dealt a word of Gold
To every Creature—that I met—
And Dowered—all the World—

When—suddenly—my Riches shrank—
A Goblin—drank my Dew—
My Palaces—dropped tenantless—
Myself—was beggared—too—

I clutched at sounds—
I groped at shapes—
I touched the tops of Films—
I felt the Wilderness roll back
Along my Golden lines—

The Sackcloth—hangs upon the nail—
The Frock I used to wear—
But where my moment of Brocade—
My—drop—of India?

"[It would never be Common]" casts the act of composition in narrative form in order to use the passage of time as a metaphor for process. That time relations are distorted throughout the poem (the shifting tenses, the expansion and contraction of moments unrelated to their duration in real time, the changing perception of duration), however, points up the fact that this process is being enacted in the poem rather than being described after its completion, and therefore that the parts of the process are not predictable and cannot be fixed.

The poem begins with Dickinson's trademark decisiveness; the first two lines assert emphatically that something has changed. Just as typically, though, *what* has changed is referred to only by "it," a pronoun with no referent here since it initiates the poem. Ordinarily, reference presupposes antecedence, a past or earlier time. But in a certain sense, there is no past time for this "it" because it *is* the inaugural moment of the poem. Thus the lack of a referent for the opening pronoun, like the ambiguous time frame, makes of the poem a process rather than a description or definition, since the poem can only be understood in its own movement not in its reference to some antecedent event or subject. Moreover, the first two lines are qualified by the fact that they are spoken, "It would never be Common—more— *I said,*" and for all their tone of ratification have only the authority of the speaker's declaration (that is, of someone mired in the process), not the poem's. Significantly, this is one of the only places in the poem where the speaker actually *speaks;* until the last stanza, she will act. That the opening lines are only direct quotation, and therefore carry the emphasis of declaration without the conclusiveness of fact, becomes evident quickly, when the commonness and bitterness that are banished with the pronouncements of stanza one return with the equivocal "or" of stanza two: "Or—if it sometime—showed." This fluctuating voice of certainty and uncertainty characterizes the prevailing tone of the poem. "[It would never be Common]" is an effort to articulate Difference rather than being a poem about Difference. Difference as a state of being is not contested in the poem; indeed, at least three stanzas are given over to descriptions of it. It is the process of expressing Difference, putting it into words, that is threatened by the action of the poem. The poem enacts the problems of speaking Difference, the risks of doing so, and finally the refusal to speak otherwise.

Here, as elsewhere, Dickinson's notion of difference is difficult to gloss. Like other crucial terms that comprise her theory of poetic language, her treatment of difference is contradictory and paradoxical because language itself is, especially such abstract language. But at least two aspects of difference can be understood from several other poems that employ the word. First, it is quite literally the distinction between herself and other people, a distinction that rests on her poetic gift (sometimes imagined as the capacity to be poetic, sometimes merely as the ability to apprehend the poetic). Difference separates her from others:

> It was given to me by the Gods—
> When I was a little Girl—
> They give us Presents most—you know—
> When we are new—and small.
> I kept it in my Hand—
> I never put it down—
> I did not dare to eat—or sleep—
> For fear it would be gone—
> I heard such words as "Rich"—
> When hurrying to school—
> From lips at Corners of the Streets—
> And wrestled with a smile.
> Rich! 'Twas Myself—was rich—
> To take the name of Gold—
> And Gold to own—in solid Bars—
> The Difference—made me bold—
>
> (P 454)

This speaker seems to have been born different, for an unspecified "it" was given to her by the gods when she was "new" and "small." She has apparently entered the world with a sense of difference that she has carefully protected, unlike the rest of us ("us," "we") who forget or lose such a birthright. The riddle of this poem is that the thing that makes her different from others is difference itself: *it* (the gift) is difference (which makes her bold enough to resist being like others). She is not tempted by the riches of the world because she recognizes her own interior wealth: "Rich!" she snorts, scoffing at the tempters, " 'Twas Myself—was rich."

In other poems, difference is gained from experience rather than received involuntarily as a gift:

Between the form of Life and Life
The difference is as big
As Liquor at the Lip between
And Liquor in the Jug
The latter—excellent to keep—
But for extatic need
The corkless is superior—
I know for I have tried (P 1101)

Oh Sumptuous moment
Slower go
That I may gloat on thee—
'Twill never be the same to starve
Now I abundance see—

Which was to famish, then or now—
The difference of a Day
Ask him unto the Gallows led—
With morning in the sky.
(P 1125)

What makes her idea of difference more than just a claim of privilege for the artistic personality is that the distinction between the speaker and others occurs in language. In these poems, difference emerges in competing definitions of things, as she says in another poem, it is "internal difference, / Where the Meanings, are" (P 258). She is different from others in how she uses language, in what words mean to her. Consequently, the distinction between the meanings of "the form of Life and Life" is discovered in the comparison between experiencing life and not experiencing it (between uncorked liquor that one has actually tasted and "Liquor in the Jug" that one has only imagined)—and she is the one who has this experience. Likewise, her definition of abundance undergoes revision once she experiences what it is to starve, just as the condemned man's definition of day can only be formulated on his last day.

The paradox of difference is that it begins in language but, once apprehended there, extends to life. The speaker in "[It was given to me by the Gods—]" draws these complicated distinctions: the people on street corners offer her richness, but she knows that she already is inwardly rich. One distinction she draws is that between taking the name of Gold and owning gold, presumably, that is, between being rich in her person and being merely materially wealthy. She does not need to own gold because she is Gold. Yet, the same lines that make that distinction also support the reading that being rich in her person is like owning material wealth, is, in fact, finally indistinguishable from it. The repetitions of "rich" and "gold" bear hearing again because they capture the paradox of difference:

> I heard such words as "Rich"— . . .
> Rich! 'Twas Myself—was rich—
> To take the name of Gold—
> And Gold to own—in solid Bars—
> The Difference—made me bold.

Given "[Between the form of Life and Life]" and "[Oh Sumptuous moment]," which associate difference with experience, we might read these last lines of "[It was given to me by the Gods]" to say that the hawkers on the street merely "take the name of Gold," while the speaker herself actually has "Gold to own." On the other hand, perhaps the name Gold is richer than the bars of gold. These distinctions reside uneasily together; we are not able to sort them out, yet we recognize that an important difference exists between the "Rich" derided in quotation marks and the speaker's claim to be rich. A third reading of these lines appropriates all forms of wealth to the speaker's difference: she is rich enough to take the name of Gold *and* to own gold in solid bars. In fact, the golden bars, like the golden lines in "[It would never be Common]," may be the bars of her song or the lines of her verse.

The fact that difference is played out in language bears upon its second feature. Difference marks a moment of abundance that is frequently traced through a moment of loss. As such, the experience of difference replicates her paradoxical experience of language that is at once inspiring (permitting her to create herself in words) and annihilating (threatening to destroy her with its unstable ability to represent). Thus, the richness given her by the gods constantly threatens to disappear either by her own growth into adulthood ("They give us Presents most . . . When we are new—and small") or by some unnamed treachery ("I never put it down . . . For fear it would be gone"). Finally, even when her definitions of words are not being threatened, she recognizes that they will always be contradicted. She and others will never agree on the meanings of words. Sometimes this will merely be isolating; sometimes, however, it will be devastating to her. Difference, then, registers meaning by articulating the traces of fullness in loss, presence in absence, poetic meaning in unpoetic meaning.[13]

The equivocations in the first two stanzas of "[It would never be Common]" are a result of difference and help in understanding the poem's larger movements. There is assertion, contradiction, and reassertion throughout, but none of these states holds final sway. The truth, like the referent for the opening "it," remains somewhere beyond the poem, not fully articulated by the poem, and it is the process of surviving these contradictions that the poem traces. The shifting focus of time in the first two stanzas suggests that time expands and contracts under the pressure of trying to narrate it from within. In stanza one Difference has just begun; the immediacy of the verb captures the sense of new resolve that the speaker wants to celebrate. In stanza two, however, Difference has supplied bliss "for all the years"—enough years in fact to assuage the bitterness that still shows itself sometimes. Nearly half the poem is dominated by Difference, yet the final stanza recalls it only as lasting a "moment." Time throughout the poem seems associated with presence rather than with duration. Wherever the speaker is, in the process of enacting Difference, is substantiated by prolonging it in time.

The status of Difference is ambiguous in the first two stanzas also. At first the speaker seems to feel that Difference eradicates the Common: "It would never be Common—more—I said— / Difference— had begun." Compression here contributes to the line's possibilities. It might be saying that "it would never be common *any more* because difference had begun" or merely that "I said it would never be common and, *moreover,* I said that difference had begun." In either case, as I have mentioned, this is the speaker's claim, not the poem's, but one still wants to know whether there is a causal relationship between the onset of Difference and the demise of the Common. The speaker then says that many bitternesses *had been*— the past perfect verb allowing the bitterness to have existed before Difference or to coexist with it, since Difference occurs in the past perfect also. Yet the verb tenses are not exactly the same since "had been" indicates an action or state completely contained within the past while "had begun" refers to one that continues from the past into the present. In any case, though many bitternesses did exist or do exist, an old sort of bitterness seems not to exist any more: "But that old sort—was done." This certainty, however, lasts only until the stanza break, after which the next stanza begins with the "Or" that will qualify the opening assertions. Even the old sort of bitterness sometimes still returns; however, the bliss—which may emanate from Difference or, paradoxically, from the Common—eases the pain of the return of the old bitterness. It is the confusing verb tense again that makes the source of bliss ambiguous. All those years of bliss that make bitterness bearable now ironically may have been the years of living in Commonness, that is, in a kind of blissful ignorance of Difference. The years of easy ignorance may have strengthened her for the more difficult experiences of Difference to come. Or the period of Difference may be so intense that the speaker describes it as lasting many years as a way of evoking its momentousness. In this case, Difference itself, which seems to have lasted forever, enables the speaker to withstand the intrusion of the old sort of bitterness associated with the Common.

Another close look at the line, not surprisingly, creates new problems in understanding the relationship of the Common to Difference, for it simply says, "Such bliss—had I—for all the years," and may not even mean "all those years of bliss." It may easily suggest that the bliss is a compensation *for* all the years of commonness and bitterness. Supporting this reading is the conditional " 'twould" which makes possible a different relationship between bliss and years, one that is compensatory rather than objective.

One cannot finally separate the boundaries of Commonness and Difference in the first two stanzas; each seems to intrude upon, perhaps even to contain, the other. Certainly the speaker claims to reject the Common, but the poem itself reveals how difficult this is to do. Nevertheless, by the third stanza the speaker is released from the struggle to separate Difference from the Common temporarily and inhabits Difference—at least briefly.

The most significant aspect of this new state is its jarring descriptions of language. Synaesthetic imagery is employed to wrest verbal authority from speech and give it over to writing. It is the blush on her cheek that "told" and the look in her eye that "publish[ed]" joy. The joy is emphatically verbal (*told*) and textual (*publish*), yet the organs for the production of these verbal and textual utterances are visual and tactile rather than vocal. It is the body that speaks here— the blushing cheek and the glint in the eye—not the voice. And the body's expression is adequate, we know, since " 'Twas needless— any speak—." But the opposition between speaking with the voice and publishing with the body is figurative, after all, and not simply meant to suggest an opposition between speaking and writing. What is actually being described here is neither speech nor writing but something that precedes both: poetic feeling or sensation. The verbal and textual metaphors anticipate the fact that this moment of poetic feeling will soon overflow, or to use Dickinson's word—explode— into poetic discourse. The polarity, we must recall, is between the Common and Difference, a distinction Dickinson elsewhere refers to as that between prose and poetry:

> They shut me up in Prose—
> As when a little Girl
> They put me in the Closet—
> Because they like me "still"—
> (P 613)

Like the prose/poetry dichotomy here or the term/golden word distinction elsewhere, the Common/Difference distinction does not refer to material differences in language. What "prose," "terms," and the "common" share is not a particular vocabulary, subject, or form; rather, they are similar in that they use language in such a way that denies the poetic, limits the meaning, and asserts the predictable and acceptable in language. The synaesthetic production of language is a trope for the speaker's entirely new relation to her own poetic vision, which she has already begun to imagine as poetic discourse.[14]

The synaesthesia that transforms language production in stanza three generates poetic production in stanza four, as traditional metrics ("The feet—I former used—") are superseded by the measure of the speaker's "feet" as she moves through this new terrain of Difference ("I walked—as wings—my body bore—"). Like the voice that need no longer speak in stanza three, the former feet are rendered "Unnecessary—now," and, even more significant, inappropriate and restrictive, "As boots—would be—to Birds—." Yet, once again, it is important to remind ourselves that the superficial opposition "former feet" and "I walked"—that is, quite literally Common Meter versus her own measure—is not exactly the point. The entire stanza, like most of the poem, is written in perfect iambic feet: the Common and Difference appear very much the same here. It is not so much the measure of a line that matters as how the speaker inhabits that measure. In this case, while the meter of the lines remains identical, the former feet plod out the pattern while the new measure glides through it. Alliteration, another self-consciously poetical device, further stresses the superficial similarity of the Common and Difference. The first and third lines that describe the speaker's new poetics alliterate *w, b,* and *n* ("I walked—as wings—my body bore—" and "Unnecessary—now to me—") while the second and fourth lines that refer to the old style alliterate *f* and *b* ("The feet—I former used—" and "As boots—would be—to Birds—"). At the same time, the interwoven alternations of the Common (the *a* and *c* lines) and Difference (the *b* and *d* lines), along with the imperfect rhyme "used/Birds" (in a poem that employs perfect rhyme much of the time) subtly hint at the dissimilarities beneath the surfaces of apparently similar poetic productions. Dickinson has given substance to Emerson's celebrated but finally vague claim that "it is not metres, but a metre-making argument that makes a poem" (200).

In the fifth stanza (the third devoted to Difference) it becomes clear that the experience of joy the speaker feels in this state is coextensive with the expression of that joy. Again the traditional devices of poetry—alliteration and iambic meter—combine with the revisionary elements of synaesthetic and tactile imagery to convey an Adamic vision of the speaker "put[ting] . . . pleasure all abroad—" and "deal[ing] . . . word[s] of Gold" to every creature she meets. Stability, coherence, and control characterize these three stanzas: they tell the untroubled story of the speaker dwelling in Difference. The very elements that were dislodged and contradictory in the first two stanzas—tense and time—are restored here by the coherent narrative that naturalizes time and subjectivity.

The sense of elation that the speaker experiences in Difference culminates in stanza six, where she envisions herself in an Adamic role, but using her new relation to language not to name creatures (as Adam did when he acquired language) but to give them each "a word of Gold." Cris Miller's argument that Dickinson's phrase "golden words" refers not to particular words but to the possibility of any word to articulate personal meaning is consistent with my claim that "[It would never be Common]" reveals the process of how prosaic language is poeticized ("Terms and Golden Words"). The tactile imagery for expression dominates here as the speaker "puts" pleasure abroad by "dealing" out words. The primary connotation of "dealt" appears to be governed by "put," both words suggesting something distributed by hand.[15] This picture of the speaker giving out golden words to every creature bears upon her use of the word "dowered" in the fourth line of the stanza. Both elements depict the speaker's benevolent relation to the world. Significantly, Difference does not rarefy the speaker's language, removing her from the common world, but enables her to bestow her words on it. In "dowered" the images of the speaker's beneficence, her relationship with others, and her power to create meaning coalesce in the vision of her as the bride of the world whose dower is her wealth of golden words. Crucial here is the way the poem imagines this poetic language to bring the speaker into a closer relation to the world. When this relationship is severed in the next stanza, it must be understood that Difference has not separated the speaker from others. Her connection to them is broken only when Difference comes under assault.

The sudden change of state in stanza six is reminiscent of the abrupt move into Difference that opens the poem: "When—suddenly —my Riches shrank—." "Riches," of course, refers to the golden words with which she had endowed the world in the previous stanza. Thus, the first thing affected by this new turn of events is the language of Difference. That the agent of this disaster is merely a goblin— that is, a malicious yet still diminutive figure[16]—underscores the vulnerability of the speaker and the uncertainty of maintaining the state of Difference. Further, the goblin does not directly attack her riches but drinks "the Dew" that apparently nourishes them. The goblin, recalling at first the puny malevolence of Austin, Higginson, and Edward Dickinson, destroys her riches indirectly by sapping her own vital source. The dew he drinks, of course, suggests the necessary liquid of life but also points toward the "drop of India" at the end of the poem. Thus the dew concerns both her general vitality—as the water that sustains living things—and, we recognize eventually, her poetic life—as the ink of writing.

Further, there is something nagging about the choice of the word "goblin" that suggests an inner demon, a form of self-doubt, perhaps about the validity of this new poetic discourse. When, in the next line, her "Palaces—dropped tenantless—" it becomes clear that the loss of the new language severs her from others and, more important, denies her own poetic vision. The palaces, edifices reared by the poetic imagination (as in Coleridge's "Kubla Khan"), are now tenant-less because her imagination has ceased to "people" them with its own creations.[17] The line indicates a failure of poetic imagination, of the capacity to project a vision, as a result of self-doubt. That doubt, we recall from the letters, has its external as well as internal sources, and the goblin provides a figure of both. Bereft of these riches, she can no longer even endow herself in the fourth line: "Myself— was beggared—too—." The grammatical uneasiness caused by sub-stituting "myself" for "I" enhances the tension between external and internal doubts. It suggests not merely that "*I* was beggared," but worse, that "My *self* was beggared, *too*"—that in losing her riches she has lost her self. Further, the reflexive pronoun standing in the nominative position confounds the causal relationships and hints at the speaker's dual role in this crisis, as object and subject. The sudden diminution of her (verbal) resources results in linguistic con-fusion and double meanings: substituting the reflexive pronoun for the personal pronoun renders the speaker the object of the action as well as the subject. In this grammatical environment, "was beggared" functions doubly as a passive verb (the speaker was impoverished by the goblin) and a predicate complement (the speaker describes herself as impoverished). These grammatical compressions create a verbal crisis that is itself a representation of the speaker's poetic crisis, with its external and internal sources.

In the next stanza, the loss of Difference has even more dramatic effects on the speaker's language. Several critics have read this stanza as representing the loss of language—an inevitable risk one runs in choosing to use poetic rather than "common" language. In this read-ing, the wilderness that overruns the edenic world of the preceding stanzas is associated with silence, or, as Cris Miller says, with "broken language." Miller concludes, "to avoid all referential language is to have no control, no point of stability in language. Absolute control is false control, and the sacrifice of absolute for a partial or temporary control is dangerous because it may fail. To regard experience as imminently interpretable or meaning as ultimately open involves risk. Doing so, at its best, brings the ecstasy of perfect exchanges . . . but it may bring 'Wilderness' as well" (59).

While Miller offers a valuable interpretation of this difficult stanza, thinking of the poem as discovering its own poetics as it writes itself—that is, as an example of the poetics of enactment—brings us to these lines in a different way. Neither silence nor chaos adequately accounts for this stanza:

> I clutched at sounds—
> I groped at shapes—
> I touched the tops of Films—
> I felt the Wilderness roll back
> Along my Golden lines—

This five-line stanza is the only one in the poem that exceeds the quatrain pattern. Much like the response we saw in the letters, while her riches shrink in one sense, they swell in another as she "mounts to the pinnacle" (L 113) when under attack. At the very least, adding more words in an extra line is an unlikely way to represent silence. Of course, this is the "crisis" stanza and the extra lines work to slow the poem down; they are shorter than the lines in the quatrain stanzas and give a halting feeling. Yet while in the first two lines she will "clutch" and "grope," perhaps chaotically, at what appears to be "broken language," (the sounds and shapes of words), in the end she "touche[s] the tops of Films," a line that recuperates the alliteration (sound) as well as the image of her tactile relation to language (shapes) that we recognize as features of the revisionary poetics elaborated earlier in the poem. Likewise, the metrical staggering back of the first two lines, both dimeter, is restored to balance in the last three lines, which alternate, as though restoring the hymn stanza, trimeter, tetrameter, trimeter. And even the end rhyme is reasserted in "Films" and "lines." Thus, while stanza seven depicts the speaker clutching and groping for language, it also finds her touching and feeling something in a way that seems to connect her with Difference once more.

Most interesting, however, and most enigmatic is the image of touching the tops of films, an action that may cause the rolling back of wilderness that follows. "Touched" achieves an effectiveness of action that "clutched" and "groped" deny, yet it also suggests contact with the surface of something rather than the penetration or actual grasping of it. "Tops" and "Films," similarly, push the level of contact to the exterior. To touch the tops of films, which are already themselves the tops of something, is to locate oneself at an extreme surface. In other poems that employ the image of the film, this surface is where one world ends and another begins, typically where mortality and immortality divide. Lines like "And when the Film had stitched your eyes" (P 414) and "The Film upon the eye / Mortality's old Custom— / Just locking up—to Die" (P 479) associate a film on the eye with death, while "The brave eyes film" (P 253), "I helped his Film" (P 616), and "The other film / That glazes Holiday" (P 504) invoke the image to suggest illness and loss. Interestingly, though, while "film" describes a barrier between herself and other people (isolation, illness, and death), it suggests an entirely different relationship between the elements it divides when it refers to language. "[The thought beneath so slight a film-]" (P 210) can be read as a statement about language as a layer that enhances rather than obscures thought:

> The thought beneath so slight a film—
> Is more distinctly seen—
> As laces just reveal the surge—
> Or Mists—the Apennine—

In this case, the film is clearly not a barrier that impoverishes or renders the speaker inarticulate. On the contrary, it appears to make thought more distinct—and it is significant that the two figures for this phenomenon place it in both the natural (mists) and the artistic (laces) domains.

That the preoccupation with the surface is not associated with broken language or silence may be understood from the way the image of that line affects the rest of the stanza. When the speaker touches the tops of the films, the wilderness rolls back along her lines. Think of a murky film covering a body of water; touching that film dispels it, *clarifying* the water as it rolls back away from the place it was touched. In this view, wilderness is associated with the clarification of what lies beneath the film—the lines. Further, it is impossible that the wilderness destroys the lines, as some readers have suggested,[18] since it rolls back *along* those very lines, like films upon the surface of a pond or, in another of Dickinson's images (less felicitous here perhaps but nevertheless helpful), like a train along its tracks—the lines give direction to the wilderness. That two things can occur in the same space without one obliterating the other has already been made clear in stanza four, where the "former feet" and the new "winged feet" proceed in the same measure. Her lines *are* altered by the wilderness rolling along them, but the change is not destructive. The films are peeled back, so to speak, and wilderness is revealed or perhaps released in the lines. Everything about this stanza implies excess rather than diminution: the extra line; the four repetitions of "I" asserting the speaker's integrity and presence; the four tactile verbs that reinscribe her revisionary relation to language; the redundancies of "touch," "top," and "films"; the release or revelation of the wilderness; and the image of the golden lines that must certainly be larger formations—not broken pieces—of the golden words of stanza five.

The last stanza returns to the opposition, Common versus Difference, that began the poem. At first glance, the quatrain highlights this contrast. The speaker is apart from the natural world of the rest of the poem; her removal is signaled by the present tense verb ("hangs") and by a shift in imagery from outside to inside. The change to the present tense and the relocation through imagery recall that the poem is enacting a process and that the speaker is still in the midst of it. She appears to be in a room, naked, refusing to don "The Sackcloth" that "hangs on the nail." The sackcloth "Frock" that she "used to wear" suggests domesticity (in the shift from the garden to the closet), plainness, mortification, girlishness, and a return to the past—elements that easily translate into the prevailing aesthetic for women's writing, and more specifically, into Dickinson's readers' expectations for her poetry. Yet, the sackcloth hanging on the nail hints at the Crucifixion, implying that the return to the Common is a sacrifice she refuses to make. This refusal gains force by a play on words when "The Frock I used to wear" generates the question "But *where* my moment of Brocade— / My—drop—of India?" The vision of the exotic brocade fabric and the Indian dye contrasts, obviously, with the coarse, plain sackcloth and refers to her lost riches. Similarly, the shift in imagery from the external landscape to the interior of a room where the frocks are marks a move from the natural setting of the traditional lyric poet to the domestic sphere of the traditional woman. It is this larger change of state that she refuses to accept.

Yet while the first couplet of the stanza recalls the Common and the final couplet invokes Difference, the quatrain as a whole embodies a third term: refusal. It does not follow for the speaker that if she cannot have her brocade she will have to wear the sackcloth. She "wears" the brocade, by virtue of the pun in asking *where* it is. In a sense, the speaker has become the poem here at the end (the shift into the present tense suggests that the speaker and the poem have arrived at the same point) and will throw open the close of the poem with a question that keeps alive the issue of Difference just as she will give the slip to the sackcloth frock by a play on language.

The escape from the domestic into the textual—what I am calling the transformation of the speaker into the poem—also occurs in the imagery of clothing that dominates the final stanza. If the issue here, as I believe it is, is female aesthetics, then the image of the sackcloth is odious not only in its suggestions of plainness, mortification, and pastness, but also in its evocation of domestic trappings. While the brocade at first seems to call up this same association, a closer reading reveals it to be a decidedly textual metaphor. First, as I have mentioned, the brocade enters the poem through a word play on "wear" and "where." Second, while the sackcloth hangs on the nail as one would expect it to do, the brocade exists in time as a "moment" rather than in space as an object. Associating the brocade with a period of time makes it descriptive of Difference in general rather than merely one of the riches acquired and lost during Difference. Third, less obvious to us, but certainly clear to Dickinson who was interested in etymology, the word "brocade" is related to "brochure," "a pamphlet or stitched book."[19] Dickinson, of course, prepared her own poems into sewn fascicles, or stitched books; "[It would never be Common]" was gathered and sewn into one of these fascicles. And finally, before going on to the more available connotations of "brocade," the "drop—of India" certainly suggests not only the pigment that was used in watercolors and fabric dye but also the ink of writing.

The distinctive features of the brocade are that it is "variegated with gold and silver, or raised and enriched with flowers, foliage, and other ornaments."[20] The gold threads woven through brocade are most obviously suggestive of the speaker's golden words and lines. Perhaps more significant, though, is that the brocade is textured with embroidered flowers and foliage, connecting it to the stanzas that are set in nature (thus, the speaker recalls that time as a "moment of brocade") as well as to the wilderness. In fact, when the wilderness rolls back along the speaker's golden lines, it reveals a continuum that encompasses the wilderness and the brocade. The brocade is, after all, the transformation of the wilderness into art. Indeed, the qualities that are contained in the pattern of the brocade and that are lost when the goblin interferes are released once again in the wilderness.

As metaphors for her poetics, if Sackcloth is the aesthetic Dickinson is repudiating and Brocade is the one she is developing, then Wilderness is an excess of the qualities of the Brocade. Like the third term, refusal, which explodes the opposition Common/Difference, Wilderness provides an alternative when Sackcloth and Brocade are opposed. Rather than write in the Common-Sackcloth style, Dickinson chooses Difference-Brocade; when her own aesthetic comes under attack—when the goblin drinks her dew or readers tell her to write like a lady—she moves to the extreme, writing the Wilderness, a style that proliferates the features of the Brocade to excess. Thus, the speaker has not lost the language of Difference in the stanza where the wilderness rolls along her lines any more than she has lost it at the end of the poem when she refuses to wear the sackcloth by asking where the brocade is. On the contrary, here and elsewhere Dickinson views this sort of verbal nakedness as preferable to unauthentic poetic artifice. In a letter to Higginson about the difficulty of writing poems, she expresses her mistrust of language in terms that anticipate this poem: "While my thought is undressed—I can make the distinction, but when I put them in the Gown—they look alike, and numb" (L 261). The final interrogative may also register the speaker's uncertainty about whether she can don the poetic mantle— but the question nevertheless throws open the end of the poem and prevents her from having to wear the sackcloth.

Recovery of the apocalyptic moment remains problematic. Even the resistances of the last stanza—nakedness, refusal, and the question—cannot recapture the moment of Difference. Her solution, made possible by her poetics of enactment, is to enclose the final dilemma, the moment of crisis, within the poem itself and in this manner to "resolve" it by representing that crisis itself *as a poetic moment,* just as Hester Prynne poeticizes her crisis, the scarlet letter, by containing it in the style of her embroidery.

"[It would never be Common—more—I said]" exemplifies Dickinson's creative process and reveals the need for poetic excess as a means of counteracting formally the internal and external pressures of language. The external constraints on writing, imposed by cultural stereotypes about women writing, were no more formidable for Dickinson than the internal pressures that dealing in words entailed.

Dickinson's excessive stylistics offended many who first read her published poems and saw depicted there both her resistance to nineteenth-century cultural norms, conventions of gender and literature in particular, and her account of the psychic and linguistic crises such resistance could involve. A catalogue of Dickinson's stylistic excesses can be drawn from reviews of her three volumes of poems published in the 1890s; though all three books were extremely popular (the first series went through nine printings in the first year), negative reviews kept pace with positive ones.[21] In the first adamantly negative review, Arlo Bates described the poems generally as "wrong in their excess" (48), a criticism that others elaborated minutely. Andrew Lang, a virulently critical British reviewer, inadvertently employed Dickinson's own figure for poetic form in his assessment of her ubiquitous failings: "It is much to be wished that her admirers will not become her imitators, defying grammar, rhyme, sense, and prosody. Critics who are asked to be candid about such effusions will be wise if they bid the writers 'drop the paste and think themselves a fool,' as Miss Dickinson puts it, for coming to the festival of the Muses in such scandalous lack of a wedding garment" (204). Outraged by Dickinson's "obscure, broken, unmelodious, and recklessly wilful" expression (204), he sensed that her poetry was not merely lacking in conventional terms but that it was operating outside those laws: "Miss Dickinson in her poetry broke every one of the natural and salutary laws of verse. Hers is the very anarchy of the Muses" (204).

Lawlessness, recklessness, willfulness: the reiterated charges of the negative reviews reveal, above all, that Dickinson's excesses broke the laws of nineteenth-century poetic decorum, and decorum for women writers in particular. Reviewers almost universally disparaged her lines as "ungovernable in form" (85), "transgress[ing] the laws of syntax and prosody and sometimes rebel[ling] against rhyme and rhythm" (286). Even more positive reviewers couldn't overlook her "apparently wilful sins against rule and convention" (70), "deliberate carelessness of poetic forms" (68), "rude and careless handling" (60), "wilful whimsicality and scorn of finish and form" (60), and felt even the "daintiest" poems to be "marred by their hysterical form" (69).

When she was not excoriated for her crimes against form, she was condescended to as ignorant and unskilled. Her formal eccentricities were then taken to be nothing more than mechanical errors, poor craftsmanship, and poverty of expression: "if Miss Dickinson had learned grammar and had known anything of the laws of metre, and had had any thought to express or any faculty of expressing them, she might have become quite a decent fifth-rate versifier" (160). Dickinson's "brocade" appears to these reviewers not as Hester's gorgeous, flamboyant embroidery but as the "rag of scarlet cloth" found rotting away in the Custom House years later; one reviewer lamented that her sometimes "breath-taking thoughts" were "disfigured by rags of grammar, tatters of rhyme and hobbling measures" (124).

Though Dickinson's meter, syntax, grammar, and rhyme received most frequent censure in the reviews, her diction, figures, personae, and meaning also came under attack. Several reviewers concluded that this wasn't poetry at all. Andrew Lang was the first to dismiss the poems *as poems,* and it is not surprising that his judgment involved a general condemnation of women writers: "Aristotle says that the ultimate Democracy is remarkable for the license it permits to women and children. Miss Dickinson, like Mrs. Browning, though she was not learned like Mrs. Browning, took great license with rhymes. Possibly the poetry of Democracy will abound more and more in these liberties. But then the question will arise, Is it poetry at all?" (108). Lang's criticisms of Dickinson's poetry are knotted up with his scorn for American literature generally, but American reviewers refused to grant Dickinson's poems the status of poetry as well: "The poetess Emily Dickinson, the latest addition to the 'startling school,' appears to be open to the criticism that one side of her Pegasus is on stilts and the other side is lame. There is a good deal of jolt in her meter that does not please all her critics. Lines cut into irregular lengths and connected by a certain amount of jingle are not necessarily poetry"

(124). A reviewer for the *New York World* referred to the poems as "experimental vagaries" and "posthumous crudities" (264), and Thomas Bailey Aldrich had to strain to keep from calling Dickinson's verses poems, referring to the contents of her volumes as "poetical chaos" (283) or "whimsical memoranda" (283) whose ideas "totter and toddle, not having learned to walk" (283). The most he would grant was that "several of the quatrains are curiously touching, they have such a pathetic air of yearning to be poems" (283), "[b]ut the incoherence and formlessness of her—I don't know how to designate them—versicles are fatal" (283). What we hear in these reviews is Dickinson's writing sequestered as women's writing and women's writing, in turn, demeaned as childlike, tottering and toddling and yearning to be poetry, but finally not poetry.[22]

The reviewers' obsession with Dickinson's "ungainly" form is reminiscent of Higginson's criticism that she should not publish because her gait was spasmodic and her lines uncontrolled. Their indignation at her lack of proportion and conformity to literary standards likewise recalls Austin's concern with female propriety and sedate deportment. Indeed, the reviews from the 1890s are important not, obviously, because they affected Dickinson (who died in 1886) but because they document prevailing attitudes toward writing, and toward women's writing, that Dickinson clearly did respond to in Austin and Higginson—and that she recognized and resisted in the literary world at large.[23] Dickinson wrote in defiance of those standards, and Betsy Erkkila has recently suggested that she declined to publish her poems precisely because she did not want to engage the literary taste of her time.[24] It is ironic that Higginson, who embodied in his own poetry and criticism these received standards of literary decorum when Dickinson first wrote to him in the 1860s, would ardently defend her poems against the attacks of the 1890s. Though his argument for her style was sometimes qualified and condescending ("After all, when a thought takes one's breath away, a lesson on grammar seems an impertinence" [14]), Higginson repeatedly defended Dickinson's poems against the very criticisms that he himself had lodged thirty years earlier. Three decades of correspondence with Dickinson and another decade of editing her poems after her death seem to have taught Higginson how to read her unorthodox verse.

Most of the traits Dickinson's first readers scorned in her poetry as "wrong in their excess" are exactly those stylistic maneuvers that I am ascribing to her aesthetics of excess. Diction, off rhyme, irregular meter, a variety of effects generated by compression, figure, persona, and rhetorical structure form Dickinson's poetic arsenal.[25] Her characteristic line, where peculiarly juxtaposed words are heaped together without connectives like boulders after an explosion, and her characteristic stanzaic progression, where the logic of the poem seems to wobble on its figurative axis until the closing stanzas fly off in different directions, are not poetic chaos but rather the orchestrations of aesthetic excess.

Though one poem claims, "I found the words to every thought / I ever had—but One—" (P 581), the speakers in the most excessive poems frequently struggle to express their thoughts against the simultaneous recalcitrance and multiplicity of language. Understanding the rhetorical moves of these speakers provides access to the workings of excess. For instance, the persona in "[Rearrange a 'Wife's' affection!]" (P 1737) is a woman whose rhetorical crisis is precipitated by the charge, registered before the first line of the poem, that her intense and unreciprocated feelings for her beloved will eventually abate:

> Rearrange a "Wife's" affection!
> When they dislocate my Brain!
> Amputate my freckled Bosom!
> Make me bearded like a man!

Like "[It would never be Common—more—I said]," the opening here refers to something not contained within the poem (we do not know the antecedent of "it" in poem 430 as we do not know who has challenged the speaker's feelings, or why, in poem 1737), and for all its emphatic asseveration, typical of Dickinson's openings, it finally offers no more stability than her uncertain endings do. The crucial thing about this boundless, unidentified challenge to the speaker's feelings, however, is that it creates a situation almost guaranteed to provoke excess: a crisis of language. The speaker must refute the notion that her feelings will fade; to do so, she must find an adequate language for the claim that her love will never diminish. Complicating her problem is the fact that she must combat the doubt that engenders the poem in words that will be able to compete with the most culturally authoritative text about love—the wedding vow.

Thus the word "wife" moves in and out of quotation marks as she wrestles with social sanctions to appropriate that title for herself.

She begins, then, with a verbal bravado that can best be described as machismo. What would it take to change my feelings for him? she challenges: you'd have to crack my skull, cut off my breasts, and make me grow a beard. Her excessive claims thematize a stereotypically masculine violence that serves two purposes: most obviously, it indicates that a change of affections would require tremendous physical force, in fact, so great a force that it would probably kill her; more important, however, it suggests that the only way to "rearrange" her affections is to change her gender. As long as she's a woman—that is, as long as she's herself—she will love him. Her point is, of course, that her feelings will never change, though she runs a certain rhetorical risk by impersonating a boasting he-man in order to say so.

The second stanza seems to compensate for the masculine excesses of the first by retreating to feminine excesses:

> Blush, my spirit, in thy Fastness—
> Blush, my unacknowledged clay—
> Seven years of troth have taught thee
> More than Wifehood ever may!

In these first two imperative lines, the speaker commands herself to adopt a more feminine mode. The blush of embarrassment suggests that the speaker, now depicted as maidenly, recoils from hearing the robust bombast of stanza one and perhaps from the original insensitivity that prompted that outburst. The speaker's style is contradictory, alternately aggressive and demure. The split in subjectivity discerned between the masculine braggadocio of the first stanza and the feminine modesty of the second suggests an internal cleaving of male and female, husband and wife, which paradoxically distinguishes and unites them in the same speaker. The external counterpart for these subjective divisions is the distinction between the legitimate wife, whose oath of marriage is publicly acknowledged, and the self-ordained "wife," whose oath must achieve its authority through rhetorical decree. That she has loved for seven years, the period of time required to establish a common-law marriage, provides some evidence for her claim. Though the speaker recognizes that she alone regards herself as a wife in the first stanza (the quotation marks around "wife's" indicate qualification), she asserts her status unreservedly in stanza two (where Wifehood is not in quotation marks), having earned the title through her long years of devotion.[26] She cleaves herself *to* her beloved rhetorically, and in doing so cleaves *apart* legitimate spouses and distinguishes herself from them by claiming a superior right to the title of wife.

The speaker's histrionics escalate in the third stanza, where her love and loyalty are transformed figuratively into martyrdom:

> *Love that never leaped its socket—*
> *Trust entrenched in narrow pain—*
> *Constancy thro' fire—awarded—*
> *Anguish—bare of anodyne!*

The imagery of physical violence and the rhetorical split between flesh and spirit culminate here in the figure of the martyr, who suffers excruciating physical pain without complaint in the hopes of a spiritual reward. The extent of her martyrdom is revealed in the fourth stanza, where she compares herself to Christ; her martyrdom is superior to Christ's because hers goes unnoticed:

> *Burden—borne so far triumphant—*
> *None suspect me of the crown,*
> *For I wear the "Thorns" till* Sunset—
> *Then—my Diadem put on.*

Though people know she's suffering, they cannot know how much she suffers because she appears to endure *only* as much as Christ endured: she wears merely the crown of thorns during the day. When the sun goes down, however, she dons her true crown. The italicized *sunset* inaugurates an entirely new order of imagery, which supersedes the figures of martyrdom. Sunset functions both as the end of day, when she can express her suffering unobserved, and as an extravagant visual phenomenon that ushers in an extravagant figure. The setting sun fills the western horizon with jewel-like colors; it is *that* celestial crown, the sunset's colors crowning the earth's horizon, that constitutes the speaker's diadem. "Big my Secret," she says in the final stanza, and it is big indeed. Having outstripped wives, martyrs, and Christ, she measures herself in cosmic terms. The cost of such greatness is, once again, tremendous suffering, captured in the unusual piece of diction, "bandaged," which renews the tension between bodily and spiritual pain:

Big my Secret but it's bandaged—
It will never get away
Till the Day its Weary Keeper
Leads it through the Grave to thee.

Here at last the speaker achieves the rhetorical authority that all these excesses have been striving toward. Ordinary wives vow to love their husbands "till death do us part"; the poem's speaker vows to love "till death do us unite." The metaphoric assaults on the physical body and the distinction between flesh and spirit have prepared the way for the final claim. In asserting a bond that defies mortality and transcends the flesh, the speaker has exceeded conventional wedding vows. Yet in modeling her oath on those conventional vows, she has accepted the terms of her culture. She is at once deeply engaged with the social institutions that dictate gender relations and deeply defiant of them. Her excesses have made this possible.

"[Rearrange a 'Wife's' affection!]" is a poem about the need for an excessive language. The speaker thrashes about rhetorically in the first three stanzas, seeking a mode of discourse that will give authority to her unsanctioned marriage vow. Her figures escalate as the poem unleashes stupendous verbal energies necessary to refute the negations threatening her utterance.

Similar escalations structure many of Dickinson's poems, especially these figurative increases that result from her poetics of enactment and her passion for abundance. Yet such structures are not necessarily excessive. In "[One need not be a Chamber—to be Haunted-]" (P 670), for example, the analogy between the mind and a haunted house is developed and elaborated methodically, using the conventions of a gothic novel to organize the poem's argument. The analogy begins inside, where the "Chamber," "House," and "Corridors" of the brain are said to surpass "Material Place" in their capacity to generate terror. The second stanza compares facing internal fears to encountering a ghost. The third stanza moves outside in order to compare the experience of unbridled fear to riding through a haunted abbey (a stock setting in gothic novels) on a spooked horse. The fourth stanza returns to the interior setting and argues that it is more frightening to discover "Ourself behind ourself" than to find an "Assassin hid in our Apartment." And the last stanza moves completely inside the mind to say that such mental horrors are finally self-destructive when "The Body—borrows a Revolver" to defend itself against the troubled mind. The stanzaic progression is fast but not furious.

In a poem like "[Grief is a Mouse-]" (P 793), on the other hand, a frenzied series of metaphors seems to confound figuration:

> Grief is a Mouse—
> And chooses Wainscot in the Breast
> For His Shy House—
> And baffles quest—
>
> Grief is a Thief—quick startled—
> Pricks His Ear—report to hear
> Of that Vast Dark—
> That swept His Being—back—
>
> Grief is a Juggler—boldest at the Play—
> Lest if He flinch—the eye that way
> Pounce on His Bruises—One—say—or Three—
> Grief is a Gourmand—spare His luxury—

Predictably, a verbal crisis is behind the need for such excess. The poem begins as though defining "grief" were a fairly easy task: stanza one asserts that grief is elusive like a mouse; stanza two makes an association between the stealthy mouse in the "Wainscot in the Breast" and a thief. Both are quiet, hidden, disturbing, and disturbed: "Grief is a Thief—quick startled." The uncharacteristic internal rhymes of "grief" and "thief," "quick" and "pricks," "ear" and "hear" pick up the pace of the lines as the poem simulates the heightened agitation of the thief. But the relationship between the "report" that the thief listens for and the experience of grief remains opaque. Like the mouse in stanza one, who "baffles quest," the *analogy* between the thief listening "to hear / Of that Vast Dark—/ That swept His Being— back" and grief baffles understanding. This is the first indication that the whole purpose of the poem will "baffle quest" since there is no adequate metaphor for grief.

Nevertheless, the poem proceeds, and the third stanza offers a third metaphor: "Grief is a Juggler," who may be associated with the thief because his occupation requires acute attention. If either "flinch[es]," he will fail: the thief will be caught (perhaps it's the "report" of a watchman's gun he listens for), and the juggler will drop his balls. The juggler's balls, in turn, are compared to bruises ("Lest if He flinch—the eyes that way / Pounce on His Bruises") that will be exposed to view if the griever flinches (as the balls will tumble to the floor if the juggler does). The three comparisons thus far employ figures who are vulnerable to exposure if they are inattentive (the mouse will be caught, the thief shot, and the juggler denounced by his audience) and indicate that the nature of grief is to hide itself. The juggler is a risky figure for such grief since his occupation is to create a spectacle; unlike the mouse and thief who keep their grief secret, he "juggles" his sorrows publicly. Yet if he is expert in his performance, he will appear to bear his grief well—another, more complicated form of secrecy. When the juggler's balls scatter, "One—say—or Three," in stanza three, the metaphor scatters as well. Instead of issuing an entire quatrain to the next figure, the poem unbalances its own established form (one analogy per stanza) by asserting in the last line of the juggler's stanza: "Grief is a Gourmand—spare His luxury." The juggler and the gourmand might be present at the same feast, and perhaps the mouse and thief are lurking there, too. The increase of the juggler's balls ("One—[two]—or Three") may suggest the gourmand's great appetite. If we return to the fact that these players are figures for grief, we can tentatively say that grief is hidden, elusive, poised, and consuming; yet it is under constant threat of discovery, exposure, loss of control, and insatiability—as the poem will inadvertently demonstrate.

The phrase "spare His luxury" involves grammatical deletions that result from Dickinson's excessive compression. Grief has a huge appetite for suffering, the line seems to begin; therefore, what? therefore, [let him have] his luxury? therefore, spare [me] his luxury? therefore, [even though he seems to consume a great deal, he is, relative to other gourmands] spare [in] his luxury? or therefore, [deny] his luxury? The final attempt to define grief, which comes in the last stanza, retroactively puts some semantic pressure on that enigmatic phrase: "Best Grief is Tongueless." Spare [the gourmand grief's] luxury [since the] best grief is tongueless. The tongue or mouth may be the link between the gourmand and this last formulation. The figurative escalations have betrayed their purpose by transforming grief from a private, silent matter into a spectacular public performance. "Best grief is Tongueless" as opposed to gourmand grief that is all mouth. *The best griever* remains silent about his suffering, even when he is burned "in the Public Square" like a martyr.

The final stanza exceeds the quatrain structure as it struggles to say what cannot be said:

> Best Grief is Tongueless—before He'll tell—
> Burn Him in the Public Square—
> His Ashes—will
> Possibly—if they refuse—How then know—
> Since a Rack could'nt coax a syllable—now.

The third line here halts at the impossible situation the poem has gotten itself into: the best grief won't talk even if you burn him in the public square; his ashes are proof of his silence; his ashes, then, paradoxically, "will" talk. This visual proof of the martyr's silence testifies to his silence *and*, in testifying, contradicts it; thus, the poem backtracks, "possibly—if they refuse." If the martyr's ashes resist interpretation as a sign of his superior grief, "How then know"? The inadequacies of such figuration are admitted in the final line, which illogically conflates two forms of torture. It is absurd to try to torture ashes on the rack in order to get them to speak, just as it is absurd to attempt a definition of grief. At last the poem acknowledges that it cannot depict grief if true grief is "tongueless." What it has been able to do, however, is enact the failure of representation. The conclusion of the poem and the recognition of failure occur simultaneously in the word "now." In one further irony, the poem succeeds in conveying something about true grief; it does so by enacting impossibility and incorporating failure into its representation of the verbal crisis occasioned by grief.

Both "[One need not be a chamber to be haunted]" and "[Grief is a Mouse]" move restlessly through a number of figures; however, the former poem's metaphors seem to meet the needs of representation while the latter poem's metaphors simultaneously approach and evade their subject. The crisis of language in "[Grief is a Mouse]" unleashes the stylistic excesses we observe there. These escalations often proceed toward complete figurative dissolution at the end of the poems, though that dissolution still functions as an emblem for what cannot be adequately represented by conventional poetic means.

The relationship between figurative excess and endings that lack closure is obvious from these poems and suggests why so many of Dickinson's poems were originally published with their difficult endings deleted (or not selected for publication at all until they were published in the complete, variorum edition in 1955). "[I felt a Funeral, in my Brain]" (P 280) was typically printed without its last stanza:

> *I felt a Funeral, in my Brain,*
> *And Mourners to and fro*
> *Kept treading—treading—till it seemed*
> *That Sense was breaking through—*
>
> *And when they all were seated,*
> *A Service, like a Drum—*
> *Kept beating—beating—till I thought*
> *My Mind was going numb—*
>
> *And then I heard them lift a Box*
> *And creak across my Soul*
> *With those same Boots of Lead, again,*
> *Then Space—began to toll,*
>
> *As all the Heavens were a Bell,*
> *And Being, but an Ear,*
> *And I, and Silence, some strange Race*
> *Wrecked, solitary, here—*
>
> *And then a Plank in Reason, broke,*
> *And I dropped down, and down—*
> *And hit a World, at every plunge,*
> *And Finished knowing—then—*

Yet, if we recognize the final stanza as a product of figurative escalations that are excessive rather than standard, we begin to understand its place in the poem.

"[I felt a Funeral—in my Brain]" begins, as so many of the poems do, with an assertion whose stability sounds unquestionable. Despite its semantic oddness, the first line is delivered with rhetorical assurance that temporarily contains its volatile subject matter. The sense of containment is not merely a product of orderly syntax and confident tone, however; it also derives from the claustrophobic setting of the funeral. Though the feeling of a funeral occurs in the speaker's brain, the analogy suggests premature burial. The mental state the speaker describes is not merely like a funeral in her brain, it is like being buried alive: the heightened awareness of sounds (treading, beating, creaking, tolling) and the sense of enclosure ("in my Brain," "they all were seated," "a Box") combine with other evidence in the poem to suggest that the mourners are conducting a funeral service for a speaker who is not yet dead ("My Mind was going numb," "creak across my Soul").

The mental state described here begins as a numbing, monotonous, claustrophobic feeling but proceeds to its opposite. If the beginning of the poem figures extreme interiority, the ending of the poem depicts an even more disturbing exteriority whose boundlessness is finally indescribable. The "Plank in Reason" that breaks in the final stanza is anticipated in the shift from interior to exterior space, as though the walls, floor, and ceiling of the room (or the sides, lid, and bottom of the coffin), all made of planks, suddenly disappear, plunging the speaker into limitless and terrifying space.

The figurative path to the complete loss of reason, and its attendant spatial dissolution, is difficult to follow. Comparison with the more logical sequence of a similar poem offers an instructive contrast. "[I felt a Cleaving in my Mind]" (P 937) employs a metaphor that describes exactly what "[I felt a Funeral, in my Brain]" enacts (that is, poem 937 *says* what poem 280 *does*):

> I felt a Cleaving in my Mind—
> As if my Brain had split—
> I tried to match it—Seam by Seam—
> But could not make them fit.
>
> The thought behind, I strove to join
> Unto the thought before—
> But Sequence ravelled out of Sound
> Like Balls—upon a Floor.

The word "cleaving" may abbreviate the contradictions of "[I felt a Funeral, in my Brain]" between the description of the mental state as claustrophobic (cleaving together) and boundless (cleaving apart). The second line establishes that the sensation being described here is some sort of mental falling apart. The orderly progression of thoughts, compared to a string of yarn or thread, cannot be knit or sewn together into a coherent sequence. On the contrary, the balls of yarn (perhaps a graphic corollary for the brain with its bundled folds and convolutions) unravel when they roll to the floor.

Not only does this poem describe the movement toward disintegration that poem 280 undertakes to depict, but it also refers to the difficulty of such representation: "But Sequence ravelled out of Sound" is not just a description of mental undoing, it is an account of linguistic failure. The sequence of mental events that leads to the disruption of rationality (another sequence) quickly moves out of verbal reach (out of sound).[27] But that one phrase is the only hint that "[I felt a Cleaving in my Mind]" cannot fully represent its subject. Its metaphors, strings of yarn torn from some knitted whole and balls of yarn unraveling on the floor, are adequate to the task they are given. The consistency of these analogies and the brevity of the poem are indices of a certain conceptual neatness.

The difference in "[I felt a Funeral, in my Brain]" is not that its metaphors are inadequate but that its subject is much more complicated and elusive than the subject of poem 937. Here the figurative increases must be followed with decreasing certainty. In stanza one, the speaker's mental state is compared to a funeral and is characterized by morbidity, monotony, and repetitiveness so oppressive that "it seemed / That Sense was breaking through." In the second stanza, the monotony and repetitiveness continue, but the sensation of motion (in the treading feet) decreases as "they all were seated." The sound of a drum replaces the treading with even more monotonous and repetitive beating until the speaker feels her mind "going numb." When, in stanza three, she "hears" the creaking of the pall bearers' steps carrying the coffin "across [her] Soul," something changes. Perhaps the movement from the interior space of the funeral service to the exterior space of the graveyard precipitates the drastic figurative change when "Space—began to toll." The tolling of a church bell to signal the burial of the dead is consistent with the metaphor thus far, as the monotony of a ringing bell is akin to the insistent treading, beating, and creaking that precede it. What is not consistent, however, is that all of "Space" is tolling, not just a church bell. At the end of stanza three, then, the setting of the initial figure is abandoned, and only the maddening sound persists to carry the metaphors of the poem forward.

Vast, undifferentiated, resounding space is the setting of lines 11 through 14, a setting, if it can any longer be termed such, of pure sound. Space tolls as [if] "all the Heavens were a Bell" and "Being, but an Ear." Whatever the speaker means by "Being," she is not included in that category, for she and "Silence, some strange Race" are [ship]wrecked in this world of sound, like two lost mariners washed up in some alien and, we discover, hostile land. "Wrecked, solitary, here" suggests shipwreck and strange lands, but we must remember that the speaker and her companion, Silence, are disembodied; and even Being, the native race of this aural world, is "but an Ear." It is worth reflecting, before proceeding to the final stanza, that the speaker has moved from the claustrophobic environment of the funeral (perhaps of the coffin) to the boundless environment of pure sound; worse, the mind-numbing experience of the beginning of the poem has reduced her to silence, rendering her strange and solitary in this world of sound. It is this strangeness and isolation that she amplifies in the final stanza.

The last stanza restores the spatial setting, at least to the limited extent that one prop, a plank, from the material world is poised precariously over this aural abyss. Balancing on the imagery of the preceding stanza, the speaker seems to be walking the plank of a [pirate] ship, the victim of a nautical execution that recurs to the funeral motif. When the "Plank in Reason" breaks, however, she plunges into space again, rather than into the sea, and thus descends through the vast emptiness that here seems to be outer space: she "hit[s] a World, at every plunge."

This dizzying perspective of the speaker tumbling through space yet colliding with whole worlds (then bouncing off of them and continuing her fall?) is difficult to *picture,* which is precisely the point of such excessive imagery. Once again the admission of failure and the end of the poem coincide: "then," like "now" in "[Grief is a Mouse]," points to a moment when the poem's formulations recognize defeat. "How then know" and "Finished knowing—then" bring their respective poem's processes of knowing to an end, though the way that "—then—" in this poem is suspended between two dashes suggests both ending and continuation: at that moment [then], I finished knowing; and, I finished knowing, [and] . . . then [I can't convey what happened then]. In either case, what the poem is able to do with words has ended.

The problem in all of these poems is how closely they can approach meaning. In many other cases, Dickinson does seem to have found the words for nearly every thought she ever had, as poem 581 claims. Yet a great number of the poems employ excess to express things that the culture or the language resists. Various manifestations of excess enable her to figure forth unspeakable things by incorporating the failure of language into such poems—that moment of "now" or "then" when sequence ravels out of sound—and presenting it as a poetic moment.

The power of excess to signify more than conventional language is related to the power of poetry to encompass more than the ordinary world:

> I reckon—when I count at all—
> First—Poets—Then the Sun—
> Then Summer—Then the Heaven of God—
> And then—the List is done—
>
> But, looking back—the First so seems
> To Comprehend the Whole—
> The Others look a needless Show—
> So I write—Poets—All—
>
> (P 569)

The speaker in this poem mocks conventional "reckoning" (when she bothers to "count at all") of the world and insists that a poetical assessment would turn up quite a different list. Poets are first in her accounting, followed by various elements of the natural and spiritual worlds. Poets, sun, summer, heaven, "and then—the List is done." But even that short list is superfluous since only the first item matters; poets contain ("Comprehend") everything else on the list, making the rest a "needless Show." "So" the speaker begins again, this time explicitly *writing,* and recognizes just one term: "I write—Poets—All."

The claim is grandiose, of course, but the poem initially presents it in a measured (in fact, ironically so) style. However, the next two stanzas veer off into excess, and it is no coincidence that the word "extravagant" seems to precipitate the swerve. After asserting that poets exceed nature and divinity, she offers evidence for her wild pretension, but her "account" of poetic excess quickly escalates into an enactment of excess:

> Their Summer—lasts a Solid Year—
> They can afford a Sun
> The East—would deem extravagant—
> And if the Further Heaven—
>
> Be Beautiful as they prepare
> For Those who worship Them—
> It is too difficult a Grace—
> To justify the Dream—

Continuing to employ the lexicon of accounting ironically, she argues for the greater wealth of poetry: the poet's summer *lasts* longer than the year's (because a summer represented in a poem is not subject to natural decline and is always available for reading), and poets can *afford* a sun that ordinary nature would think *extravagant* (because their imaginative description of sunrise can exceed the natural event in beauty and drama). These reasonable claims, however, apparently cannot approach the true extravagance of poetry, which is not pictorial but conceptual.

The very notion of extravagance, as I have said, seems to ignite a deeper excess in the poem. The coordinating conjunction "and" prepares us for a third example of the superiority of poetry; however, instead of adding one more figure to a list that is quickly becoming another "needless Show," the poem begins a performance of excess that is almost impossible to account for.

If the "Further Heaven," as opposed to the "Heaven of God," is as beautiful as poets represent it to their devoted readers . . . Even subduing the lines like this does not smooth the way to the last two lines: "It is too difficult a Grace— / To justify the Dream—." The speaker appropriates religious diction ("Further Heaven," "worship," "Grace") to elevate literary relations above theological ones, yet the effect is confusion of poet and deity, poetry and liturgy, rather than distinction—despite the comparative "further" in this stanza and the unambiguous distinction between the poet and God in stanza one.

Dickinson recorded a flurry of variant words for these difficult lines: for "Further," she proposed "Other" and "final"; for "prepare," "Disclose"; for "For," "to"; and for "worship," "Trust in" and "Ask of" (435). And though her first editors adopted four of these changes, none of them finally clarifies the meaning of the last five lines of the poem:

> And if the final Heaven
> Be beautiful as they disclose
> To those who trust in them,
> It is too difficult a grace
> To justify the dream.

Whether the heaven of line 12 is "Further," "Other," or "final," it still stands in contrast to the "Heaven of God" in line 3 and to the heaven of nature, the east, in line 11. To disclose beauty suggests something more visionary than to prepare people for beauty, but to trust in or ask of poets is less grand than to worship them. These variants do not resolve the contradictions of the end of the poem; rather, they record the poem's struggle to find an analogy for poets that captures their superiority without deifying them—since even the divinity is comprehended by the poet. The language offers God and heaven as the supreme being and transcendent place; the poem, however, wants something more.

What it is able to register is that "Poets" cannot be accounted for—certainly not by ordinary reckonings and not even by poetical ones. The speaker's third attempt to give an account of her occupation is finally just as reductive as the first two lists. The "if"-clause in the last sentence has no completing "then"-clause; this may indicate that the conditional logic is abandoned when the speaker acknowledges that all of her attempts to account for poetry will inevitably fail. Since poetry is "All," efforts to define it will be deficient. In this reading, "It" in the penultimate line refers to the preceding formulation about poetry, to the speculation that if the "Further Heaven" is as beautiful as poets say, then something substantial about poetry can be asserted. Instead, the final two lines refuse to complete the formulation and "for a moment—swung," so to speak. The reckoning term "justify" in the last line is at once self-mocking and sobering. One cannot justify poetry as an accountant justifies columns of numbers (or a printer justifies pieces of type in setting a poem); a poet cannot justify her occupation by describing it in worldly terms.[28] What she can do, however, is incorporate the refusal to do so into her poem. She can represent the moment of crisis, the "now," "then," and even the deferred "then" here, and poeticize it as a moment of brocade.

CHAPTER 3

Gertrude Stein

A Crazy Quilt of Style

Rose is a rose is a rose is a rose.

$\mathcal{I}$t is difficult to imagine two poets less alike than Emily Dickinson and Gertrude Stein. The nineteenth-century New England recluse who confined herself to her own home and wrote nearly all her poetry in the hymn stanza makes an initial impression very different from the worldly grande dame of Paris modernism who abandoned conventional poetic forms entirely. Yet their similarities as women poets are striking. Thornton Wilder was probably the first to compare the two poets when he suggested that both had kept "the idea of an audience at bay" by writing in isolation (Mellow 390). Certainly neither poet made concessions for the sake of an audience. Antagonistic readers made Stein, like Dickinson, even more determined to pursue the excesses of her own unorthodox style rather than capitulate to the pressures of a prospective readership. In fact, Stein's first audience, and the model for her future audiences, was also, like Dickinson's, a critical, uncomprehending older brother.

Gertrude and Leo Stein had been close companions since early childhood, spending all their time together to avoid what they considered to be their uninteresting older siblings and tyrannical father (Brinnin 10). While they apparently never shared their private emotional concerns, and though Stein may have asserted herself more freely when she was alone, they were good friends even during periods of separation—when Leo went away to college, when he spent a year on a world tour, and when he first settled in Paris. But after Stein joined him there, they lived congenially only as long as she was content to listen to his incessant, long-winded proclamations about modern art. Once she began producing art herself, their relationship slowly disintegrated. In *Everybody's Autobiography,* she links her absorption in her own writing to her inability to continue listening to him: "by that time I was writing and arguing was no longer to me really interesting" (76–77). Their estrangement was complete when he, in turn, failed to recognize the value of her work: "it destroyed him for me and it destroyed me for him" (77). Indeed, Leo's domineering personality and dismissive attitude toward his sister—he now claimed she was "basically stupid" (Brinnin 311) and considered her writing "damned nonsense" (Mellow 202)—may have precipitated more than their separation. Shari Benstock speculates that Stein instituted her solitary late-night writing habits in order to escape Leo's scrutiny: "one wonders whether another, unspoken and perhaps unacknowledged, reason for these nightly vigils was the certain knowledge that Leo Stein was asleep. His repressive presence safely removed, she perhaps felt free to explore her own consciousness and to continue the experiments in writing that were to lead to *Three Lives* and *The Making of Americans*" (152). In the first biography of Stein expressly dedicated to Stein's family relations, Linda Wagner-Martin confirms Benstock's speculations that Stein attempted to elude Leo's critical scrutiny: "To avoid his observation and advice, she began writing in the atelier late at night" (*Favored Strangers* 62).[1] John Malcolm Brinnin even suggests that writing itself—not just when she wrote but *that* she wrote—was for Stein an act of rebellion against Leo: "Turning to writing at this early stage appears to have been her most natural means of breaking away from Leo's paternalistic domination. . . . Somewhere along the line Gertrude apparently realized that only when she became an artist in her own right and on her own terms might she escape her brother's overzealous control" (54).

Leo's oppressiveness may bear on her writing style as well as her writing habits. First escaping him by writing rather than listening to him, and then by writing in the middle of the night when he could not distract her, she may also have eluded him by writing in a style that Leo could not penetrate. A passage from "A Vocabulary of Thinking" in *How To Write* hints that Stein developed a hermetic style in order to avoid being criticized and dismissed in precisely the way Leo was likely to do: "Having undertaken never to be renounced never to be diminutive never to be in consequence never to be with and delayed never to be placing it with and because it is an interval it is extremely difficult not to make sense extremely difficult not to make sense extremely difficult not to make sense and excuse" (293). One reading of this simultaneously repetitive and elliptical passage suggests that she attempted to write unintelligibly in order to avoid being criticized, but she found it impossible to put words together without producing sense. Thus, she cannot absent herself (be excused) from the problem of hostile readers by claiming that her words are meaningless (by making excuses).[2]

Like Dickinson, Stein may have discovered in the very writing strategy that enabled her to balk at a hostile reader a poetics that would support much grander and more important writing experiments. This discovery must have been a turning point for Stein: the language that would shield her from criticism turned out to be a language that would still make sense, inevitably. And a writing practice that could simultaneously disrupt conventional sense and generate new meanings implied a poetics that could at once reject and renew literary language, repel and engage readers. This paradox would prove to be the basis of Stein's poetics of excess.

The passage above associates this significant development in Stein's writing to the discovery of the "interval" between words. When any two words appear together, they create an interval—that space between them—which inevitably generates meaning. "Because it is an interval," that is, because it marks the space between words, it mediates their meanings both by bridging them together and by keeping them apart. In a 1946 interview with Robert Hass, which appears as an afterword to *What Are Masterpieces,* she restates this more explicitly: "I took individual words and thought about them until I got their weight and volume complete and put them next to another word and at this same time I found very soon that there is no such thing as putting them together without sense. It is impossible to put them together without sense. I made innumerable efforts to make words write without sense and found it impossible" (101). The words and their interval compose a unit that exceeds each word's "individual weight and volume"; meaning cannot be controlled, as the interval both reinforces and undermines the denotative aspect of words as well as blocks and facilitates the flow of connotative associations between them. Thus, in an expression like "tender buttons," the denotative meaning of each word hardens in resistance to the incongruity of the phrase and yet crackles with potential for new significance. Clearly her verbal experimentation was not, as many have suggested, a mere language game in which words are plastic forms, devoid of their semantic content. Rather it was a strategy to generate, not to evacuate, semantic content. Indeed, the new way of writing proved far more capable of articulating Stein's personal and literary concerns than traditional writing. It gave her a unique language in which to verbalize her unorthodox relationship with Toklas,[3] and it enabled her to launch a critique of the dominant literature without implicating herself in it by employing its forms and conventions.

In fact, Stein's most frequently quoted line of "nonsense," "Rose is a rose is a rose is a rose," first appeared in a poem that combines these unorthodox personal and literary concerns. The poem, "Sacred Emily," (*Geography and Plays* 178–88[4]) is a kind of wedding vow in which the poet composes and consummates her marriage on the double bed of textuality and sexuality:

> *Compose compose beds*
> *Wives of great men rest tranquil. . . .*
> *I love honor and obey I do love honor and obey I do.*
> *(178)*

Stein often described her partnership with Alice B. Toklas in terms of a heterosexual marriage, Toklas being the wife and Stein the husband. This traditional paradigm served not only to structure their relationship but also, and perhaps more important, to explain Stein's greatness, for she believed that genius was limited to men.[5] In "Sacred Emily," however, the heterosexual dimension that would make marriage "a firm terrible hindering" (178) is countered in the poem by the pleasing details of their female world. In the following passage, for example, the phrase "wet spoil" briefly disturbs the domestic order achieved in the progression "Door. / Do or. / Table linen," where the "door" opens, as it were, in the middle of itself ("Do or"), like the double doors of a formal dining room, to reveal the table inside, set with its linen:

> Door.
> Do or.
> Table linen.
> Wet spoil.
> Wet spoil gaiters and knees and little spools little spools or ready silk lining.
> Suppose misses misses.
> Curls to butter.
>
> (187–88)

"Wet spoil" intrudes mischievously, spoiling the scene with dripping gaiters. Yet in the fourth line, the verbal eye appears to move up from the puddle to the gaiters to the knee—where it begins an alternate, more positive string of associations. Sheer verbal play turns "spoils" into "spools," but the knees themselves may be like little spools, or perhaps the speaker is recalling the spools of thread used in making (or attaching) the gaiters. "Ready silk lining" pursues the imagery of sewing, but may in fact hint at the "red," silky interior of the garment (possibly the gaiters) or even the interior of the body wearing the gaiters. At any rate, many passages contain such disruptive or resistant phrases, but the easy, rhythmic accumulation of domestic details manages them with the grace of a hostess who restores order after someone has entered the room with dripping gaiters or knocked over a glass of water on the table linen.

The serene mood for this setting is created through an array of unusual devices. For instance, clusters of words establish a tone exclusively through sound, while adjacent lines "translate" these sound-tones into conventional expressions:

> Murmur pet murmur pet murmur.
> Push sea push sea push sea push sea push sea push sea push sea push sea.
> Sweet and good and kind to all.
>
> (178)

In the first line here, "murmur pet" offers approximately equal parts of sound and sense as the intimate repetitions of "murmur" (created by the muffled *m*'s and the short *u*'s), the image of whispering lovers, and the familiar term of endearment ("pet") reinforce one another. The next line, however, seems to give itself fully to the sensual auditory sibilance of "push sea," though the erotic motion of advancing and retreating waves (and thus of lovers moving together or experiencing waves of pleasure) can certainly be read there, too. The final line clearly awakens from these hypnotic sounds to articulate the sexual beneficence that the passage exudes: the lover is sweet and good and generous (or perhaps the lover makes the speaker feel this way). Internal rhyme exploits sound in yet another way: "Ink of paper slightly mine breathes a shoulder able shine" (184). Other passages deemphasize this kind of lyricism and instead use repetition to permit the sheer semantic weight of words to accrue: "Happy happy happy all the. / Happy happy happy all the" (182). The abundance of domestic images and the frequent rhetorical sachets overtake the conventional view of marriage and create a context in which the solemn vows to love, honor, and obey ring with a new delight and playfulness.

The process of feminizing matrimony begins with the speaker's assertion of her own presence and authority—as a lover and a writer—in the marriage: "I am not missing. / Who is a permit" (178). The traditionally feminine vows to love, honor, and obey will not here inaugurate a "firm terrible hindering" (178). Significantly, the men's names that seem at first automatically generated by the marriage context—Philip, Henry, Willie, and Jack—drop out of the poem as women's names proliferate instead—Lizzie, Ethel, Susie, Emily, Anne, Susan, Anna, Rose, Pussy (Stein's nickname for Toklas), Louise, and Jane. James R. Mellow rightly calls the poem a "domestic idyll" (259) in which the daily doings of the Stein-Toklas household are enumerated and celebrated. But it is important to note that these details are interwoven with elements from a writer's studio, inextricably linking the domestic and the artistic worlds:

> *Ink of paper slightly mine breathes a shoulder able shine. . . .*
> *Put something down some day in my.*
> *In my hand.*
> *In my hand right.*
> *In my hand writing.*
> *Put something down some day in my hand writing.*
> *Needles less.*

Never the less.
Never the less.
Pepperness.
Never the less extra stress.
Never the less.
Tenderness.
Old sight.
Pearls.
Real line.
Shoulders. . . .
Search needles.
All a plain all a plain show.
White papers.
Slippers.

(184–85)

Distinctions between writing, housekeeping, and lovemaking blur as the words that represent them overlap and shift so that new emotional and domestic arrangements represent a new poetics. For instance, the literary "Cunning saxon symbol. / Symbol of beauty" is translated into the homely "Thimble of everything" (186) in the next line by a play on initial sounds that turns "symbol" into "thimble." A series of puns reveals how familiar language can be made to express new possibilities. The title of the poem itself, "Sacred Emily," may be a playful revision of the traditional "Sacred Matrimony"—in which the institution of marriage is replaced with the name of a particular woman. In this new marriage, they are both "one and indivisible" (180) and yet recognizably individual: Stein (the husband who is "so great") and Toklas (the wife who "sews" and "grates" food). The paradox of being at once indivisible and individual is embodied in the homonyms "so great" and "sew grate" that register crucial differences in meaning despite their identical sounds:

Sudden say separate.
So great so great Emily.
Sew grate sew grate Emily.
Not a spell nicely.[6]

(182)

The last line here can be taken to abbreviate Stein's whole literary project—not to "spell nicely"—as well as to refer to the spelling game she plays with homonyms throughout the poem. Likewise, the only

"Mrs." this wedding produces is in the pun "suppose misses misses" in which repetition permits two single women to achieve the aural status of a married woman ("misses" is a homonym for "Mrs.") as well as her domestic bliss without being subjected to the limitations of a traditional marriage—since by remaining misses they can "miss" becoming Mrs. This development gives new resonance to the speaker's claim in the opening of the poem—"I am not missing" (178).

It is only a felicitous coincidence that Stein's poem about the union of women bears the name of America's premier female poet, links sewing to writing (as Dickinson did in sewing her poems into packets), and lists Susie and Susan among the litany of women's names (Susan "Susie" Gilbert Dickinson was Emily Dickinson's best friend and sister-in-law), for we have no evidence that Stein read Dickinson (and in 1912, when "Sacred Emily" was written, few recognized Dickinson's importance). It is not coincidental, however, that Stein links sexuality and textuality in a poem that makes sacred the union of women. In "Poetry and Grammar" she explains that she began writing poetry precisely in order to articulate this love, through an anecdote about her brother:

> I remember very well when I was a little girl and I and my brother found as children will the love poems of their very very much older brother. This older brother had just written one and it said that he had often sat and looked at any little square of grass and it had been just a square of grass as grass is, but now he was in love and so the little square of grass was all filled with birds and bees and butterflies, the difference was what love was. The poem was funny we and he knew the poem was funny but he was right, being in love made him make poetry, and poetry made him feel the things and their names, and so I repeat nouns are poetry. (*Lectures in America* 236)

Elsewhere in the essay, Stein explains that falling in love with Toklas made it necessary for her to write poetry because only in poetry— the genre that, for Stein, employs nouns—could her new feelings be named. And, as the anecdote about her brother underlines, naming feelings is essential to experiencing them since the relationship between love and poetry is mutually creative: "poetry made him feel the things and their names." Falling in love with Toklas and writing poetry were likewise events in Stein's life that reinforced each other, a fact that her poetics reflect.

"Sacred Emily"—the text that generated Stein's most famous "nonsense" line—is a poem that legitimizes femininity. The repetitions of "Rose is a rose is a rose is a rose" comprise an abbreviated statement of a stylistics and thematics of excess that are deeply linked to this legitimization. First, Stein turned to writing as an act of self-assertion and developed her peculiar style as an act of self-preservation. Second, she began writing poetry in order to articulate what the culture's language left unnamed or misnamed—love between women. Third, she feminized the institution of marriage in the poem by renaming it "Sacred Emily." Fourth, she appropriated what is probably the key symbol in Western literature for the female object of love, the rose. And fifth, she reworked that symbol by means of a device she called "insistence," a phenomenon of language that she learned about from listening to her aunts:

> When I first really realized the inevitable repetition in human expression that was not repetition but insistence when I first began to be really conscious of it was when . . . [I] came to Baltimore and lived with a lot of my relations and principally with a whole group of very lively little aunts who had to know anything.
>
> If they had to know anything and anybody does they naturally had to say and hear it often, anybody does, and as there were ten and eleven of them they did have to say and hear said whatever was said and any one not hearing what it was they said had to come in to hear what had been said. That inevitably made everything said often. I began then to consciously listen to what anybody was saying and what they did say while they were saying what they were saying. This was not yet the beginning of writing but it was the beginning of knowing what there was that made there be no repetition. No matter how often what happened had happened any time any one told anything there was no repetition. (*Lectures in America* 168–69)

The passage posits the speech patterns of gossiping women as a model for poetic language, a remarkable formulation considering that women's talk was universally viewed as trivial and unartistic.[7] The famous rose line, then, embodies her resistance to Leo specifically and to the received literary tradition more generally, it places the traditional symbol of objectified femininity at the center of this resistance, and it enacts the poetics of excess that distinguish her entire literary enterprise.

For Stein the rose line became the motto of her life project—
to invigorate Western literature by renewing language.[8] In 1935 in
Chicago, where she was giving a special course for Thornton Wilder,
in response to the inevitable teasing about it, Stein explained part of
the significance of the line:

> Now you have all seen hundreds of poems about roses and you know
> in your bones that the rose is not there. All those songs that sopranos
> sing as encores about "I have a garden; oh, what a garden!" Now I don't
> want to put too much emphasis on that line, because it's just one line in
> a longer poem. But I notice that you all know it; you make fun of it, but
> you know it. Now listen! I'm no fool. I know that in daily life we don't
> go around saying "is a . . . is a . . . is a . . ." Yes, I'm no fool; but I think
> that in that line the rose is red for the first time in English poetry for a
> hundred years. (*Four in America* vi)

Excess is what enables the rose to be red (and therefore "read") again
for the first time in a century. The line is, of course, a parody of those
like Robert Burns's "My luve is like a red, red rose" (178). The effect of
the first repetition is to challenge the role of referential language (the
first "Rose" in Stein's line is a proper noun). In "Poetry and Grammar,"
she doubts the authority of words that refer to things: "A noun is the
name of anything, why after a thing is named write about it. A name
is adequate or it is not. If it is adequate then why go on calling it, if it
is not, then calling it by its name does no good" (*Lectures in America*
209–10). She believed Shakespeare had acknowledged this in his
famous line: "They the names that is the nouns cannot please, because
after all you know well after all that is what Shakespeare meant
when he talked about a rose by any other name" (212–13). The four
repetitions, ironically, reverberate with the hollowness of the name.

The larger goal of the line is to replace metaphor with repetition.
"Rose is a rose" confounds the metaphor by rendering its vehicle
and tenor identical. The first equation, then, "Rose is a rose," sub-
verts both reference and metaphor. Like Pablo Neruda's revealing
tautology,

> *por las calles la sangre de los ninos*
> *corria simplemente, como sangre de ninos*
> *(through the streets the blood of children*
> *flowed simply, like the blood of children),*
> *(118–19)*

the repetition confronts the failure of words, referential or metaphoric, to capture the fullness and immediacy of meaning. For Stein, in fact, meaning is extraordinarily elusive for two contradictory reasons: because words are simultaneously fixed by habit and history and yet capriciously susceptible to context, sound, punning, and other forms of verbal play. Repetition becomes a way of clinging to thought while one struggles to articulate it: "Most people destroy their thought before they create it. That is why I often repeat a word again and again—because I am fighting to hold the thought" (Mellow 420). In a typical Steinian paradox, however, repetition allows her to hold on to a thought at the same time that it permits the thought itself to keep changing. "Insistence" is her term for the fact that each time something is repeated, it is altered: "insistence is always alive and if it is alive it is never saying anything in the same way because emphasis can never be the same" ("Portraits and Repetition," in *Lectures in America* 171). Thus, the repetitions of the word "rose" acknowledge the emptiness of language and the weariness of metaphor, and at the same time they arouse the line into motion, "we have now, a movement lively enough to be a thing in itself moving" (171). Like Dickinson's vehement acquiescence—"as *simple* as you please, the *simplest* sort of simple"—Stein's rose line does not stop at subverting meaning but continues, in its repetitions, to proliferate it. The repetitions shake out the language, like a dusty rug whose pattern reemerges as the layers of dirt are beaten from it. When Stein asserts "Rose is a rose is a rose is a rose," the old associations are cast off by the fourth "rose." Formulating the connotative effects of this passage sequentially, we can say that the first rose is the noun that can no longer name, the second rose is the metaphor that fails to figure, the third rose is the insistence that keeps the word signifying, and the fourth rose is a renewed word produced by the proliferation of namings. All of these effects are echoed in each "rose." It is crucial that the disruptions of reference and metaphor are followed by the continuing signification of insistence because excess is, above all, a refusal of silence.

"Rose is a rose is a rose is a rose," emblematic of Stein's style, has engendered emblematic critiques of the excesses of her style. Brinnin's biography, for example, is called *The Third Rose* and opens with an anecdote about the title in which a friend of his says, "I can go along with those first two roses of hers all right . . . but when she gets to that third rose she loses me" (xiii). The friend is saying exactly what Stein's reviewers said from the beginning—her style goes too far. Pierre Roche, a contemporary of Stein, associates her literary excesses with her femaleness: "Quantity! Quantity! Is thy name woman?" (Brinnin 150).[9] His outburst, of course, echoes Hamlet's famous complaint about his mother (who was also named Gertrude), "Frailty, thy name is woman." Yet Roche significantly inverts Hamlet's declaration into a question, for as surely as Hamlet is defining femininity by the deficiencies of his mother, Roche is doubting Stein's femininity because of the excesses of her work. He suggests she condense it by "60 to 90%" (150), and he is not alone in thinking her work excessively long. Edmund Wilson considers her style a dilution of content when he says that "the psychological truth is still there, no doubt, but it is in a solution of about one percent to the total volume of the dose, and the volume is enormous" (*Axel's Castle* 240–41). Publishers, reviewers, and readers alike lamented the excesses of her style: length, repetitions, opaqueness. William Carlos Williams issued the most complete insult against her "quantity" when she showed him her many unpublished manuscripts and asked his advice about what to do with them. According to his *Autobiography* he answered, "If they were mine, having so many, I should probably select what I thought were the best and throw the rest into the fire" (254). More recently, Bridgman has characterized the diversity of her writing as "a crazy quilt of style" (50), an image that depicts Stein's work as haphazard and uncontrolled (and that, incidentally, associates Stein's writing with the cottage *craft* of women—thus dissociating it from high art).

Viewing Stein's writing as an opposition between quantity and quality encourages readers to excerpt only those words or phrases they judge to be the quality.[10] Her critics and readers frequently do to her texts what she would not do—cut out that other 90 percent (and more)—by quoting, explicating, and perhaps reading only a fraction of her work. The fact is, however, that though her works are long, repetitive, and difficult to read, they constitute a process, rather than a static product, that makes excerpting lines extremely problematic.[11] In order to comprehend the event that a Stein text stages, one simply must read it through. Otherwise the relationships between lines, the shifting from words that signify to words that do not, the accumulation of words as objects, the movement of sound-tones, and the emerging argument will be lost. Stein recognized that her style would alienate readers and publishers, but she refused again and again to compromise the project. In "Saving the Sentence" she says outright, "It is easy to say it another way. I will refuse" (*How To Write* 19). This refusal is elaborated in her work as a poetics and thematics of excess.

Stein actually uses the word "excess" in print at least twice, once straightforwardly in a letter and another time enigmatically in a poem. In a letter to *Atlantic* editor Ellery Sedgwick that responded to B.F. Skinner's accusation that the eccentricities of her style were the result of automatic writing (which she had practiced and written about years before as a psychology student), she writes, "I think I achieve [my style] by [e]xtra consciousness, [e]xcess" (Mellow 404). She associates excess positively with the aspects of her writing that Skinner was attacking—incantatory repetition, nonreferential language, and inordinate length. Second, in *Useful Knowledge* the word appears in a suggestive environment, surrounded by other key Steinian terms like "rose," "authority," and "pieces," but its role in the passage is unclear:

> First religion. Roses are necessary and they are given away in this way.
> First religion. And now for an address.
> Second religion. And for redress.
> Third religion. And for excess.
> Fourth religion. And for authority.
> Fourth religion. I have neglected I have not neglected she has not neglected nor has she been neglected nor indeed does she neglect it.
> Third religion. Extra pieces here and there, extra pieces are here and extra pieces are there and she can care for the extra pieces.
>
> *(200)*

It is notable that Stein pairs "extra" and "excess" here (by listing both words under the Third religion) since she also does so in the letter to Sedgwick. She had often mentioned that one of the special gifts of genius was a heightened consciousness that enabled her to speak and listen at the same time (*Lectures in America* 135); perhaps the extra consciousness she refers to in the letter is in part this superior awareness. The "extra pieces" in the last line must be connected to the pieces of words that she recovers after breaking down conventional language into reusable parts. Taken together, the two entries for the Third religion connect the heightened consciousness of the genius and the "leftover" pieces of language, those remaining after conventional writing has used up everything else or maybe resulting from her own demolition of traditional writing. At any rate, the extra pieces represent some sort of verbal surplus that only someone like Stein can "care for."

The roses at the beginning of the passage trigger at least an initial association with the famous rose line and consequently hint that we are in the realm of her revisionary poetics. Without being certain exactly what kind of process we are involved in, it is still possible to sense a four-part movement in the formulaic phrases "And now for an address," "And for redress," "And for excess," "And for authority," especially since each one is successively aligned with a higher degree of religion from first through fourth. Thus, there appears to be some progression from "address" to "authority." If we take the four key words to concern writing (as words like "roses" and "pieces" would indicate), then we have a progressive linguistic movement from address (direct communication) to redress (verbal remedy) to excess (literary superfluity) to authority (power, source, or, quite literally, authorship). We might venture to say that the four religions, like the four roses, move language along a kind of purifying path until it is usable again. "Address," then, is equivalent to simple reference, "redress" to the rectification of literary language (like subverting metaphor), "excess" to insistence, and "authority" to the renewed word. It is, after all, the fourth rose that is finally red/read once more, that, in the terms of this scheme, would have verbal authority.

This reading, though speculative, hazards the view that Stein thought of her own poetics in terms of excess. Like Dickinson's poetry, however, Stein's writing embodies excess rather than expounds on it. Nevertheless, unlike Dickinson she does have a great deal to say about the aspects of her work that are excessive: the length, the repetition, and the opacity (resulting from nonreferential language, omission of punctuation, and disjunctive structure and syntax). And while much scholarship on Stein has already focused on her stylistics, I intend to review Stein's own account of her writing practices in order to demonstrate her consistent argument for poetic excess.

The most frequent charge against Stein's works, of course, is their length. Publishers considered her long manuscripts too expensive to print, and readers felt they were too tedious to read.[12] Yet publishers and readers obviously have accepted long books for centuries; in fact, the view that a poet's career cannot be fully established until he has written an epic-length poem is a commonplace of literary studies. Certainly Stein's fellow modernists were concerned with writing long works. Eliot's *The Waste Land* realized the modernist concern with length that had been gradually building, and one poet after another launched his own magnum opus in response to it. When *The Bridge* was only half finished, Hart Crane expressed his delight that it was "already longer than *The Waste Land*" (*Letters* 268–76). The basic distaste for Stein's long works was not solely a literary issue, I think, but one of gender. The great length struck people as unladylike just as Dickinson's literary excesses struck Austin as breaching the limits of "female propriety and sedate deportment." In fact, Stein's detractors often criticized her literary output in metaphors that seem inspired by her physical largeness. In "The Somagrams of Gertrude Stein," Catherine R. Stimpson analyzes the public obsession with Stein's weight and rightly uncovers the inherent misogyny in it: "To [Stein's detractors], her physical fatness is nothing less than proof of a hideous cultural and psychological overrun" (184) of the "monstrous qualities of the female body" (183). In fact, even more can be said: many of the reviewers conflate the writer's body and the body of writing in their concern with size. Wyndham Lewis epitomizes this conflation when he personifies Stein's style, creating the illusion that the reader's eye passes over the writer and not merely the writing: "slab after slab of this heavy, insensitive, common prose-song churns and lumbers by" (55). The equation is obvious: the length of her works, like the size of her body, was unfeminine and therefore unacceptable.

Stein herself may have unwittingly made this association between a massive literary output and her own defeminization, though she would have ascribed a positive connotation to it. Writing lengthy works was one way she could maintain her literary voice in an environment that threatened to squelch her. If she wanted to be recognized as equal to the male "geniuses," she would have to produce a substantial corpus of writing—an unladylike production. Further, she chronically feared writer's block (an understandable worry considering she was stifled first by Leo's verbosity and later, in some sense, by the symbolic muteness of her own unpublished manuscripts), and many of her experiments with new styles originated as attempts to overcome the inability to write. Amassing manuscript pages consoled her; she mentions again and again when she anticipates that a piece will be long and even named one work *A Long Gay Book*—perhaps revealing a causal connection between book length and her own optimism.

Yet far more important are the aesthetic motivations for Stein's lengthy works. In "The Gradual Making of The Making of Americans," she gives three reasons that that book grew to be a thousand pages. First, she was writing a history of people; in order to comprehend them, she had to learn their "bottom natures" (84). By listening to people say things over and over, she began to know what was really inside them. As she had explained in *The Making of Americans,* "When you come to feel the whole of anyone from the beginning to the ending, all the kind of repeating there is in them, the different ways at different times repeating comes out of them, all the kinds of things and mixtures in each one, anyone can see then by looking hard at any one living near them that a history of every one must be a long one" (128). Personal histories would, by her definition, be very long. Second, world history also necessitated a long format:

> In describing English literature I have explained that the twentieth century was the century not of sentences as was the eighteenth not of phrases as was the nineteenth but of paragraphs. As I explained paragraphs were inevitable because as the nineteenth century came to its ending, phrases were no longer full of any meanings and the time had come when a whole thing was all there was of anything. . . . And so it was natural that in writing The Making of Americans I had proceeded to enlarge my paragraphs so as to include everything. (158–59)

Only in long works could the emptiness of phrases be counteracted and the depths of a person and the completeness of history be expressed. Third, and perhaps most convincing, casting her narratives in what she calls the "continuous present" inevitably made them long (148). By continuous present she means two things. First, it is a narrative tense that undermines the balance of beginning, middle, and end in traditional plots by starting again and again. It progresses by minutely shifting ruminations and restatements that continually loop the thread of the narrative backward. The precursor to the continuous present was the prolonged present, in which she first experimented with stretching out narrative moments; in the continuous present these elongated moments combine with incessant recapitulation to disrupt rather than merely slow down linear movement. In addition to beginning over constantly, the continuous present "us[es] everything"—presumably since there is unlimited time and space to elaborate bottom nature and world history. In "Composition as Explanation" Stein equates these narrative principles with excess, and excess, in turn, with length:

> In this beginning naturally since I at once went on and on very soon there were pages and pages and pages more and more elaborated creating a more and more continuous present including more and more using of everything and continuing more and more beginning and beginning and beginning.
> I went on and on to a thousand pages of it. (*What Are Masterpieces* 32)

Finally, the continuous present is a notion that throws the emphasis in writing on the ongoing process of creation.

The length of Stein's works is also obviously the result of what many readers find the most irksome feature of her style, repetition. Repetition manifested itself in almost every stylistic development she pursued. At times it seems almost a primal structure in her imagination, a technique she had the most basic kind of trust in. It enabled her to invent the continuous present by beginning again and again, and it proved revelatory of the bottom nature. Insistence, the style that generated the rose line, is an extension of these techniques. Marianne DeKoven characterizes insistence as "a reduced, simple vocabulary, emblematic key words, incantatory rhythm, and above all, repetition" (51). Stein, of course, would have rejected the use of the word "repetition," calling it instead insistence, duplicating, doubling, or reusing.[13] Her terms for repetition convey its kinetic property—the feature that allows for constant change; thus, the four roses do not represent static repetitions of the same word but insistent variations each constituting a new word.

Finally, in "Poetry and Grammar" she explains her most radical reason for repeating words. After avoiding nouns in prose (in favor of the verbs, adverbs, and prepositions that she considered to be less definitive and static than nouns), she discovered that poetry "has to do with vocabulary just as prose does not" (*Lectures in America*

230). In poetry she at last had to confront nouns, but she was still determined to reject their tyranny. Her answer to this dilemma was to "refuse" nouns by using them, a method that depends on the double entendre in "refuse" (as a verb, to reject) and "refuse" (as a noun, waste material)—and possibly on a third pun, "re-fuse" (to fuse again, to generate new energy in words): "I resolutely realized nouns and decided not to get around them but to meet them, to handle in short to refuse them by using them" (228). Not surprisingly, Stein cites "A rose is a rose is a rose is a rose" as one result of her "using losing refusing and pleasing and betraying and caressing nouns" (231).

Repetition also figures in the third manifestation of her poetics of excess: opaqueness. Many readers feel that from the time she began writing portraits around 1906 (after *Three Lives*) until the late twenties (when she wrote *Lucy Church Amiably* and "Four Saints in Three Acts") her works are hopelessly hermetic. Repetition plays a key role in making words appear devoid of meaning. To many readers, the incessant repetitions knock the sense out of words, as it were, making them numb and inexpressive. For Stein, however, the experience of writing the portraits was enlivening and highly expressive. Ironically, as readers lost touch with her words, she felt she had gotten a hold of them. In "Portraits and Repetition," she writes:

> I became more and more excited about how words which were the words that made whatever I looked at look like itself were not the words that had in them any quality of description. This excited me much at the time.
>
> And the thing that excited me so very much at that time and still does is that the words or words that make what I looked at be itself were always words that to me very exactly related themselves to that thing the thing at which I was looking, but as often as not had as I say nothing whatever to do with what any words would do that described that thing. (*Lectures in America* 191–92)

She recognizes that she is using language in an unusual way—non-referentially—but she feels that this manner of composition is nevertheless precise, "very exactly related."[14] In addition to emptying words of their ordinary associations so they can be used anew, repetition breaks words down into pieces. The pieces become the raw materials for a renewed literature. Similarly, "refusing" nouns is a way of breaking them into pieces, it "[breaks] the rigid form of the noun the simple noun poetry which now [is] broken" ("Poetry and Grammar" 237).[15]

Stein's lack of punctuation (and, more rarely, her unorthodox punctuation) is another stylistic element that contributes to her opaqueness. A brief part of her elaborate treatise on punctuation makes clear that conventional punctuation would undermine the struggle that she wants readers to have with her texts:

> A long complicated sentence should force itself upon you, make you know yourself knowing it and the comma, well at the most a comma is a poor period that it lets you stop and take a breath but if you want to take a breath you ought to know yourself that you want to take a breath. . . . The longer, the more complicated the sentence the greater the number of the same kinds of words I had following one after another, the more the very many more I had of them the more I felt the passionate need of their taking care of themselves by themselves and not helping them, and thereby enfeebling them by putting commas in. ("Poetry and Grammar" 221)

Clearly, she views both conventional writing and typical readers as enfeebled. Insistence revives deadened language, and the omission of punctuation works prophylactically to prevent words and readers from becoming weakened by habit. Furthermore, the lack of punctuation throws stress on the words themselves—and on their relationships—and calls attention to the ways in which Stein has ordered language instead of allowing readers to impose familiar grammatical patterns that would enervate her writing.[16]

Repetition, nonreferential language, omission of punctuation—all of these aspects of Stein's style contribute to the disjunctiveness of her work, the final feature of her opacity that concerns excess. An anonymous reviewer depicts his violent sense of disjunctiveness after reading "Portrait of Mabel Dodge at the Villa Curonia": "After a hundred lines of this I wish to scream, I wish to burn the book, I am in agony. It is not because I know that words *cannot* be torn loose from their meanings . . . It is not because I see that this is a prime example of the 'confusion of arts.' No, my feeling is purely physical. Someone has applied an egg-beater to my brain" (Hoffman 38–39). Stein would probably be gratified at the violence of his response since it confirms that her style is disrupting the habituated relation of reader to text. While most of Stein's literary innovations aim at purifying the language, disjunction serves to purify the reader. Lisa Ruddick recognizes one instance of this in *Tender Buttons:* "Stein . . . has various ways of recreating innocence in the reader. First, she undoes the symbolic order by using words noninstrumentally; even where we can identify discursive content, there is an element of verbal play that distracts us. . . . To force us to appreciate the texture of words, Stein uses puns, . . . repetitive or rhythmic sounds, syntactic distortions, and paradoxically, a sheer overflow of reference that makes the text obscure rather than transparent" ("A Rosy Charm" 236). What Ruddick calls "innocence" Stein refers to as "foreignness." In "An American in France," she examines the benefits of cultural dislocation. "You are you and if you are you in your own civilization you are apt to mix yourself up too much with your civilization," while being in a foreign country allows a person to "have freedom inside yourself" (*What Are Masterpieces* 63). This freedom allows us to escape our confining histories and languages. Stein had learned this herself when she first moved to Paris. In *The Autobiography of Alice B. Toklas,* she explains that being in France among people who did not speak English (and being unable to speak French herself) brought her to a new sense of her own language: "One of the things that I have liked these years is to be surrounded by people who knew no english. It has left me more intensely alone with my eyes and my english. I do not know if it would have been possible to have english be so all in all to me otherwise" (66). She advocates foreignness in both books as a means of sharpening our identities and renewing our relationship to language.

Early in her career, Stein had been admonished by William James: "complicate your life as much as you please, it has got to simplify" (Haas 34). Her own formulation in "Poetry and Grammar" of her urge to include everything condenses his observation into an adage: "Complications make eventually for simplicity" (220). The simplicity she sought was a purified language. The complications she invented to achieve this comprise a manifesto of poetic language; but unlike other aesthetic treatises that outline a program for poetry in prose, Stein's theorizing proceeds in the poetry as well. The poems refer to their own revisionary project through the enactment of the poetics of excess, and they must be read by different criteria than poems that make more static claims.

A theory of reading Stein would itself have to be a kind of crazy quilt. Its considerations would include verbal surfaces (words as objects, words as space, lines, sentences, and paragraphs), insistence, wordplay (spelling games, sounds, puns, double entendres, coinages, proper names), figurative language (the refusal of metaphor, the use of synecdoche, metonymy, imagery, symbolism), nonsense, difference (foreignness, disjunction, refusal), syntax (word order, questions, definitions, sentence diagramming), intimacy (eroticism, messages to Alice, private jokes), "translations," intertextuality, instrumental and noninstrumental usages, literary allusions and "pieces," dialogic voice, and the quotidian. Most important, it would have to apprehend both the autonomy of the pieces and their place in the larger patterns that they compose.

Though Stein's extensive writings on art and composition issue an elaborate poetic theory, the task of reading a Stein poem remains formidable. Her aesthetic of excess, which renders most of the poems long and difficult, places heavy demands on the reader. An example of the kind of writing Stein's theories produce is the crucial poem about aesthetics, "Patriarchal Poetry." This poem is her counterpart to Eliot's *The Waste Land,* Pound's *Cantos,* Williams's *Spring and All* and *Paterson,* Crane's *The Bridge,* and HD's three long *Trilogy* poems in that it is at once a rejection of the Western literary past and an attempt to erect a new literature on the ruins of that demolished culture. Written in 1927, it falls between the hermetic lyricization of daily life and love that *Tender Buttons* inaugurated and the gradual return to referential language and conventional narrative during the thirties and forties—especially after World War II when she recognized the urgency and necessity of the literal. This forty-page poem, consisting of more than a thousand lines and hundreds of "paragraphs,"[17] troubled readers from the beginning. In the preface to *Bee Time Vine,* the volume in which it appears, Virgil Thomson admits "I have not the slightest idea what it means." In the next breath, however, he is more optimistic: "Perhaps one day I may find the meaning in it. Gertrude Stein's lines do sometimes give up their secrets over the years" (vi).

Unfortunately, few of her lines have imparted their secrets in the years since they were written, principally because Stein's poetic canon has been shrouded under the critical assumption that it is not—and was not intended to be—readable.[18] Even a book on Stein's experimental language claims that "[m]ost of 'Patriarchal Poetry' not only defies interpretation, it defies reading" (DeKoven 138). Others have suggested that "Patriarchal Poetry" is not about patriarchy at all and that the pun in the title and throughout the poem on "patriarchal" and "patriotic" is too pointed actually to mean anything. Still others have guessed that Stein chose the title of the poem because she liked the alliteration of the *p*'s or because she "found the phrase both amusingly pretentious and suggestively absurd" (DeKoven 168)— as though any of these motives for the title would also preclude its meaning something.[19]

More recently, Harriet Scott Chessman makes her way well beyond the title to offer a stimulating reading of the poem as a revision of Genesis: "In rewriting Genesis, Stein's meditation links monotheistic creation with a monologic and authoritarian literary form allied to historical and narrative linearity" (126).[20] Chessman's analysis gives us the best indication so far of what reading a poem like this entails and also of the rewards for doing so. My analysis will in some respects amplify Chessman's study, but in treating much more of the poem, I hope to demonstrate that "Patriarchal Poetry" offers a grand aesthetic program that *includes* a revision of Genesis but does not stop there.

In fact, this poem is at the center of Stein's poetics. "Patriarchal Poetry" is a treatise on male-dominated Western literature and Stein's problematic relationship to it. It offers an exposé of literary history and a critique of literary convention at the same time that it advances her own revisionary poetics. Indeed, "Patriarchal Poetry" makes clear that excess is the only remedy for an ailing literary tradition. The poetics of excess revitalize a calcified literature, create space in an overcrowded literary history, disrupt literary tradition, and restore the excluded feminine to language and literature. Further, these stylistics carry forth an argument about patriarchal poetry that analyzes its failures, parodies its conventions, and dismantles its forms in order to prepare the way for new literatures.

"Patriarchal Poetry" is a kind of mock epic, launching itself, as Joyce, Pound, and even Eliot's works had done, back toward the beginnings of Western poetry where the heroic quest for a new literature might logically be taken up. Stein's journey will not retrace the footsteps of this literary history but will instead strike out from that starting point in an entirely new direction. Her allusions to the beginnings of patriarchal poetry are far more oblique and fragmented than her contemporaries' references to earlier literary odysseys because she is not attempting to recapitulate literary history by shoring fragments against ruins or trying to write Paradise.[21] What Stein captures in her muted echo of Homer in the opening verse paragraph is the sense of backward movement, a gesture that for her, quite unlike for them, represents the closed, predictable, repetitive nature of patriarchal poetry: "As long as it took fasten it back to a place where after all he would be carried away, he would be carried away as long as it took fasten it back to a place where he would be carried away as long as it took" (254). The vague phrase "he would be carried away" obliquely suggests Odysseus's departure from Ithaca to fight in the Trojan War, his captivity on Calypso's island, and his escape and return journey home. That Stein uses the same pallid phrase for different adventures suggests that they are of a piece. Several features in the passage suggest an allusion to the *Odyssey;* the opening *in medias res,* the passiveness of being "carried away" like Odysseus at the mercy of the gods, the sense in the opening phrase "as long as it took" that a great deal of time passing does not weaken the plot's backward imperatives, and allusions elsewhere in the poem to later literature all indicate that Stein is beginning with Homer. The repetitions of the opening, in fact, reproduce what for Virgil was the problem with the Homeric plot: the validation of the homeward journey, the return to origins rather than progress toward a new destiny.[22]

If indeed this passage can be associated with the *Odyssey,* it is an *Odyssey* stripped of plot and character, an archetypal story of male adventure in which the hero is inevitably carried away and, however long it takes, inevitably carried back again. The curious word "fasten" links this obsessively repeated tale with any attempt to think about or write literature, as though literature itself were inextricably connected to such structures of ritualized masculinity. The second stanza appears to break out of this narrative grasp[23] by unleashing poetic excess in the form of "lively words" and insistence. "For before let it before to be before spell to be before to be before to have to be to be for before to be tell to be to having held to be to be for before to call to be for to be before to till until to be till before to be for before to be until to be for before to for to be before will for before to be shall to be to be for to be for to be before still to be will before to be before for to be to be" (254). "Lively words"—prepositions, verbs, adverbs, and conjunctions—are, for Stein, words that are "on the move" ("Poetry and Grammar" 212) because, unlike nouns and adjectives that are tyrannical in their naming functions, these words are easily mistaken, shifting, flexible. Thus, the lively words in the second stanza cause a kind of verbal flood that dislodges the more "fastened" language of the opening. Further, once the words are in motion, insistence renders them even more capable of change since words are never merely repeated but altered with each reiteration. And these are not just random words being set free here, but echoes of the static literature—"let there be" from the Bible and "to be [or not] to be" from *Hamlet.* Even isolated words, like "spell" and "tell" (and possibly "call") appear to concern literature in their reference to verbal communication.

The frequency of the word "before" reveals that Stein's epic will sweep back further than these fragments of Western literature can take us—perhaps even before "spell" (language) and "tell" (literature).24 Yet "before" is in counterpoint with "until" and "till," creating a sense of history (spanning from "before" to "until") that involves both past and future literatures in this great upheaval of words.

These first two stanzas of "Patriarchal Poetry" introduce one of the sources of the poem's volition: her revisionary poetics act as a powerful verbal flood. In this surge of words we see allusions to the dislodged dominant literature bob to the surface as they are swept along by the tremendous energy and movement of excess— insistence, lively words, noninstrumental language, and the omission of punctuation. The detritus of this tradition is recycled as the raw material of the new poetry when Stein puts into play the word "leaving," which will come to be the root word for a cluster of related terms that all address her role in the process of renewing language: "Little pieces of their leaving which makes it put it there to be theirs for the beginning of left altogether practically for the sake of relieving it partly" (254).

The poem's most obvious attack on the received literary tradition employs these pieces in the form of parodic allusions to patriarchal poetry. While allusions to Western literature are never permitted to distract us, one senses the presence of Odysseus, Hamlet, and Macbeth; hears echoes from the Bible and fairy tales; catches references to

Homer, Shakespeare, the Romantics, and even the Moderns.[25] Most of these references are fractured and oblique, and rightly so, since the new poetics has demolished such literary monuments. Normally, it is only their pieces that Stein employs—elemental, purified bits that can be used for the new literature without polluting it. At one point, however, the poem encounters a parodic representative work of patriarchal poetry en masse, ironically permitting its totality to enact its own deficiency. "A Sonnet" appears midway through the poem as one such artifact of the exhausted tradition, intact but fossilized:

A SONNET
To the wife of my bosom
All happiness from everything
And her husband.
May he be good and considerate
Gay and cheerful and restful.
And make her the best wife
In the world
The happiest and the most content
With reason.
To the wife of my bosom
Whose transcendent virtues
Are those to be most admired
Loved and adored and indeed
Her virtues are all inclusive
Her virtues are beauty and her beauties
Her charms her qualities her joyous nature
All of it makes of her husband
A proud and happy man.

(272)

The poem, of course not technically a sonnet, is reminiscent of that form in its celebration of love, obsession with the female object, and valorization of the lyric speaker. The content of the poem, in fact, is what is at issue, and thus its refusal of form is what makes the deficiencies of content so glaring. In it a male speaker praises his wife's beauty and virtues. She is the charming woman who makes him proud, yet he credits himself with her qualities, believing his own worthiness makes her "the best wife in the world." This "sonnet" reveals that love poems of this sort celebrate unequal relations between men and women and exploit the female object of love as a means of validating the male speaker.

Yet the tensions of sexual difference, if we can call them tensions here, obviously need not produce such flat poetry. Indeed, in the tradition of sonnet sequences to which this poem weakly refers, the pretext for the poem is desire—not satiation. Such sonnets were inspired by and addressed to a woman one could not have, an ideal, unattainable lover who served as muse rather than as mistress.[26] The state of desire that frequently engenders the sonnet, then, is replaced in Stein's poem by contentment bordering on torpor. Complacency, rather than desire, motivates this speaker, and his stasis embodies the larger poem's charge that the conventions and concerns of sonnets are trite, abstract, and empty. It is striking, especially since Stein considered poetry the noun's genre, that the speaker in "A SONNET" uses almost no concrete nouns: instead, he deals in empty abstractions like "happiness," "virtues," "beauties," "charms." Even his string of superlatives is lifeless—"best wife," "happiest," and "most content"—and his explanation for them, "with reason," is utterly flaccid. Similarly, inert generalizations like "everything," "transcendent values," "all inclusive," and "all of it" reveal their speaker's profound lethargy. The language of this sonnet, like its form, has disintegrated almost completely. Stein's parody ridicules patriarchal poetry, revealing that its forms, conventions, and concerns have become a parody of themselves.

Since Stein is no traditional sonneteer, she can allow the poem to function both as a parody of patriarchal poetry and as a ditty to Alice B. Toklas (Toklas typed Stein's handwritten manuscripts every morning when she had retired after a long night of writing; here and elsewhere, Stein sprinkles her work with little messages and greetings to Toklas). That Stein feels free to make an analogy between their unorthodox lesbian relationship and the traditional heterosexual one depicted in the poem suggests how unconstrained she felt by the patriarchal model. Indeed, it is ironically only in the context of an unconventional marriage that these orthodox abstractions once more have some force. Here, for instance, lines like "[May he] make her the best wife / In the world" ring with playful ambiguity: Stein *as husband* (she in fact referred to herself as such) is vowing to *be* a good wife as well as to celebrate the goodness of her wife. That even a parody of love poetry can function, in Stein's revisionary practice, as a romantic ditty indicates the potential of such "leavings" of the exhausted literary tradition. Everything is reusable in Stein's poetic vision.

But Stein's critique of patriarchal poetry goes deeper than these parodic allusions can suggest. Her analysis uncovers two related problems. Broadly speaking, the first concerns patriarchal poetry as a closed system; here she argues that the noun's tyrannical urge to define and delimit words is reciprocated in the poet's (and publisher's and reader's) attempts to define "good" poetry and delimit the literary canon. The second issue also formulates patriarchal thinking in terms of what Stein perceives as the problem of poetic language. Stein contends that metaphor—the cornerstone of poetic language—has lost its ability to figure difference. The metaphors of patriarchy have become predictable and hollow and thus fail to put words into new relations with each other, fail to vitalize poetry.

There is no doubt that Stein intended "Patriarchal Poetry" to refer to patriarchy, as phrases like "following dukedom duke" (255), "first it was the grandfather then . . . the father . . . and then she . . . not as good as that" (272) suggest.[27] "Signed by him" (274), and "Men many men many how many many many many men men men said many here" (280) establish the patrilineal character and the sheer maleness of literary tradition. Likewise, "patriarchal" implies "privileged," as many other phrases make clear: it is a poetry that has been "having an advantage all the time" (254), that even from a distance "still bears their name" (264), a poetry that "makes it be theirs" only when it is "Allowed allowed allowed" (275).

Because these grandfathers, fathers, and sons have privileged access to the canon, it has become a closed, inbred system that enfeebles itself with its own lack of diversity. One stanza formulates this problem through the rhymes "chose" and "close," two words that suggest selection and exclusion: "Patriarchal poetry means and close patriarchal means and chose chose" (29). When such a system chooses its members so selectively, it naturally closes itself to others. Thus, Stein acknowledges her own position late in the poem when she asserts that "Patriarchal Poetry includes not being received" (289), an ironic turn of phrase that says she is "included" in the tradition only in the sense that it "includes [excluding]" her. Throughout the poem she has commented on the dominant literature's exclusion of unorthodox poetries: "they please themselves indeed" (275) by "not letting half of it be by" (255); or "If he is not used to it, this is the beginning of their singling singling" (262); they will only "include cautiously" (273) and their "selecting . . . is very well thought out" (284) because patriarchal poetry is "their place their allow" (290) that they have "filled to method" (287) and "obtained with seize" (287).

The word "seize" signals that patriarchal control of the canon has been achieved and maintained by force. This point is connected to the theme of militarism that surfaces several times throughout the poem. But the militarism, though obliquely menacing (the ominous sound of marching in "patriarchal poetry left left left right left" [294] or the hint of war in "Patriarchal Poetry is the same as Patriotic poetry" [264]), is distinctive for its stiltedness rather than its violence. We first hear the arid monotony of traditional poetry early in the poem when one of the many definitions of "patriarchal" sounds like a textbook description or field report: "Patriarchal in investigation and renewing of an intermediate rectification of the initial boundary between cows and fishes" (258). Indeed, another section confirms that patriarchal poetry is reasonable, administrative, reserved, "interdiminished," and regular (271); and a few pages later, it is again described as usual, accountable, and reasonable (274). In such passages, lines that register its monotonous qualities are interwoven with lines that count numbers to suggest further the tedium of the closed system:

> Patriarchal poetry makes it as usual.
> Patriarchal poetry one two three.
> Patriarchal poetry accountably.
> Patriarchal poetry as much.
> Patriarchal Poetry reasonably.
> Patriarchal Poetry which is what they did.
> One Patriarchal Poetry.
> Two Patriarchal Poetry.
> Three Patriarchal Poetry.
> One two three.
> One Patriarchal Poetry.
> Two Patriarchal Poetry.
> Three Patriarchal Poetry.
>
> (274)

In addition to this almost bureaucratic stiffness and monotony, patriarchal poetry has become weak and ineffectual because of its refusal to include poets and poetries that would invigorate it. She seems to associate this failure to develop with a fundamental childishness or immaturity. When Stein says that "Patriarchal Poetry is used with a spoon" (271), she suggests that it has become a kind of pabulum—the bland, smooth diet of readers, writers, and publishers who prefer sameness to difference, who "never like to bother to be sure" (260). The numbers, then, convey not only the repetitive, mechanical, measured nature of such poetry but also its elementary, primer-like sensibility. Passages like "One divided into into what what is it" (278) or "Three thousand divided by five" associate patriarchal poetry with a schoolboy's lessons. Still others give it the sound of nursery rhymes or children's counting games: "Two make it do three make it five four make it more five make it arrive and sundries" (263) is reminiscent of the rhyming jingles that aid children in remembering their numbers; "One little two little one little two little one little two little" (276) recalls "One little two little three little Indians," another counting game; "Forty-nine more or at the door" (279) echoes counting rhymes like "Not last night but the night before, twenty-four robbers came knocking at the door." She considers catering to infantile tastes in order to perpetuate the status quo "negligence" (291) and insists "they do not do it right" (291), "Patriarchal Poetry does not make it never made it will not have been making it" (293).

Given what we know of Stein's theory of language, the poem's most condemning assessment of patriarchal poetry may be that it "makes no mistake"—it is a poetry of convention that worries about making mistakes, a poetry dominated by its rules (263). If we recall that prepositions are Stein's favorite type of words because they can be mistaken, then the many references to the fact that this literature makes no mistakes confirm its lack of spontaneity and its inflexibility. This rigidity in poetry is, of course, parallel with the canon at large; the same kind of thinking that appreciates static language also prefers a stable canon. Thus, this authoritarian sensibility protects its own interests by defining and conserving the canon. Not surprisingly, the "best" work is that which is most static: "Patriarchal poetry makes no mistake makes no mistake in estimating the value to be placed upon the *best and most arranged* of considerations" (272; emphasis added). The measured certainty and predictability of the numbers, as well as their suggestion of something very elementary, capture this complex paradoxical portrait of a literature that is at once childish and tyrannical, that squanders all its energies on monitoring itself and reserves nothing for continued growth and innovation.

Stein's most devastating argument against patriarchal poetry, however, is her critique of metaphor. She had rejected using metaphor as a staple of literary language years before, of course, in the famous rose line, but this poem constitutes an unrelenting diatribe against it. The argument is pursued in the form of a question that asks, "What is the difference between [A] and [B]." In the space of forty pages, the question is raised at least thirty times. The poem often answers the question, but sometimes it does not; and, in any case, the answers are rarely the same since the question is intended to provoke investigation into figurative language, not to resolve the issue.

One point the poem makes in asking this question is that figurative language is often completely detached from its literal foundations. In their concern with being "poetical," writers have lost touch with the original meanings of words. In her word portraits Stein had used words in such a way that would restore a sense of "their weight and volume complete"; here, too, she emphasizes the word as elemental entity. For example she asks, "What is the difference between right away and a pearl there is this difference . . . a pearl is milk white and right away is at once" (270) or "What is the difference between a fig and an apple. One comes before the other" (276). The first answer suggests that each word must be recognized independently from other words; the pearl is a concrete noun and can be described in figurative language—it is "milk white"—but the phrase "right away" is abstract and less susceptible to figuration. On the other hand, the pearl is static because it is a noun, while "right away" suggests movement and speed. To ask what the difference is between these two words (a question that always also assumes a similarity) is to link two different species of words. For the purpose of creating a metaphor out of them, there is little to be gained from asking what their difference is: they are too obviously different. However, setting them side by side accentuates their limits and possibilities, forces a reappraisal of their "weight and volume," their potential as elemental words. The second answer focuses attention on context; from this perspective, the most superficial difference between this fig and this apple is that "fig" appears first in the sentence and "apple" second. In using these two particular words to illustrate the authority of context, Stein is disregarding (or implicitly denying) the powerful literary precedent that links them—in Genesis, Adam and Eve must cover themselves with fig leaves for the sin of eating the apple (in that context, of course, the apple comes before the fig). By denying their intertextual lives, Stein is forcing the issue of context, insisting that this very sentence bears upon their meanings. Each time a word is "reused," its other associations must be "refused"; the trick in understanding this is to remember that to refuse a word means both to reject it *and* to recycle it (the double entendre on the noun "refuse" allows the leavings of one word to be the raw material of the new). These two examples warn that the elemental meaning of a word can be suppressed by its association with other words. Stein's overly literal answer to the question "what is the difference" removes the two terms from their metaphorical context and restores their independent significance.

Another problem with metaphor is that it encourages poets to see difference where there is none, to create artificial or even tortured relations between terms. The poem asserts, "There is no difference between having been born in Brittany and having been born in Algeria" (265), and asks "What is the difference between Elizabeth and Edith. She knows. There is no difference between Elizabeth and Edith that she knows" (278) or "What is the difference between two spoonfuls and three. None" (286). Of course, one can find any number of differences between these pairs, but Stein is asking us to consider whether marking their differences gets us anywhere. Moreover, the differences between Edith and Elizabeth result, as that passage continues, from changes in syntax. The stanza operates as an exhibition of sentence diagramming in which "What is the difference between Elizabeth and Edith. She knows" becomes "What is the difference between Elizabeth and Edith *that* she knows" (there may be differences between them, but it asks for the particular difference that she knows). She mockingly refers to poets who contrive useless metaphors as the ones who "know the difference between instead and instead" (264). And, in a more troubled passage that may touch on her "differences" with her own brother, she asks, "Does she know how to ask her brother is there any difference between turning it again again and again and again" (265).

Ironically, certainly for Stein there is a difference between "again again" and "again and again"; the first phrase is akin to her style of writing in which the omission of the conjunction allows each word to push its meaning forward independently and permits the two words together to operate on the principle of insistence; the second phrase, however, functions within a traditional syntax in which the conjunction signals mere repetition. Similarly, "the difference between ardent and ardently" (279) is that "ardently," an adverb, is a lively word, while the adjective is not. Thus, just when she persuasively shows that it is silly to tease out the difference between "instead and instead," she just as convincingly shows that it is useful to consider the difference between "ardent and ardently." Clearly her purpose is not to eradicate the metaphor's preoccupation with difference but to render it more subtle and attentive.

Related to this interrogation of difference is the recognition that "Patriarchal poetry is the same" (77, 275)—the most condensed, devastating, anticanonical line in the poem and one Stein repeats intermittently. Metaphors should figure difference, but patriarchal poetry (in addition to its problems apprehending difference with keenness and insight) has degenerated into mere repetition. The following example adroitly shows not only the formulaic quality of traditional figures but also the difficulty of distinguishing them from each other: "A hyacinth resembles a rose. A rose resembles a blossom a blossom resembles a calla lily a calla lily resembles a jonquil and a jonquil resembles a marguerite a marguerite resembles a rose in bloom a rose in bloom resembles a lily of the valley a lily of the valley resembles a violet and a violet resembles a bird" (270). In patriarchal poetry, all the various flowers blur into the unitary concept of Flower because they are all used in exactly the same way. And even worse, the staple images of poetry (especially birds and flowers) have become indistinguishable from one another: "a violet resembles a bird." Patriarchal poetry is all "the same" because it slights the crucial distinctions that would give comparisons life. Instead of providing visual and thematic vitality, these images slide automatically into the catchphrases of Western literature such as "rose in bloom" and "lily of the valley." Yet one of the ways Stein assures language will be excessive is to prevent the passage from being wholly constrained by the limits it is describing. It also works affirmatively (like the rose line does) to "refuse" and "reuse" the enervated images of the dominant literature. The flowers transforming into women's names, the aural and visual interest the words themselves exude (*as words*—hyacinth, calla lily, jonquil, marguerite—these are all unusual and sensual words), the staggered gait of the repetitions (a equals b, b equals c, c equals d), and the final comparison fluttering from flora to fauna all affect the passage in an entirely different way. One comes away from a Stein poem—when she writes like this—struck by both the hopelessness of patriarchal poetry and the potential for a new literature.

The final stage of figurative exhaustion comes when the second term of the comparison drops out (perhaps because it has become indistinguishable from the first term) and the literature simply obsessively repeats its own weary images. Stein mimics this degeneration when she urges, "Compare something else to something else" and then answers with a block of words that repeats "Such a pretty bird" over sixty times instead of drawing a real comparison. Stein's excessive repetitions of "such a pretty bird" capture the childish monotony of patriarchal poetic practice; yet like those four roses, or the flowers in the previous passage, the repetitions eventually become (or inherently are) "insistent" and can in the end work to reclaim the image of the bird for literature. Stein's "ode" to a pretty bird rattles numbingly toward unexpected renewal:

> . . . and such a pretty bird and to and to and such a pretty bird and to and such a pretty bird.
> Was it a fish was heard was it a bird was it a cow was stirred was it a third was it a cow was stirred was it a third was it a bird was heard was it a third was it a fish was heard was it a third. Fishes a bird cows were stirred a bird fishes were heard a bird cows were stirred a third. A third is all. Come too. (258)

Rhyming questions disturb the monotony of the "such a pretty bird" litany with fresh cadences and complete syntax, as though the poem itself "come[s] to," emerges from exhaustion and stupor in these suddenly more pleasing lines. The questions don't, of course, achieve conventional meaning, but they do break the spell of the preceding block of words and suggest that significance is possible. Excess seems to provide the last means for regenerating figurative language.

Finally, "what is the difference" also functions as a rhetorical question: it asks "who cares" or "what does it matter." In *Allegories of Reading* Paul de Man discusses the contradictory meanings this question produces: " 'What's the difference' [does] not ask for difference but means instead 'I don't give a damn what the difference is.' The same grammatical pattern engenders two meanings that are mutually exclusive: the literal meaning asks for the concept (difference) whose existence is denied by the figurative meaning. . . . we cannot even tell from [the] grammar whether he 'really' wants to know 'what' the difference is or is just telling us that we shouldn't even try to find out" (9–10).[28] Stein exploits both the literal and figurative sides of this question in "Patriarchal Poetry," insisting that writers attend to each possibility. Asking "what is the difference" restores the literal weight and volume of words even in figurative contexts. And for Stein, asking the question repeatedly is the only way left to register it with writers and readers who are indifferent to difference.

Stein's critique of metaphor, like her analysis of the tyranny of naming, has political as well as rhetorical implications. Each stylistic point provides an illustration at the level of poetic language of the overarching problem with patriarchal poetry: its suppression of difference. "Thank you for the difference in me" (*How To Write* 21) is Stein's declaration, spoken to Toklas as lesbian lover and to herself as experimental writer, that "It will never be Common—more." Above all, Stein does not want to become like the patriarchal poets; her repeated attacks on their poetry are only partly a corrective aimed at them. She is also speaking for her own benefit and must establish again and again her separateness from them—because she has read and enjoyed them all her life, she has defined her work in relation to them, and she recognizes the aesthetic appeal of their tradition. In its parody of Western literature, "Patriarchal Poetry" is her "How-Not-To-Write," a poetical counterpart to her treatise on writing, *How To Write*, a key intertext for this poem.[29] Like her notion of refusing by reusing, Stein's rejection of the dominant literature is not a disengagement from it but rather a deeply ambivalent engagement.

Her ambivalence is overwhelmingly clear: she both "Wish[es] for Patriarchal Poetry" (255) and "Wish[es] to be . . . not like the rest" (257). These contradictions offer another implication of that reiterated question, "What is the difference?" The poem repeatedly questions its relationship to the dominant literature and admits its powerful connections to it: "It was not without some difficulty" (270), "Not only requested but desired" (273), "To like patriarchal poetry as much as that is what she did" (273), "To never blame them" (282),

"Patriarchal Poetry tenderly" (282), "This is mine left to them in place of how very nicely it can be planted" (283), "Did she patriarchal poetry" (285), "feeling at once to be in the wish and what is it of theirs" (291) are just some instances of the nagging concerns throughout the poem that reveal tenderness and longing. She confronts her own reluctance to dissociate herself completely from them: "Patriarchal Poetry if patriarchal poetry is what you say why do you delight in never having positively made it choose" (292). And she admits from the outset that she bears a tenderness for patriarchal poetry that it does not reciprocate: "These words containing as they do neither reproaches nor satisfaction may be finally very nearly rearranged and why, because they mean partly to be left alone. Patriarchal poetry and kindly, it would be very kind in him of him of him to be as much obliged as that" (265). Her refusal to join the dominant literature must be viewed in the context of her ambivalence about it.

Given Stein's ambivalence about her relationship to patriarchal poetry, it is not surprising that she employs excess as a means of rejecting the tradition as well as a way into it. In many lines she appears to refuse it categorically. She expresses "a wish to be not like the rest" (257) and determines "never to have followed farther there" (263), "never to be sent" (270), "never to think of patriarchal poetry at one time" (275). Recognizing that "Patriarchal poetry might be withstood" (281) and that "Patriarchal poetry might be what is left" (282), she can assert "this is mine" (282) and distinguish her work from theirs. She uses lively words and insistence to carry her work past that depleted canon because "Once sleepy one does not need a lullaby" (294). "Letting it Letting it Letting it alone" (284) puts gerunds to work on unfastening that crucial concept signified by the cluster of words around "leaving(s)"—leave, let, left. Similarly, insistence gives force and vitality to her determination "Never to do never to do never to do to do to do never to do . . . to be certain to let to let it to let it alone" (286).

At the same time, however, Stein deploys the techniques of excess in order to storm the castle of patriarchal poetry and get inside.[30] Her style becomes "louder louder to be known" (255), and she is "determined determined . . . re-entered which means entered again and upon" (275).[31] The recurring phrase that articulates her contradictory relation to traditional literature is "Patriarchal poetry in pieces" (281), a line that expresses her paradoxical goal to dismantle the literature and to contribute to it. Breaking apart the word "masterpiece" in order to reveal how the received tradition authorizes itself, Stein proposes to renew poetry by unfastening its "pieces" from its "masters": "Patriarchal Poetry should be this without which and organisation. It should be defined as once leaving once leaving it here having been placed in that way at once letting this be with them after all. Patriarchal Poetry makes it a master piece like this makes it which which alone makes like it like it previously to know that it that that might that might be all very well patriarchal poetry might be resumed" (281). Here as elsewhere, the leavings theme connects the demise of patriarchal poetry to the exclusion of different poetries; yet this, in turn, can be used (reused) to revitalize it. The pieces, here and elsewhere in the poem, are surely the "leavings" of patriarchal poetry that she will reuse "for the sake of relieving it partly"—that is, in order to unburden literary history of itself. Breaking patriarchal poetry down into elemental pieces and then using those pieces to create a new poetry constitutes one wave of her revisionary poetics released in this poem.

"Leaving" is one inflection of a verbal paradigm Stein develops to formulate the relationship of her words to those of patriarchy. The cluster of words associated with "leaving" is complex. First, it refers to the "leavings" of traditional literature, both its own remainders (metaphors and symbols that have become clichés, and language uses it has never even imagined) and the pieces left over after she has demolished it. Second, it signifies the verb "to leave," a word that cuts two ways, in one direction toward the dominant literature that leaves her out and in the other toward her own work that, in turn, leaves traditional literature behind. This inflection generates the related word "left"; again, they have left her out and she has left them behind.[32]

Further, "leave" sometimes means "allow" and when it does, it refers to the complex causal relationship between the fact that literary history excludes her, yet she wants it to give her "leave" to create her own kind of literature. That these contradictory meanings find their expression in one and the same word perfectly and economically captures her ambivalence about a literary tradition she wants to be both recognized in and liberated from. This manifestation of the "leavings" theme builds slowly through the first fifteen pages of the poem—in phrases like "She might be let it be let it be here as soon," "leave her hear she leave her hear," "Leave it with it let it go able to be shiny so," and "Leaving left which is why they might be here be here be here" (261–62)—until it escalates into one of the rare crescendos of the poem. In a burst of repetition that depends significantly upon the imperative form of the verb, "let," the poem demands a place for her in literature through an overwhelming display of verbal excess. Only the full passage can demonstrate the effects of the repetition and resolution of the sequence:

> Let her be to be to be to be let her be to be to be let her to be let her to be let her be to be when is it that they are shy.
> Very well to try.
> Let her be that is to be let her be that is to be let her be let her try.
> Let her be let her be let her be to be to be shy let her be to be let her be to be let her try.
> Let her try.
> Let her be let her be let her be let her be to be to be let her be let her try.
> To be shy.
> Let her be.
> Let her try.
> Let her be let her let her let her be let her be let her be let her be shy let her be let her be let her try.
> Let her try.
> Let her be.
> Let her be shy.
> Let her be.
> Let her be let her be let her let her try.
> Let her try to be let her try to be let her be shy let her try to be let her try to be let her be let her be let her try.
> Let her be shy.
> Let her try.
> Let her try.
> Let her be
> Let her let her be shy.
> Let her try.
> Let her be.
> Let her let her be shy.
> Let her be let her let her be shy
> Let her let her let her let her try.
> Let her try.

Let her try.
Let her try.
Let her be.
Let her be let her
Let her try. Let her to be let her.
Let her be let her let her try.
Let her try.
Let her
Let her try.
Let her be shy.
Let her
Let her
Let her be.
Let her be shy.
Let her be let her try.
Let her try.
Let her try.
Let her try.
Let her let her try
Let her be shy.
Let her try
Let her let her try to be let her try.
Let her try.
Just let her try.
Let her try.
Never to be what he said.
Never to be what he said.
Never to be what he said.
Let her to be what he said.
Let her to be what he said.
Not to let her be what he said not to let her to be what he said.
Never to be let her to be never let her to be what he said. Never let her
to be what he said.
Never to be let her to be never let her to be what he said. Never let her
to be what he said.
Never to let her to be what he said. Never to let her to be let her to be
let her to be let her what he said.

(268–70)

The sequence begins as the feminine pronoun erupts between the stuttered "to be to be" that carries over from earlier in the poem. Behind this phrase, of course, is Hamlet's dilemma, "To be or not to be," which, though it represents his problem, at least also admits of a choice. The female to whom the "her" refers, on the other hand, has clearly never been allowed such a choice. "To be" she must be given an opportunity to try, as the lines make utterly clear, "Let her be. / Let her try." The repetitions tell as much as the words themselves, for the passage conveys above all the necessity of verbal excess: it is the only way she will be heard. The two-page litany constitutes an argument made eloquent more by its size than its sense.

But even this revisionary language has internalized a dismissive view of women that the lines deploy against "her": "Let her be shy." This point of view is momentarily disrupted as the passage reaches its culmination, when the poem seems almost to spit out the lines "Just let her try. / Let her try" with a vengeance. Supporting this attempt to speak for herself are the three repetitions of "Never to be what he said," presumably refusals of the stereotyped definitions of "her" that are abbreviated here in the word "shy." Again, however, the demand to be self-defining is undermined: "Let her to be what *he* said." But this, in turn, generates a new effort to repudiate that point of view, "*Not* to let her be what he said." The next two lines record the continuing struggle over definition as "Never to let her to be" (possibly meaning, "he will never let her be what she wants to be") is elaborated into "Never to let her to be what he said" (a line that vacillates between meaning "he will never let her be what she wants to be" and "*she* will never allow *her* [herself or another woman] to be what he said"). And throughout the section the words "let her" blur into a pun on "letter" that provides a suggestive background hum: all of the verbal shiftings in the passage occur because of the malleability of language's little pieces, letters.

This shouting match between herself and the dominant discourse is at last ended when the intrusion of female erotic imagery disrupts the male/female dialogue with a wholly female discourse:

> Near near near nearly pink near nearly pink nearly near near nearly pink. Wet inside and pink outside. Pink outside and wet inside wet inside and pink outside latterly nearly near near pink near near nearly three three pink two gentle one strong three pink all medium medium as medium as medium sized as sized. One as one not mistaken but interrupted. One regularly better adapted if readily readily to-day. This this this readily. Thursday.
> This part the part the part of it.
> And let to be coming to have it known.
> As a difference.

(269–70)

The "his/her" binarism that has given this section its tension and volition is replaced here with a new opposition that resolves that tension yet still generates energy for the poem. "Wet inside and pink outside" introduces a binarism (inside/outside) that locates femaleness on both sides of the opposition, for it is obviously a description of a woman's body. Likewise, the color pink represents female sexuality both literally, as descriptive of her body, and figuratively, as a color traditionally associated with femininity and as a color that Stein in particular associates with the feminine.[33] The erotic tensions upon which much of Western literature is predicated and the creative energies that such conflicts generate for art are unfortunately the same gender conflicts that tend toward the exclusion of women's artists; here, however, those tensions are superseded by an erotic paradigm that makes women central.

The imperative form of the verb, "let," that gave force earlier in the passage to her demands for inclusion shifts in this section to its other inflection, "allow," and signals the easing of tensions.[34] "And let to be coming to have it known. / As a difference" conveys some cluster of meanings that includes permission (the fulfillment of her request to "let her try"), arrival (both in coming into existence, into the canon, and "coming" in sexual orgasm), recognition (being acknowledged by "them" and being known carnally), and difference. Everything she wanted that she could not get from "them" is supplied in this passage where the sexual and the textual permit and even generate sustaining differences that patriarchal poetry lacks.

The intrusion of a female voice, ordinarily excluded by the dominant literature, occurs elsewhere in the poem. One large repetitive passage ends with "Settle it pink with pink. / Pinkily" (277) as though the introduction of something female "settles" or interrupts the stream of words that characterizes patriarchal poetry. Elsewhere, a play on the word "ruffle" links the gathered edging of a feminine garment to the disruption (ruffling) of the dominant literature: "Return Patriarchal Poetry at this time. / Begin with a little ruff a little ruffle" (288). Many lines simply exude the warmth and tenderness that Stein often associates with women. "She says I must be careful and I will" (264), "it is very warm here" (276), and "It is very nearly a pleasure to be warm" (280) are just a few of the lines that convey this

dimension. Her connection to women emerges in more overt ways
as well: "to be which never separates two more two women" (255),
"having decided not to abandon a sister" (291), and "All the way
through dedicated to you" (266) declare this commitment. Further,
Hamlet's "to be or not to be" goes through another revision in a long
passage that builds upon the phrase "to be to be we" (262–63), a
change that implies that "not being" can be overcome by "being we"
with another woman.

Similarly, passages of sheer nonsense (verbalizations that are not
actual words) also signal the intrusion of an antipatriarchal voice that
is expressly female. Near the end of the poem, for example, a block
of lines all tediously beginning with "Patriarchal Poetry" is finally
interrupted by a stanza of pure nonsense:

> Patriarchal Poetry left.
> Patriarchal Poetry left left.
> Patriarchal poetry left left left right left.
> Patriarchal poetry in justice.
> Patriarchal poetry in sight.
> Patriarchal poetry in what is what is what is what is what.
> Patriarchal poetry might to-morrow.
> Patriarchal poetry might be finished tomorrow.
> Dinky pinky dinky pinky dinky pinky dinky pinky once and try. Dinky
> pinky dinky pinky dinky pinky lullaby. Once sleepy one once does not
> once need a lullaby.

> (294)

Significantly, the assertion that patriarchal poetry might be finished
tomorrow is followed by the eruption of nonsense, as if to enact its
decline by articulating something decidedly unpatriarchal. But, of
course, Steinian nonsense is always rich in significance. The "dinky
pinky" that follows the fatal prediction might just be the first symp-
tom of its decline—the diminished phallus—or a mocking recitation
of its refusal to grow, a baby-talk translation of patriarchal poetry.
"Dinky pinky" is a term poised between the poem's rigid masculinity
(recalled here in the militarism of "left left left right left") and its playful femininity. The "pink" in "dinky pinky" calls up the female sexual
imagery that "finished" patriarchal poetry earlier in the poem.[35]

"Patriarchal Poetry" does not proceed by structured argument or
causal organization. It contains few moments where its tensions reach

a peak and then resolve. Instead it progresses by uneven, contradictory rantings and ruminations. These contradictions do not exactly negate one another because they proceed from different sources and argue conflicting perspectives. For instance, one line asserts that "patriarchal poetry makes no mistake" (272), and this is apparently an indictment against its inflexibility—in addition to being its own inflated claim. Later, though, another voice will say that "Patriarchal poetry makes mistakes" (280), speaking just as critically. The second instance does not reverse the first, but clarifies it: any literature that prides itself on not making mistakes is in fact woefully mistaken. These contradictions emerge because the poem is attempting to understand the problems of patriarchal writing while it is in the very process of writing itself.

Perhaps the single most revealing line, very near the end of the poem, that captures Stein's ambivalence toward such an endeavor comes when she says, "I defy any one to turn a better heel than that while reading" (292). One imagines the speaker approaching patriarchal poetry and then coyly turning a heal on it at the last moment. To admit that she does so "while reading" is to acknowledge her engagement with the very poetry she is rebuffing. Certainly the many allusions to the dominant literature throughout the poem have confirmed that she had read it; yet to reproach patriarchal poetry in the same motion as she approaches it reveals a continuing engagement with it. This involvement is what gives her "leave" to "refuse" it, but the genteel, playful tone of her rebuff gives a whole new cast to her refusal.

The final line of "Patriarchal Poetry" compresses this tone of contrary commitments into a resounding, high-spirited, good-humored affirmation of the poem's success in getting the best of the dominant literature: "Patriarchal poetry and twice patriarchal poetry" (294). Here, in its last repetition, the poem achieves a satisfying balance between refutation and celebration. This terse little line says, "two cheers for patriarchal poetry," as though praising it, *and* "patriarchal poetry, going once, going twice," as though auctioning it off. It is at once the belligerent battle cry and the patronizing pat on the back. Technically, in its brevity and its contracting repetitions, the line closes the poem with a snap of finality. This one line provides emphatic closure to a poem that seemed, for nearly 1,500 lines, to have no shape at all.

While Pound, Eliot, and Williams were "breaking the pentameter," Stein was much more radically "breaking the noun."[36] Their project eschewed literary conventions, as the reference to English prosody reveals; it did not challenge the whole cultural order. Stein desired to do much more—to dismantle literary form and language as a means of renewing culture. *Her* revolution was meant to disrupt the primacy of patriarchal poetry—not to recur to it. Her arsenal consisted of poetic excesses that would prove relevant for later literary revolutions as well.

CHAPTER 4

Sylvia Plath

Splitting the Seams of
Fancy Terza Rima

MY WRITING IS MY WRITING IS MY WRITING.

*I*n her journal in 1958, Sylvia Plath echoed Gertrude Stein's famous rose line, formulating her own private poetic struggle in the same manner Stein had used to formulate what she viewed as a widespread poetic dilemma: "MY WRITING IS MY WRITING IS MY WRITING" (255). For Stein, of course, the repetitions were one strategy for overcoming the inertia of patriarchal poetry. For Plath, the emphatic capitalized sentence was an attempt to wrest her writing from the people she believed were using it—her dead father, mother, husband, teachers, benefactors, and publishers—as a measure of her success and, therefore, of their affection for her. Though Plath only sometimes identified this as a conflict of gender, it is evident that her struggle to earn approval through writing was at bottom the problem of being a woman poet in a man's world: "Being born a woman is my awful tragedy. From the moment I was conceived I was doomed to sprout breasts and ovaries rather than penis and scrotum; to have my whole circle of action, thought and feeling rigidly circumscribed by my inescapable femininity" (27).[1] Again and again the journals record a fundamental recognition: "I am jealous of men" (32). Despite the familiar abbreviation of this conflict in terms of anatomical difference, she obviously desired men's privilege and power, not their physiology. She envied men their ability to be "active and doing, not passive and listening," their physical and sexual independence, and their "freedom to live a double life," to have both a career and a "sexual and family life" (32). Worse still, she knew that as a woman she would have to channel her resources away from herself in order to provide men this double life: "I must pour my energies through the direction and force of my mate" (21).

Though she recognized that writing, even her writing, could offer an escape from the traditional female role, it could not release her from the system of values that drove her to excel at conventional womanhood as well as at writing—and therefore to strain too hard at both. Every problem she ponders in the journals—health, beauty, love, self-confidence, productivity, finances, fulfillment—finds its solution in writing: "Names, words, are power" (236). Yet for most of her life even her best writing only reinforces the image of "inescapable femininity" that haunts her and, ultimately, threatens her writing. A journal entry from 1959 captures these contradictions with frightening clarity:

> It is now almost 11. I have washed two sweaters, the bathroom floor, mopped, done a day's dishes, made the bed, folded the laundry and stared in horror at my face: it is a face old before its time.
>
> Nose podgy as a leaking sausage: big pores full of pus and dirt, red blotches, the peculiar brown mole on my under-chin which I would like to have excised. Memory of that girl's face in the med school movie, with a little black beauty wart: this wart is malignant: she will be dead in a week. Hair untrained, merely brown and childishly put up: don't know what else to do with it. No bone structure. Body needs a wash, skin the worst: it is this climate: chapping cold, desiccating hot: I need to be tan, all-over brown, and then my skin clears and I am all right. I need to have written a novel, a book of poems, a Ladies' Home Journal or New Yorker story, and I will be poreless and radiant. My wart will be nonmalignant. (260–61)

This chain of associations, punctuated with the colon that sets up each descriptive phrase as the inevitable next unit of this paradoxical equation, links her own imperfect face in the mirror with the image of the doomed woman in the medical school movie about cancer: both are mortally flawed. The perfection she fantasizes about, however, is not achieved through washing and tanning (this makes her merely "all right") but through writing. Her work, then, far from liberating her from the demands of conventional femininity, is monstrously in the service of the very ideal that makes writing such a difficult career for a woman to pursue. Not surprisingly, the two magazines that figure in her equation for beauty, health, and success each represent one side of her predicament: the *Ladies' Home Journal,* a domestic women's magazine on the one hand, and the *New Yorker,* a worldly, professional magazine on the other.[2]

The tremendous contradictions Plath felt between being a perfect woman and a great writer are well documented in her journals and letters and richly analyzed in biographies and critical studies.[3] Whereas Dickinson adapted and subverted the role of conventional womanhood and Stein parodied and rejected it, Plath struggled most of her short life to embody it. In *Homeward Bound: American Families in the Cold War Era,* Elaine Tyler May historicizes the "domestic revival" (11) of the 1950s, arguing that the domestic ideology of the Cold War period "emerged as a buffer against [the] disturbing tendencies" of the time. The post-World War II environment, with its threat of nuclear destruction, anti-Communist hysteria, secularism, materialism, bureaucratic collectivism, and consumerism drove people into the perceived safety of the traditional family. Plath's desire to excel at conventional womanhood must be understood in this larger context, a historical circumstance that gives further urgency and importance to her personal and professional ideals. On July 9, 1962, however, the dream of domestic bliss as the groundwork of professional success was shattered irrevocably (though certainly it could never have been realized) when she intercepted a telephone call to her husband that confirmed he was involved with another woman. Two days later she had completed a poem about the incident and titled it "Words heard, by accident, over the phone":

> *O mud, mud, how fluid!—*
> *Thick as foreign coffee, and with a sluggy pulse.*
> *Speak, speak! Who is it?*
> *It is the bowel-pulse, lover of digestibles.*
> *It is he who has achieved these syllables.*

What are these words, these words?
They are plopping like mud.
O god, how shall I ever clean the phone table?
They are pressing out of the many-holed earpiece, they are looking for a
listener.
Is he here?

Now the room is ahiss. The instrument
Withdraws its tentacle.
But the spawn percolate in my heart. They are fertile.
Muck funnel, muck funnel—
You are too big. They must take you back!

(202–3)[4]

"Words Heard" is not, as critics have termed it, merely an occa-
sional piece written by Plath in response to the phone call from her
husband's lover, though that incident surely ignites the poem.[5] It
is not simply confessional but uses the excruciating vividness and
immediacy of the confessional mode to depict the material force of
language. Related to this view of language is the poem's fascination
with hearing, overhearing, and listening to words. In an essay entitled
"Listening," Roland Barthes distinguishes between hearing (a physiological phenomenon) and listening (a psychological act) and identifies three distinct types of listening. The first listening is an alert activity that does not separate animal from human since both are attuned
to significant environmental sounds. The second listening, however,
is deciphering, in which "the ear tries to intercept certain *signs*";
here, he says, human listening begins. The third listening, "does
not aim at—or await—certain determined, classified signs: [what is
important is] not what is said or emitted, but who speaks, who emits:
such listening is supposed to develop in an inter-subjective space
where 'I am listening' also means 'listen to me' " (245–46). Barthes's
formulations identify two relevant aspects of listening *to language,*
as the title of Plath's poem specifies—to *words* heard. First, the act
of listening requires interpretation. Barthes says, "Listening [once
it involves language] is henceforth linked (in a thousand varied,
indirect forms) to a hermeneutics: to listen is to adopt an attitude of
decoding what is obscure, blurred, or mute, in order to make available
to consciousness the 'underside' of meaning" (249). Second, listening
"brings two subjects into relation" (251). The telephone becomes

for Barthes, as it clearly is for Plath, the symbol of such listening because it excludes all other forms of communication: "the archetypal instrument of modern listening, the telephone, collects the two partners into an ideal (and under certain circumstances, an intolerable) inter-subjectivity, because this instrument has abolished all senses except that of hearing: the order of listening which any telephonic communication inaugurates invites the Other to collect his whole body in his voice and announces that I am collecting all of myself in my ear" (251–52).[6] Moreover, a point crucial for understanding both Plath's poem and its particular importance in her canon is that the telephone translates the speaker and the listener into sheer language.

The poem stresses this, of course, in its title where we immediately learn that the words are "heard . . . over the phone," received as disembodied signs of the secret this "accident" reveals. Because the persona has no recourse to other modes of communication (gestures, facial expressions, eye contact), the force of these words is greatly increased. The word "accident" is also extremely important, suggesting as it does both the sense of chance and passivity (the persona does not intend to hear these words) and of calamity. Plath clearly considers the persona's passivity central to this event; this is obvious from the passive verbal construction of the title that allows the subject (the one who hears) to remain unnamed and the object (the words) to ascend to the place of grammatical subject. This intercepted phone call, then, unlike the ideal intersubjectivity of Barthes's telephone conversation, threatens the persona; the circuit of self and other that this call seeks to establish is meant to connect only the two lovers—the husband and caller—and the poem must create a subject position for the third party, the listening persona, as well.

Plath had articulated this sense of passivity years earlier in her journal where she recounts overhearing a conversation between one of her male colleagues and a female student. Hearing his "silly, pretentious, . . . fatuous" chatter, which she recognizes as flirting, she thinks of his wife—the person their flirtation must suppress. Then she specifies her own relationship to the speakers, "Ha, I thought, listening, or rather, hearing" (210). What she is trying to define here by substituting "hearing" for "listening," as well as in the title of her poem, is *overhearing,* a phenomenon that is irresolutely poised somewhere between the involuntary physiological event of hearing and the willed psychological act of listening. Overhearing is distinctive because it begins without the consent of the listener, it enthralls the listener with its sudden relevance, and it imprints itself on the listener. In the case of overhearing something upsetting, the listener experiences a double violation: one is first forced to hear something without giving consent, and one takes in what is heard and can then never afterwards un-hear it.

The analogy the poem finds for such overhearing is rape. The phallic "instrument [which] / Withdraws its tentacle" leaves "spawn [that] percolate in [her] heart"; and the spawn, like the semen of the rapist, "are fertile." Overhearing that marks or imprints the hearer is like rape that impregnates the victim—again pointing to the dual atrocities of the event and its issue. The violent and tortured exclamation "Muck funnel, muck funnel," surely an anagrammatic construction, suggests both visually and aurally the persona's outraged cry of something akin to "fuck you" against her violator as well as her startled realization that she is being "fucked" in some sense by the telephone receiver—the funnel that emits muck. Further, to say "fuck you" to one's rapist is to implicate oneself in the act, a rhetorical equivalent to the way one becomes enthralled by overhearing and begins to listen.

The imagery of rape is further supported by a subtler dimension of the poem. The first two stanzas describe both the caller and the one receiving the call as "he." "Who is it?" the first stanza asks; the answer is "It is he who has achieved these syllables." We might at first assume this refers to the husband; however, in the second stanza, the first "he"—the caller—asks to speak to the second "he"— the husband, "Is he here?" In the actual phone call on which this poem is based, the lover pretended to be a man so she would not be found out. Plath nevertheless recognized the woman, who continued to lower her voice even more and refused to abandon her disguise.[7] Thus the voice Plath heard was "thick" and "sluggy" and spoken by someone who had to impersonate a man to "achieve" her effect. In the logic of the poem, the lover's adoption of the male voice is supremely appropriate because the pain she causes the persona issues from a masculinity that links sexuality and violence—both the husband and his lover are the wife's rapists.

While the metaphor of rape registers a devastating assault on the persona, it also puts her into relation with the two speakers. As their victim, she is no longer the negated overhearer, the deposed subject of the passive sentence. What she has accomplished is wholly verbal: she has transformed their conversation which excluded her into a metaphor that includes her. This move at once harnesses their sexuality and redirects it toward herself—they are no longer making love to each other but raping her. Through the image of rape, their words enter her; further, they fertilize her, and she, in turn, becomes creative. The declaration "They are fertile" precipitates her own creative outburst in the final lines of the poem when she, at last, can articulate: "Muck funnel, muck funnel— / You are too big. They must take you back!" Her demand may at first seem futile since the words of the lovers can never, strictly speaking, be taken back; however, in the idiom of the playground from which this expression derives, words can be taken back if she can force the lovers to recant them. Assuming the voice of a bully, then, in the last line of the poem, the speaker ends with a tone of authority and energy. She may force a renunciation by brute strength or devise ways to make them wish they had never spoken. In either case, she will overpower them verbally. This newfound access to language is empowering and creative; the poem itself is proof of that. She has penetrated the ideal intersubjectivity of their phone call by listening to them. Moreover, listening to them has inaugurated her own (albeit intolerable) intersubjective relation to them: "the listener's silence will be as active as the locutor's speech: *listening speaks,* one might say" ("Listening" 252). In the course of the poem, then, the persona moves from passive hearing to active listening and consequently to verbalizing, for it is she, finally, "who has achieved these syllables" by containing their words within her own.

Both the persona in the poem and the poet writing it achieve syllables with "Words heard." The poem marks a dividing line in Plath's canon just as its subject marked a dividing line in her life. That phone call was a decisive event for the poet and the woman. Even though they are edited carefully to tell only a partial story, the available journals and letters reveal that Plath had long suspected her husband's infidelity, with the woman on the phone that night and with others before. In fact, on the occasion when Plath had overheard her colleague's flirtation with his student, she was looking for her own husband, who was not where he said he would be waiting to celebrate her last day of teaching at Smith College. When she finally located him, he was in much the same situation as her colleague. She records the event in her journal as a thoroughly visual experience:

> I had one of those intuitive visions. I knew what I would see, what I would of necessity meet, and I have known for a very long time, although not sure of the place or date of the first confrontation. Ted was coming up the road from Paradise Pond, where girls take their boys to neck on weekends. He was walking with a broad, intense smile, eyes into the uplifted doe-eyes of a strange girl with brownish hair, a large lipsticked grin, and bare thick legs in khaki Bermuda shorts. I saw this in several sharp flashes, and his smile, though open and engaging as the girl's was, took on an ugliness in context. His stance next to [her male colleague's] clicked into place, his smile became too white-hot, became fatuous, admiration-seeking. He was gesturing, just finishing an observation, and explanation. The girl's eyes souped up giddy applause. She saw me coming. Her eye started to guilt and she began to run, literally, without a good-bye. (211)

She calls her precognition about her husband and the girl a "vision" and says she knew beforehand what she "would see"—formulations that emphasize the visual quality of her discovery. Even the relationship between the husband and the young woman proceeds by sight: his "eyes [looking] into the uplifted doe-eyes" of the student. Emphasizing the visual nature of the experience further, Plath employs the metaphor of photography: "I saw this in several sharp flashes." Finally, the passage ends with an extended description in which the girl becomes an eye, and her apprehension of the wife (like the wife's of her) is therefore thoroughly visual: "The girl's eyes souped up the giddy applause. She saw me coming. Her eye started to guilt."

Concluding the long journal entry that describes both stories of a husband's infidelity, Plath feels that acknowledging the painful facts at least restores her sense of self. Rendering the event visual once again, she uses the image of the mud, which she will later develop much more fully in the poem, as a figure for his deceit and her lack of recognition: "my intuition clears for me like a pool of clearing water after the mud settles" (213). Other passages in the journals and letters about suspected betrayals similarly rely on visual more often than on verbal evidence. And she apparently invariably *overlooked* what she had seen. Contributing to the significance of the July 9 incident may be the fact that it was purely verbal. More powerful than any indication of infidelity she had witnessed, the words she overhears possess a blunt materiality that she finds undeniable. The poem is able to capture the force and palpability of the words heard over the phone through a style of excess that had already become Plath's trademark in *The Colossus.*

I begin with "Words Heard" for several reasons. First, it raises the inevitable question of whether Plath is "merely" a confessional poet, confronting the problematic correlation between her biography and her poetry. Second, "Words Heard" marks a shift in Plath's poetic canon away from what have been called her apprentice poems in *The Colossus* toward what most readers consider her masterful and authentic *Ariel* poems.[8] And finally, the poem employs stylistic and thematic excess in order to articulate and control its unwieldy subject matter.

Plath rejected confessionalism in poetry as an end in itself. Recording several of her most famous "confessional" poems—"Purdah," "Lady Lazarus," "Cut," "Medusa," "Daddy"—in October 1962, she also commented on her use of personal experience:

> I think my poems immediately come out of the sensuous and emotional experiences I have, but I must say I cannot sympathize with these cries from the heart that are informed by nothing except a needle or a knife, or whatever it is. I believe that one should be able to control and manipulate experiences, even the most terrifying, like madness, like being tortured, this sort of experience, and one should be able to manipulate these experiences with an informed and an intelligent mind. I think that personal experience is very important, but certainly it shouldn't be a kind of shut-box and mirror-looking, narcissistic experience. I believe it should be *relevant,* and relevant to larger things. (*Plath Reads Plath*)

The publication of her *Letters Home* and her *Journals*—where she presumably records her experiences with less artistic intent than in her poetry—has confirmed her claim that autobiographical details are manipulated in her poetry by "an informed and intelligent mind."[9] But the poems, of course, must make their own case for their relevance to larger things. In the final essay of a 1977 collection of Plath criticism, Irving Howe concludes that they do not succeed in this, that her thematic and stylistic excesses limit her poetic vision; his concerns are echoed by many other critics.[10] Howe poses what he considers "the hardest critical question remain[ing]" about Plath's work: whether her vivid evocation of emotional extremity constitutes an adequate poetic vision (235).

If this is the hardest critical question that remained in 1977, then it should have been answered in 1981 with the publication of *The Collected Poems*, for there at last it became clear that Plath's *Ariel*, as opposed to Hughes's published version, was not in fact her death knell in verse. In his introduction to *The Collected Poems*, Hughes divulges the astonishing history of the *Ariel* manuscript almost non-chalantly, as though innocent of its enormous significance. He writes, "Some time around Christmas 1962, she gathered most of what are now known as the 'Ariel' poems in a black spring binder, and arranged them in a careful sequence. (At the time, she pointed out that it began with the word 'Love' and ended with the word 'Spring.' . . .) The *Ariel* eventually published in 1965 was a somewhat different volume from the one she had planned" (14–15). As Marjorie Perloff has demonstrated in her crucial essay "The Two Ariels: The (Re)making of the Sylvia Plath Canon," Plath's *Ariel* tells a narrative of rebirth while Hughes's *Ariel* presents a narrative of inevitable suicide (11). Thus, the question that Howe thinks will stump Plath admirers— Is the suicidal state of mind ground for high valuation?—must be revised. Is the suicidal state of mind the final vision of *Ariel*? The answer, we have only recently realized, is no.[11]

Likewise, if "Words heard" raises the question whether Plath is merely a confessional poet, the answer here and elsewhere is that she clearly employed that mode as one particularly rich and pro-ductive poetic vein. Further, this poem signals a crucial moment of development in Plath's writing—a moment that helps us reassess the relationship between Plath's biography and poetry, between her early and late work, and between her stylistic and thematic excesses.

The consensus among Plath's readers is that her first book, *The Colossus*, contains her apprentice poems while her second book, *Ariel*, contains her masterpieces. *The Colossus* exhibits an infatuation with formal devices such as rhythm, rhyme, alliteration, assonance, dissonance, syllabics, and stanzaic patterns; consequently, the voice of the poems sounds highly controlled and distant—as though it has been transmitted through some intricate technolyrical machinery. Further, the *Colossus* poems are frequently imitative of the poets she admired: Wallace Stevens, Theodore Roethke, Dylan Thomas, and others.[12]

In "When We Dead Awaken: Writing as Re-Vision," Adrienne Rich, one of Plath's contemporaries and a writer she intensely envied and admired, explains her own early formalism as a means of distancing herself from the volatile suppressed content, the "glimpses of the split . . . between the girl who wrote poems, who defined herself in writing poems, and the girl who was to define herself by her relationships with men" (40). Formalism, she says, was "like asbestos gloves, it allowed me to handle materials I couldn't pick up barehanded" (40–41). This may also help explain Plath's early tortured formalism. Both poets seem to rely on a strained formalism in their early work where their subject matter has not yet found its native form. Several years before she was able to confront her own disturbing recognitions in writing the *Ariel* poems, Plath had chafed against the limitations of her excessively strict formalism: "I am splitting the seams of my fancy terza rima" (*Journals* 137). At the time, she longed to write a novel, thinking that poems—which she termed "moment's monuments" (137)—constricted her by their demand for brevity and precision. She acknowledged that even her best early poems were "too fancy, glassy, patchy and rigid" (221); and she scoffed at an editor who rejected one of her poems because of what he called its lack of technical finish, insisting that "my main flaw is a machinelike syllabic death-blow" (277). Yet only with the *Ariel* poems did she discover that what she needed was not the greater length of the novel but a more direct treatment of disturbing, often feminist content. John Frederick Nims has suggestively described this new style as "almost excessively simple" (52).

"Words heard, by accident, over the phone" is a poem that inaugurates the bare-handed directness so striking in *Ariel*. What Plath seems to have taken away from that telephone call is a sense of the brute materiality of language—its fierce potency and oppressive weight, its perniciousness and ineluctability. The only way to control such words was to snatch them by their throats, to make them speak for rather than against her. The necessity of the poem, written almost immediately after the phone call, was to revise and redirect the awful words that could never be rescinded. Such a task demanded grappling with language formally in order to manipulate it; she was already an expert wordsmith. Yet it also demanded confronting devastating themes head on so as not to obscure or distance them; this was her new challenge. In "Words heard" Plath uses language to lay theme bare rather than to conceal it. Her long apprenticeship in stylistic excess serves her well as she begins to discover the force and eloquence of thematic excess, too.

Thus, related to its analysis of overhearing—that is, related to its concern with theme—the poem investigates language as matter, for Plath was confident of her ability to manipulate forms. Making the overheard words palpable through stylistic excesses would support the themes of rape and defilement. By the first line of the poem, the speaker has already recast the "words heard" as mud—that central figure from which all other images in the poem derive. The journal entry about infidelity makes obvious that the mud is a metaphor for deception, but here it is elaborated and complicated in important ways. First, of course, the mud signifies that the words of the lovers are vile. Further, the opening line establishes the almost overwhelming fact of their words with its apostrophe to the mud, which dramatizes its physical presence, and the repetitions, which intensify it: "O mud, mud." Additionally, the transcription of the abstract and passive "words heard" in the title into the concrete and urgent exclamation in the first line captures the persona's experience of the immediacy and substantiality of these words.

The image of the mud operates on two levels—the domestic and the scatological—where the mud, coffee dregs, voices, words, excrement, and semen disturbingly intermingle. This not only enables the speaker to express how the lovers have defiled her marriage but also allows her, in turn, to debase their relationship.

The first use of the metaphor depicts the voices coming through the telephone receiver as mud oozing through the "many-holed / earpiece." This conveys the speaker's shock and repugnance as the thick, sluggy mud pulses out of the receiver in a domestic nightmare in which common household appliances become menacing instruments of terror. In the second stanza, the words that are "like mud" threaten the order and cleanliness of the housewife's world, and she wonders, "how shall I ever clean the phone table?" Isolated, this line may at first seem trivial: an obvious and even predictable figure for the notion that the domestic sphere has been sullied by the extramarital affair. However, the surrounding lines give a special charge to her fear that the telephone table will never come clean, for they suggest that though the fluid is *like* mud, it is not merely mud—but excrement.

The excremental imagery insinuates itself into the poem through a series of overlapping similes. The mud of the first line is compared to foreign coffee in the second line—a crucial comparison since coffee triggers the association between mud and muck (excrement): the words are like mud, and the mud is like coffee; the thick coffee not only resembles mud but also stimulates the sluggy "bowel-pulse" and transmits the words of the "lover of digestibles." The telephone line—because of its shape and function—is imagined as an intestinal tract in which words are digested into syllables that pulse through the telephone receiver to be finally plopped onto the phone table. The onomatopoetic "plopped" contributes, with the "many-holed" earpiece, to the excremental imagery. But the caller, too, is associated with this process because she is foreign, like the coffee, and because she is devouring the wife's marriage. "Who is it?" the wife asks, "It is the bowel-pulse, lover of digestibles." The coffee both stimulates digestion and resembles its waste products. This scatological dimension pushes the imagery of defilement to an extreme. The words she overhears are now permanently degraded by the analogy with excrement just as the phone table can certainly be cleaned up but can never be cleansed of such vile associations.

In the third stanza, the speaker's fury at the intrusion of the lover's words inspires an outburst that reveals another dimension of the metaphor: the anagrammatic "muck funnel." The telephone had already been viewed as a phallic weapon, a funnel that produces the fertile spawn. The rearrangement of letters causes semen and excrement to commingle in overlapping "fuck" and "muck." "Muck" is, of course, not simply mud now but dung or manure and is, paradoxically, fertilizer for her impending creative outburst. The succession of juxtapositions—"fertile," "muck," and "too big"—in the final three lines suggests rampant, uncontrollable growth, like the spawn that percolate in her heart or perhaps her own voice that begins to boom at the end of the poem.

Further, the spawn percolating in her recall the "foreign coffee" of the second line since coffee is one thing in the poem that percolates. It is significant that the coffee is foreign because the husband's actual lover was part Russian and part German. Her exotic name, Assia, is surely held up for scorn in the first line of the third stanza, "Now the room is ahiss." The steam escaping from the percolator, the gaseous emissions of the digestive tract, the menacing sound of a snake are all evoked here.[13] But beyond the mere word play of Assia and "ahiss," it is important to note in the last stanza that the lover— whether in the form of words, muck, hissing sounds, or infidelity— has penetrated the house of the speaker. Even when the "instrument / Withdraws its tentacle," that is, even when the phone has been hung up (or, as in the actual case, when the telephone cord has been ripped out of the wall), the devastating results remain. All of the images come together in new ways in the word "percolate"; it suggests the straining or sifting action of coffee, the flow of mud, or the expulsion of excrement. Worse, the verb joins these nouns in uneasy combinations—coffee, telephone receiver, mud, excrement. At the very least, "percolate" acknowledges that the words have permeated the speaker in some perverse way. On the other hand, "percolate" suggests, more colloquially, to become lively, like the bubbling action of percolating coffee. The spawn, then, have not merely penetrated the persona but are becoming active in her. "They are fertile," she says, meaning, of course, that she has been invaded and infested by the terrible words but also that she is able to make something of them.

"Tentacle" is another crucial word that deserves attention. It anticipates the famous line—"Off, off, eely tentacle!"—of "Medusa," a poem written three months later during Plath's most prolific period in October 1962. In that poem, the tentacle is again a connecting cord between the speaker and the woman who threatens to destroy her: "Old barnacled umbilicus, Atlantic cable, // Tremulous breath at the end of my line" (225).[14] The oceanic imagery in "Medusa" may offer another way to view the mud imagery of "Words heard"; perhaps both tentacles reach out of some primordial pool that is at once threatening and fertile. This reading accommodates the fertile spawn that teem in the semen, mud, muck, and even in the suspicious, thick foreign coffee (especially since the spawn "percolate").

Finally, it is clear that language has become fully personified during the course of the poem when, in the last line, the speaker addresses the words instead of the lovers: "You are too big. They must take you back!" Speaking directly to the words ("you") and referring to the lovers in the third person ("they"), the wife deflects attention from the lovers just as their conversation has slighted her. The speaker has suppressed the lovers but emphasized their words with this maneuver, making her own relationship to the words she heard over the phone the central one of the poem.

This is the incident that precipitated the breakup of Plath's six-year marriage, and this may be the poem that inaugurates her new poetics. There has been much discussion about the shift in Plath's writing from her first book to her second and a great deal of analysis about where the change in style can first be seen.[15] I choose to view "Words heard" as a pivotal poem in the Plath canon not only because it demonstrates the stylistic excesses of the early period and the thematic excesses of the late writing but also because it evinces an awareness of both poetic strategies. And parallel to this, the poem marks a turning point because it represents the first utterance of the poet following the destruction of one half of her contradictory dream. In "Words heard, by accident, over the phone" the great writer rises from the ashes of the perfect woman. In saying this, I am not suggesting that Plath's poetic development is owing to her husband's infidelity. I am arguing that Plath responded to the shattered dream of conventional femininity by redirecting her psychic, imaginative, and material resources toward her poetry. This new dedication to a single purpose—writing—resulted in the production of her best poems.

I make this point using the analogy with the phoenix (and, of course, Plath's powerful image at the end of "Lady Lazarus") in order to stress that Plath has not cast off her early formalistic style in writing the *Ariel* poems; rather, she has consumed it. Thus, her early and late styles can be acknowledged as noticeably different without being considered discontinuous. While Dickinson developed a poetics of excess in response to particular readers' attempts to stifle, feminize, and domesticate her writing; and while Stein cultivated an aesthetics of excess as a means of revitalizing an exhausted literary tradition; Plath employed excess for more complex reasons.

First, as a fledgling writer, she generated a poetics of excess to bolster a style she felt was too "stifled, weak, pallid, mealymouthed, and . . . absurd" (*Journals* 30) to compare with the "great" writers, most of whom were male. In her journals and letters she repeatedly worries about having no worthwhile subjects (since she considered her own concerns as a young person and a woman too trivial) and realizes that she tries to make up for this lack of content with greater attention to form. She links her "bitty, scatty, tawdry" (237) vision to her lot as a woman, fearing that her sphere of experiences will never prepare her to "bod[y] the world in words" (237) as D.H. Lawrence does, for example. Worse, she recognizes that her nascent talent will more likely be squelched than encouraged because she is a woman: "Some pale, hueless flicker of sensitivity is in me. God must I lose it in cooking and scrambling eggs for a man" (30). Consequently, she imitates great poets by writing in traditional forms—villanelles, sonnets, odes, terza rima. Yet these very efforts to substantiate her poetry by gilding it in form devitalize it even further: "I began a poem . . . but set up such a strict verse form that all power was lost: my nose so close I couldn't see what I was doing. An anesthetizing of feeling" (269). Clearly her early "syllabic death-blow[s]" (277) were meant to pound out a place for herself as a woman poet in a man's world. Later, however, when she has abandoned the effort to disentangle her gender from her writing, that is, when the stylistic excesses are no longer necessary to suppress her gender and strengthen her skills, she adopts a thematics of excess. Perhaps it is more accurate to say that the early stylistic excess seeps into the themes like kerosene saturating the wick in a lantern. The early and late poetic sensibilities are the same, but as Plath confronted the failure of her dream of being a perfect woman, the hardships that culture imposes on a woman, the burdens of being a single parent, and the difficulty of penetrating the London publishing scene without the influence of her husband, she found excess most articulate at the level of theme. Moreover, she no longer needed to restrain dangerous subjects with a muscular style. The shift in her aesthetics of excess from style toward theme (which is just a shift in balance after all) enabled her to address and refute not only the words of the dominant culture but her own complicity in words as well.

One of the most fascinating ways she consumes her own previous writing (and, significantly, that of her husband) is by "overwriting" it. Susan R. Van Dyne, working with the Plath manuscripts at Smith College, notes the distinctive composition practice of the *Ariel* poems, Plath's "habit of drafting her first handwritten copies and earliest typescripts of each poem on used paper":

Plath worked out the first stages of these poems on the back of a typed draft of *The Bell Jar*. Whether it was frugality, a rage for order, or the dictate of her headlong muse, Plath's earliest drafts are recorded on the [reverse] of *The Bell Jar* papers with hardly a page skipped or used out of its numbered sequence. So consistently and carefully does Plath re-use the novel manuscript for her poems throughout this sequence that the rare occasions she uses pages out of sequence seem peculiarly resonant. Thus I'm tempted to attach special meaning to the fact that within consecutive drafts for "The Bee Meeting," "The Arrival of the Bee Box," and "Stings" several pages from the novel turn up in unexpected places. These disordered, or consciously chosen, pages include evocative material about birth, poetry, and sexual infidelity. ("Manuscripts" 157)

Van Dyne wisely speculates that Plath used the *Bell Jar* sheets as sympathetic magic to empower her new efforts; *The Bell Jar* represented proven good writing, and it treated themes the new poems would also take up (158).[16]

Additionally, I think, Plath may have been attempting to override her previous words by overwriting them. Van Dyne points out that Plath occasionally used the backs of Hughes' manuscript pages for her new poems as if she wanted, in some sense, to cancel out what he had written (159). Further, Wendy Owen, also working with the Smith collection, discovered that Plath wrote on one side of the sheet with self-conscious attention to what was on the other side. Owen describes being puzzled by what seemed to be an intrusive image of a hare in one Plath poem; when Owen held the page up to the light, she saw that the hare had entered Plath's writing from a Hughes' poem on the backside of the sheet. The hare was Hughes' totem for his muse, often for Plath in that role, and Owen suggests that Plath is reappropriating herself as muse in this borrowing.[17] If Plath was attempting to repudiate Hughes' work, then it is likely that she would also want to override some of her own previous words. She does not reject or repress her former writing, but she reuses it in order to fuel something entirely new. *Ariel*, then, is layered over *The Bell Jar* as if to supersede her former struggles, values, and accomplishments. Moreover, *The Bell Jar* is composed on Smith College memorandum paper, which she had stored up for that use with determination and relish.[18] These layers—the aspiring Smith girl, the superwoman (writer-wife-mother)—represent selves that the poet consumes in her drive to become at last a "genius of a writer" (*Letters* 468).

Plath was finally sure of her genius in mid-October 1962, just after completing the Bee sequence, when she wrote to her mother that she was ready to start a new life: "I am a writer . . . I am a genius of a writer; I have it in me. I am writing the best poems of my life; they will make my name" (468). Though the poems that would ultimately make her name came a few days later—"Daddy," "Ariel," and "Lady Lazarus," among others—she obviously felt that the Bee poems were ones on which she could build her poetic reputation. There is no question that she considered the Bee poems her culminating poetic statement in addition to her best work. She placed them at the end of her second book of poems, giving them precedence over the other poems in the volume. If we have only recently discovered the importance of the Bee sequence, it is partly because Hughes demoted it to the middle of the book when he put together his version of *Ariel* and partly because the sequence contradicts the myth of Plath as suicidal poet churning out her greatest poems to meet a frighteningly literal deadline.

Plath wrote the five Bee poems, which she initially titled "Bees" and conceived of as a sequence, in less than a week in October 1962 as her marriage was breaking up. They are unified by their subject matter, bees and beekeeping, and by their five-line stanza pattern, though each poem works its own unique variation of the general theme and form. They reveal a concern with self-assessment and redefinition, both personally and poetically, and proceed by scrutinizing relationships between the speaker and her world. The sequence moves from community, in "The Bee Meeting," to solitude, in "Wintering," as the speaker settles her relations with others and with her own former selves. This trajectory from an external preoccupation with others to an inward concern for the self has formal reverberations. Plath's characteristic stylistic excess eases during the course of the sequence as the speaker retreats from the pressures of the external world, especially the world of gender conflicts, to the inner rhythms of her own exigencies. As the influence of the exterior world diminishes, the stylistic agitation seems to abate as well.

In the first poem, "The Bee Meeting" (211–12) the speaker finds herself in the midst of other people. The long, Whitmanian lines sprawl horizontally to accommodate the crowd of villagers, "The rector, the midwife, the sexton, the agent for bees" and later "the butcher, the grocer, the postman, someone I know." There may be a pun in the title of this first poem (and in the running title for the sequence) since the word "bee" itself refers to a group of neighbors. In an interesting etymological loop, the word "bee," meaning a meeting of neighbors who unite their labors for the benefit of one of their number (as in a barn raising bee or a quilting bee), is an allusion to the social character of the insect. This sense of "bee" may account for the fact that the villagers all appear to be doing something specifically to or for the speaker and may qualify the speaker's paranoid response to their attentions toward her.

The place and time of the meeting suggest that the speaker is at a transitional stage. She meets the townspeople "at the bridge," a symbolic place of connection between divided locales and, therefore, a site of change. The way the speaker is dressed confirms the time of the year is summer, a season traditionally associated with the final harvest that precedes decline. Further, the sequence itself moves from summer to winter—and even beyond since the final poem promises spring. Many readers are fond of emphasizing that Plath's *Ariel* began with the word "love" and ended with the word "spring" (*Poems* 14–15), but none has stressed the significance of summer in this culminating sequence. She began the Bee poems shortly after moving to the country cottage she had dreamed of, giving birth to her second child, losing her husband to another woman, seeing her first book of poems in print, and finding a publisher for her first novel. Clearly, the new volume of poetry would reap the sweet and bitter fruits of these recent events. The Bee poems assess the speaker's relation to her neighbors, children, husband, other women, and herself, as well as her place in history. The summer season hints that one phase of her life is ending, and so it is an appropriate time for reevaluation and change.[19]

The most distinctive feature of "The Bee Meeting" is its gothic tone. If this is a poem about transition, then the speaker finds change extremely disorienting—even nightmarish. The speaker's paranoia is conveyed through her confused and incessant questions, inability to recognize familiar people, stuttering repetitions, monstrous personifications, and obsession with violence and death. Likewise, the bizarre setting is created through imagery and metaphors of violence, a mixed atmosphere of the ritual, the carnival, and the funeral, and mythic allusions. These elements are intensified rhetorically with alliteration, assonance, and dissonance. Noticeably, then, the formal features that lend the poem its gothic tone are the staples of Plath's poetics of excess. In this expressionistic landscape the speaker must begin to puzzle out her relationship to others. Significantly, the task demands that she control her overactive imagination, that is, that she see through the thematic and rhetorical trappings of excess that she herself has contrived.

The poem opens and closes with questions and is riddled with questions throughout. Of the eleven stanzas, all but two have at least one question and most have more. Through much of the poem, the speaker tries to answer them herself; but when the last line closes the poem with yet another question, obviously it cannot be answered (at least not within this poem). Consequently, it is the one inquiry in the poem that is not punctuated with a question mark as though the atmosphere of enigma and uncertainty has been naturalized in this perplexing setting, and the interrogative is now as definitive an utterance as she can formulate.

Her first questions concern the people around her and what they are doing: "Who are these people at the bridge to meet me?" "Which is the rector now, is it that man in black? / Which is the midwife, is that her blue coat?" "Is some operation taking place?" "Is it the butcher, the grocer, the postman, someone I know?" and finally "what have they accomplished?" The manuscript drafts from this poem reveal that Plath changed many of these questions from straight declarative sentences apparently in order to intensify the speaker's confusion and disorientation.[20] Her sense of alienation from her neighbors naturally serves to emphasize her isolation, but this is a larger point than we may at first realize. A central issue of the Bee sequence is the speaker's autonomy; the sequence, in fact, works to separate her from others. In itself, isolation is not a problem; on the contrary, it is a state the speaker must achieve in order to know herself, gather her resources, and pursue a new direction. The anxiety and dislocation she experiences in "The Bee Meeting" suggest it is the community of neighbors—not isolation—that the speaker cannot tolerate. She receives their attempts to help her, well-intentioned though they may be, as assaults upon her. She feels vulnerable ("In my sleeveless summery dress I have no protection"), effaced by their efforts to protect her ("here is the secretary of bees with her white shop smock, / Buttoning the cuffs at my wrists and the slit from my neck to my knees. / Now I am milkweed silk, the bees will not notice."), forced to conform ("they are making me one of them"), and yet finally betrayed ("The villagers are untying their disguises, they are shaking hands. / Whose is that long white box in the grove, what have they accomplished, why am I cold"). However, there is no evidence in the poem that the villagers actually behave suspiciously. Instead, what should be obvious is that participating in the collective life of the village has disastrous effects on the speaker; clearly, she is not "one of them," and thus she finds their attempts to include her extremely threatening.[21]

It is not only in her dealings with the townspeople that the speaker's perceptions are distorted and exaggerated. She views the setting with the same expressionistic sensibility that informs her apprehension of the villagers. Stanzas four and five depict a dangerous and frightening landscape:

> Strips of tinfoil winking like people,
> Feather dusters fanning their hands in a sea of bean flowers,
> Creamy bean flowers with black eyes and leaves like bored hearts.
> Is it blood clots the tendrils are dragging up that string?
> No, no, it is scarlet flowers that will one day be edible.
> . . . .
> They are leading me to the shorn grove, the circle of hives.
> Is it the hawthorn that smells so sick?
> The barren body of hawthorn, etherizing its children.

All elements of the scene are personified, exacerbating the confusion of who's who, in the opening stanzas, with what's what here. The contraptions for warding off plant foragers (strips of tinfoil and feather dusters) present an image every bit as alien as the townspeople in their apiary gear; indeed, they are "like people" but only in the respect that they are as weird and ominous as the villagers. The "eyes" of the bean flowers are black, as though bruised; their leaves are like pierced hearts; their flowers like blood clots; and the hawthorne tree kills its own offspring. These personifications compare the elements of the landscape to a monstrous humanity and thus have the effect of dehumanizing the whole environment.

On the other hand, the speaker depicts herself as inextricably bound in her own humanness. Throughout the sequence she alludes to Daphne, who metamorphosed into a laurel tree to elude Apollo, in contrast to her own human vulnerability. In this poem she imagines herself becoming "milkweed silk" and "cow-parsley" so that the bees will not attack her. In the second poem, "The Arrival of the Bee Box" (212–13), she employs the Daphne myth more explicitly, again as a fantasy of protection from the bees: "I wonder if they would forget me / If I just undid the locks and stood back and turned into a tree." The desire to transform from the human to the vegetable reveals a longing to escape sexual oppression. In Ovid, the source for this allusion, Daphne's father wants his daughter to marry and have children (specifically male children): " 'Daughter, you owe me a son-in-law . . . you owe me grandsons!' " (1:37). But Daphne resists: " 'O father, dearest, grant me to enjoy perpetual virginity" (1:37). Though she is granted her wish ("He, indeed, yielded to her request" [1:37]), she remains prey to the male sexual privilege that marriage would institutionalize. Daphne's physical vulnerability, like the speaker's here and in "Stings," is captured in the image of her bare arms: "[Apollo] marvels at her fingers, hands, and wrists, and her arms, bare to the shoulder" (1:37). Surely the speaker resembles Daphne in this: in "The Bee Meeting" she says, "In my sleeveless summery dress I have no protection," and in "Stings" again she is "Bare-handed . . . the throats of [her] wrists brave lilies." The emphasis on physical vulnerability is crucial since elsewhere in mythology, as in the myth of Daphne and Apollo, the transformation into a tree is effected in order to escape sexual assault.

Moreover, the metamorphosis into a plant concerns the definition and boundaries of the human. One could change into a god or an animal, but these beings are still sexually vulnerable. Only by relinquishing all creaturely claims can Daphne escape sexual assault. For the speaker of the Bee sequence, however, such a metamorphosis is simply another conceit and one she must give up in order to achieve the self-awareness and new self-definition of "Wintering" (217–19). Significantly, then, the allusion occurs early in the sequence in the two most technically wrought poems with their personifications, myths, alliterations, repetitions, and what has been termed their "manic metaphor-making" (Van Dyne, "Manuscripts" 168)—"The Bee Meeting" and "The Arrival of the Bee Box." By the last poem, "Wintering," the association between the woman and the plant is merely analogous, not metamorphic. She is clearly human, knitting over the cradle of her child (and therefore no longer like the virginal Daphne):

> The woman, still at her knitting,
> At the cradle of Spanish walnut,
> Her body a bulb in the cold and too dumb to think.

One might be tempted to say that the baby is encased in the Spanish walnut like Daphne in the laurel tree and that the woman too is becoming a plant, no longer even able to speak. However, the walnut tree merely serves the mother and child, by being fashioned into a cradle, in the same way that the metaphor of the bulb serves the poet, by providing an image for her hibernation. Her ability to control these plant metaphors attests to the progress she has made since the beginning of the Bee sequence. These are distinctions the earlier poems fail to make. Such restraint is still far off in "The Bee Meeting" where personification and metamorphosis are employed to heighten the speaker's strangeness, vulnerability, and confusion.

Even so, the speaker recognizes that the myth of metamorphosis, like the other conceits in the poem, is an inadequate solution to her problem; however, her moment of clarity is brief at this point. In the crucial and distinctive seventh stanza, she confronts the hysterical tone and the surrealistic allusions to Daphne, "I cannot run, I am rooted, and the gorse hurts me / With its yellow purses, its spikey armory," and says flatly, "I could not run without having to run forever." Her separateness from others—the real issue in the sequence—would pursue her even into the Daphne myth; when she becomes "rooted," that is, transformed into the tree to evade the bees and villagers, the other vegetation now assails her: "the gorse hurts me / With its yellow purses, its spikey armory." And significantly, the flowers and prickles of the gorse are imagined as both female (purses) and male (armory) just like the communities of the villagers or the bees. Abandoning all tropes in the sanest line of the poem, she admits, "I could not run without having to run forever." Fleeing the actual scenes and causes of her anxieties is futile, but she still has not given up the attempt to escape into literariness. After this bald avowal, she appears to delegate the Daphne imagery to the hive: "The white hive is snug as a virgin, / Sealing off her brood cells, her honey, and quietly humming." The lines recall Daphne's metamorphosis: "her soft sides were begirt with thin bark. Her hair was changed to leaves, her arms to branches. . . . Her gleaming beauty alone remained" (1:41). The contracting assonance of the long *i*'s that signals the shutting up of the hive ("white hive") and the whispered alliterations of *s*'s and *h*'s ("snug," "sealing," "cells" and "honey," "humming") betray the speaker's lyric responsiveness to the bees. The self-containment and contentment that the hive achieves at the end of stanza seven is short-lived, however, just as the speaker's moment of sanity was; in stanza eight when the bees are smoked out of the hive, they (and the speaker) once again take flight of their senses: "Here they come, the outriders, on their hysterical elastics." Their fear ignites hers, and she reverts to her earlier fantasy of metamorphosis by trying to "stand very still, [so] they will think I am cow-parsley."

Feeding this impressionistic mood is the speaker's inability to perceive accurately, to rein in her hyperactive imagination and hone her vision. Like the paranoid questions that can be answered reasonably ("Who are these people at the bridge to meet me? They are the villagers" or "I am nude as a chicken neck, does nobody love me? / Yes"), the speaker must revise her first impressions of the landscape: "Is it blood clots the tendrils are dragging up that string? / No, no, it is scarlet flowers that will one day be edible." The repeated emotional burst of "No, no" as she realizes the red clots are only flowers suggests that the simple reassuring answer is as unnerving to her as the alarming question because their contrast is a measure of her extremity. Her task in this poem is to liberate herself from both the bizarre and the mundane. She will confront more directly in "Stings" (214–15) that she does not want to end up as the queen, the extraordinary but fated center of the hive; yet she also does not want to become the drudge, one of the "unmiraculous women" whose "strangeness evaporate[s]" from a life of domestic labor. Her vacillations from the bizarre to the mundane, from the surreal to the real, from suspicious questions to matter-of-fact answers are finally what exhaust the speaker by the end of the poem—"I am exhausted, I am exhausted"—though she, like many readers of the poem, blames the villagers.

The frequency with which readers of "The Bee Meeting" conclude that the villagers fiendishly draw the innocent speaker into their demonic ritual attests to the poem's success in evincing the speaker's point of view.[22] Yet, the townspeople appear menacing because her fantastic imagination distorts perception. It is true, as nearly every reader points out, that the first list of villagers includes the town officials—the rector, the midwife, the sexton, and the agent for bees—and therefore suggests some sort of public ritual. Yet the second list, an even more important one since it enumerates the people who might be the central mysterious "surgeon" performing the ritual, is noticeably composed of common, insignificant, and thus innocuous characters: the butcher, the grocer, the postman, and most vaguely, "someone I know." Moreover, the setting of the mysterious ritual is borrowed, like the Daphne imagery, from literature and thus gives the poem self-conscious literariness rather than emotional veracity. The event is modeled on Nathaniel Hawthorne's short story, "Young Goodman Brown," in which the title character, like the speaker here, has a nightmarish meeting with his neighbors in a shorn grove. That Plath wants to tap the literariness of this allusion rather than merely its theme and mood is obvious in the more playful, embedded references to Hawthorn—the hawthorn tree in the grove and the "scarlet" flowers that recall *The Scarlet Letter.* Like Young Goodman Brown, the speaker of "The Bee Meeting" is a dubious judge of the intentions of the villagers.

In some ways, her position in relation to the villagers is very much like that of the bees. The townspeople do not intend to harm the bees; they merely want to divide the hive into three hives and save the queen bee from the virgins. Yet the bees misinterpret the smoke (that is used to drive them out so the hives can be moved): "Smoke rolls and scarves in the grove. / The mind of the hive thinks this is the end of everything." Likewise, the queen hides from the people who are trying to help her: "The old queen does not show herself, is she so ungrateful?" The intensely lyrical quality of some of these passages (the long *o*'s that almost seem to loop and curl like the smoke they are describing—"Smoke rolls and scarves in the grove"—the long *i*'s that tighten and enclose the bees in a unity of sound—"The mind of the hive") again belies the speaker's sympathetic identification with the bees. Strategic repetitions further link the speaker to the bees; she says of herself, "They will not smell my fear, my fear, my fear" and of the queen, "She is old, old, old." This connection between the speaker and the bees must be read carefully, however, for its purpose is to separate her from the villagers every bit as much as it is to associate her with the bees. She is like the bees primarily in that she is unlike the townspeople. Further, the bees themselves are similar to the villagers in some ways (in their group function, in their hierarchy, in the threat they pose to the speaker). This point is more important than it first appears. Many readers interpret the sequence, especially the third poem "Stings," as a work in which Plath attempted to create an image of herself from the bees, whether as victimized wife (the drudges) or victorious poet (the queen bee). Yet the larger success of the sequence depends on the speaker's recognition that the hive is an unsatisfactory model for human social relations (indeed, the metaphor of the hive amounts to a critique of heterosexual social relations) and that the bees are outside of her, as everything that oppresses her is. Distinguishing herself from her conceits makes possible the relationship to the bees she acknowledges in "The Swarm" (215–17)—"How instructive this is!" Here at the end of "The Bee Meeting" she still confuses herself with the bees, "Whose is that long white box in the grove . . . why am I cold," and experiences a foreboding of death (an early draft of this line read "that coffin, so white and silent" [Van Dyne, "Manuscripts" 165]). Yet, like the bees, she must learn that this is not "the end of everything." By the last poem, she has established her autonomy as well as her connection to the world; despite the fact that Plath changed the sequence title from "The Beekeeper" and "The Beekeeper's Daybook" to "Bees," the speaker is aware in the last poem that she is a beekeeper not a bee. When she says in "Wintering," "It is they [the bees] who own me," she does not mean that she cannot distinguish herself from them—only that she is connected to them by their dependence upon her, a relationship she assents to: "This is the time of hanging on for the bees." Thus, the speaker's rhetorical and emotional identification with the bees in the first poem, like the other intensely imaginative elements, stems from excesses that the sequence as a whole works to overcome.

Another aspect of "The Bee Meeting" that often diverts critical attention from the speaker's unreliability is the penultimate stanza in which the new virgins

> Dream of a duel they will win inevitably,
> A curtain of wax dividing them from the bride flight,
> The upflight of the murderess into a heaven that loves her.

The appeal of this stanza, of course, is that it prefigures the violence of the bride flight in "Stings" and is consistent with the theme of vengeful self-destruction that is said to monopolize Plath's imagination. And, indeed, it does foreshadow the third poem of the sequence in its vision of "recovering" a queen, as "Stings" will say. However, much more important here is the fact that the bride flight remains merely a dream. This poem ends with exhaustion and uncertainty not, like "Stings," with energy and self-assurance. And, as might be expected, the speaker recedes even further into the unreality she has been struggling throughout the poem to cast off.

The failure of her effort to distinguish between the real and the surreal is anticipated in the opening of the final stanza that signals her defeat, "I am exhausted, I am exhausted," and confirmed in the last line where three accusing questions give vent to her worst fears, "Whose is that long white box in the grove, what have they accomplished, why am I cold." She sees what appears to be a coffin, realizes something has ended, and feels the chill of the grave already upon her. Yet the box, the sense of accomplishment, and the iciness of death all derive directly from her own metaphor in the preceding lines. When she claims to be a "Pillar of white in a blackout of knives. / . . . the magician's girl who does not flinch," she is, in effect, conjuring up her own box and stepping into it. Reneging on all the other images for herself the poem has contrived, this last metaphor makes passivity a performance and tinctures the funereal atmosphere with the carnival. Embracing virginity with a vengeance, she becomes the magician's "girl"—both daughter and assistant—who participates in the trick of Sawing the Lady in Half.[23] The box, then, is the prop that makes the optical allusion possible. She is the "pillar of white in a blackout of knives" because she is the stoical girl in the box who remains unscathed even as the phallic knives appear to pass through her, a variation of Daphne who becomes the unfeeling tree in order to avoid Apollo's sexual assault. The knives do not cut her because they are merely a "blackout," that is, an optical illusion. The term is taken from the theatrical expression "blackout," meaning to dim the lights while a scene changes or, in a magician's act, to allow a trick to be accomplished under the cover of darkness; it is also a word that suggests the magician's occupation, "black art." She is unflinching, not because she is brave, but because she is in on the trick. The shock at the end of the poem that inspires the final three questions is her surprising realization that she is the only one left performing. "The villagers are untying their disguises," but the speaker is still caught in hers. While the townspeople were carrying out their chores, and there is no evidence in the poem that they were doing otherwise, the speaker has nailed her own coffin, so to speak, with her fantastic imaginative constructions. Moreover, her role as the magician's girl associates *her* with witchcraft since it allies her with sorcery as well as with illusion.

The exhaustion she feels at the end of the poem makes her unable to answer the last battery of questions. This is appropriate since the voice of the poem is expert at heightening rather than allaying fears and uncertainties. She will, however, approach the last enigma from another angle in the second poem. "The Arrival of the Bee Box" (212–13) must be understood as responding to her demand in this first poem to know "Whose is that long white box in the grove."

The first stanza of "The Arrival of the Bee Box" provides, in some measure, a corrective to the excesses and exaggerations of "The Bee Meeting." The speaker is now able to answer her own earlier question about the box; in fact, overcoming her former passivity, she even takes responsibility for it, "I ordered this, this clean wood box." Seeing it more clearly in her present state of mind, it is no longer the long, white virgin's coffin feared to be *for* her but a prosaic "clean wood box" that she herself owns. As if to demonstrate the unequivocal reality of the box, she says it is "Square as a chair and almost too heavy to lift." The choice of "chair," the classroom philosopher's favorite object for exhibiting the "real," is good-humored and appropriate. Further, the rhyming phrase, "square as a chair," gives aural substance to the box, and the word "square" suggests honesty, directness, and exactitude. In three words, then, she has overturned the hallucinatory tone of the first poem.

Yet her fine control over words diminishes rapidly, and she concocts a quick succession of odd metaphors for the box—"I would say it was the coffin of a midget / Or a square baby." The subjunctive "I would" testifies that she is aware even before she generates them that her metaphors are contrived. These self-conscious tropes preview the numerous metaphors and similes that this poem will hazard. Even when she claims to leave off making metaphors, she slips immediately into another sort of verbal play, "I would . . . were there not such a din in it." The humming sound created by the three short *i*'s of "din in it" attests to irrepressible linguistic production. But the difference between "The Arrival of the Bee Box" and "The Bee Meeting" is that here the speaker remains fully aware that she is using poetic language to shape her experience.

In fact, one could read this as a poem about poetic language. If the box represents form and the clamor inside of it represents content, then "The Arrival of the Bee Box" may best be read as a poem in which the speaker explores the relationship between her "asbestos gloves" and her incendiary subject matter.[24] In this view, the two aborted metaphors, the coffin of the midget and the square baby, can be understood as descriptions of poetic content that becomes malformed or remains undeveloped when cramped into conventional structures. In this sense, her first attempts to describe the box were accurate. "The box is locked" because its contents are "dangerous," yet the speaker "can't keep away from it." As she examines the box and considers opening it, she is faced with the threat that what is inside may destroy her.

This is a box she has approached elsewhere in her poetry. In each case it seems to represent the conflict between rigid outer forms and a suppressed inner life. It is, of course, the long, white box she fears in "The Bee Meeting" that will trap her in a premature grave; but it is also the hive box in an earlier poem, "The Beekeeper's Daughter" (118). There, in a line she will recycle for "The Arrival," the daughter of the beekeeper, like the present speaker, tries to look into the box: "Kneeling down / I set my eye to a hole-mouth and meet an eye / Round, green, disconsolate as a tear." The eye of the daughter recognizes in the eye of the queen bee a reflection of her own dejection. Both are isolated by their special bond to the father/beekeeper and trapped by structures of power in which they are defined completely by their relation to him. Here, however, the bees are "furious" rather than disconsolate, and she can see nothing of them. When the effort to see fails, "I put my eye to the grid. / It is dark, dark," she must take recourse in listening, "I lay my ear to furious Latin." Here again, as in "Words heard," the persona finds her own voice by hearing the voices of others.

Naturally, then, she begins to create metaphors for the sound in an attempt to understand it. Over the course of the next three stanzas she proposes three analogies for the contents of the bee box, each one an image of power and oppression. First it reminds her of "the swarmy feeling of African hands / Minute and shrunk for export, / Black on black, angrily clambering." Here her role in relation to the box is that of slave trader or colonizing exporter. The power of the colonizer (exporter/poet) over the colonized (African hands/poems) results in the diminution of the latter, which are "Minute and shrunk for export"; the contents of the box are once again imagined as dwarfed and deformed as the whole notion of containment through forms is repeatedly called into question. The bees (and, we can infer, the poems) resent their captivity and agitate to escape. In this analogy, she is right to feel that the bees are dangerous. Next "It is like a Roman mob, / Small, taken one by one, but my god, together!" Echoing again that line from "The Beekeeper's Daughter," she says, "I lay my ear to furious Latin." Relinquishing power over this mob because she cannot understand them, she admits, "I am not Caesar." Almost inadvertently, these first two metaphors for the din in the box employ exemplary instances from history of domination: the slave trade, white colonization of nonwhite countries, and autocracy. These political structures, then, are related to the formal structure that controls and contains content. This is the role she rejects in claiming not to be Caesar. Finally, she tries to speak more directly, but even this effort produces a metaphor: "I have simply ordered a box of maniacs." This line is a continuation of her preceding disclaimer: I am not a tyrant who wants to dominate the bees; I simply ordered a bee hive, but it has turned out to be more than I bargained for. Further, however, it too offers a metaphor of power relations—the mental asylum—this time one that the speaker can perhaps identify with more easily since, in "The Bee Meeting," she felt herself becoming the maniac in the box.

Realizing now that she is obliged to the box at least for the night, she senses the danger she is in and toys first with the idea of abdicating her power, "They can be sent back" (the passive voice construction is not accidental), then immediately with the idea of exerting it, "They can die, I need feed them nothing, I am the owner." Clearly, the poem views such power as corrupting, for as soon as she assumes the position of authority ("I am the owner"), she becomes aware of her total control ("They can die").

Fortunately for the bees, the role of autocrat is not one she relishes; thus, instead of executing her control over them, she wonders "how hungry they are"—a line that reveals she is probably not capable of withholding food from them. (Even the syntax of the line that proposes not to feed them is contorted to throw emphasis on the likelihood that she will care for them: the affirmative phrase "I need feed them" comes first and then, as an unconvincing afterthought, the negative word "nothing.") Indeed, she would like to feed them, or better, to set them free, but she cannot tell how they will treat her if they are liberated. Turning again to the protective myth of Daphne, she tries to imagine freeing them without harm to herself:

> I wonder if they would forget me
> If I just undid the locks and stood back and turned into a tree. . . .
> They might ignore me immediately.

These lines are actually quite strange. She does not wonder if the bees will attack her but if they will "forget" her, as though her connection to them is more profound and binding than that of a customer who has just purchased a hive. Likewise, the choice of the word "immediately" suggests a concern with duration rather than with the imminent event of their assault. This language also indicates that she has some prior connection to the bees. In the reading I am pursuing, this connection parallels a career of writing that shuts up her imaginative vitality in rigid forms. The bees, then, represent her own repressed feelings, and she dreads the possibility of being overcome by her own memories and outrages. Would she ever be able to forget the slights and injustices? Would the feelings immediately consume her? The "unintelligible syllables" causing the commotion in the box are the sounds of her own anger and fury, and it is her inability to articulate an outrage that she can nevertheless hear that "appalls [her] most of all."

The allusion to Daphne in this poem is not merely an image for the speaker's isolated problem; rather it represents other women as well. She recognizes precedents for the metamorphosis: "There is the laburnum, its blond colonnades, / And the petticoats of the cherry." Here for the first time she detects the traces of other women in these trees, their blondness and their petticoats. To refuse the metamorphosis is to attempt to remain in the world as she is, an extremely vulnerable position for a woman (even more so for a woman writer). It necessitates protective gear that is hardly less alienating than bark and leaves, a "moon suit and funeral veil." Moreover, the gear that is meant to protect her human vulnerability seems instead to dehumanize her (the moon suit suggests her strangeness).

In a last effort to find a way to release the bees without risking injury, she reasons that since she is "no source of honey," they have no cause to attack her. Yet she overlooks the irony that whoever liberates the bees must inevitably be exposed to danger. This point is conveyed through the verbal play on "honey" and "sweet": "I am no source of honey / So why should they turn on me? / Tomorrow I will be sweet God, I will set them free." Ironically, by being sweet she will be like the honey that the bees are after; in fact, it is her sweetness—her desire to help and her willingness to release the bees—that makes her so vulnerable. On all levels of the poem, the beekeeper opening the box, the woman giving vent to repressed emotions, or the poet uncovering her real subjects, the liberator will likely get hurt.

"The Arrival of the Bee Box" is the only poem in the sequence that exceeds the five-line stanza pattern. It closes with an extra line—significantly, a line about form that the form of the poem is not able to contain—that asserts "The box is only temporary." This final utterance not only announces the inevitable displacement of the box but also outstrips the formal boundaries set by the poem (and the sequence). The speaker will release the bees. The content will exceed the form. More important, of course, the hand that penned the apocalyptic last line will remove its asbestos glove.

The third poem of the Bee sequence, "Stings" (214–15) fulfills this prediction. Not only have the bees been set free (they now dwell in and around their hive) but the speaker, too, we learn in the first word of the poem, is "bare-handed." In some ways, "Stings" is another bee meeting, but this time the speaker and the bee seller are equals—working together and similarly attired for the job: "Bare-handed, I hand the combs. / The man in white smiles, bare-handed." The short fifth line, containing only the pronouns "he and I," and the stanza break that follows it with a gulf of white space, suggest the insularity and detachment of the two workers. The basis of their relationship appears to be the orderliness of their work. There is something sterile in their association yet also something undeniably tender:

> Bare-handed, I hand the combs.
> The man in white smiles, bare-handed,
> Our cheesecloth gauntlets neat and sweet,
> The throats of our wrists brave lilies.
> He and I
>
> Have a thousand clean cells between us,
> Eight combs of yellow cups,
> And the hive itself a teacup,
> White with pink flowers on it,
> With excessive love I enameled it
>
> Thinking 'Sweetness, sweetness.'

The imagery makes clear that there are no more battles, even parodic ones, as there were in "The Bee Meeting." Taking up an image of armor from that poem, "Breastplates of cheesecloth knotted under the armpits," "Stings" reworks it, infusing it with the tender tidiness that characterizes these opening stanzas, "Our cheesecloth gauntlets neat and sweet." Similarly, the ghastly image of feeling "nude as a chicken neck" finds its delicate counterpart here in "The throats of our wrists brave lilies." The inside and the outside of the hive alike exude domestic refinement and charm when they are compared to china teacups that are "yellow" and "white with pink flowers." Everything about this passage is "sweet"—the relationship between the workers, the honey, the hive, the paintings, and, most of all, the speaker's former love.

"Stings" is so renowned for its ferocity that it is easy to forget this painfully tender opening. The aspects that are said to give it vehemence—the speaker's refusal to remain a drudge (and the jealousy among the female figures this decision supposedly sets off), the drudges' attack on the scapegoat, and the queen's "violent" bride flight—are simply not enough to negate this gentle beginning. Plath drafted and finalized "Stings" on the backs of her husband's own writing work sheets. She began the poem two months before the burst of writing in October that produced the Bee sequence when the pain of losing Hughes was probably sharpest. Further, the earliest drafts of the poem were written on the reverse sides of several of Hughes's poems about the birth of their first child (Van Dyne, "Manuscripts" 159); these were pages that documented their lost happiness. Thus, she began the poem in a period of acute pain and on the very papers that could only serve to intensify her misery. The threat of stings in this passage comes less from the bees than from the evocation of the "excessive love" the speaker recalls as she performs her beekeeping tasks. The stings the scapegoat receives from the bees can be nothing compared to the stings the poet experiences in writing under these conditions or those the speaker evokes in remembering her former relation to the hive. At the very least, the sensitive opening must give another resonance to the title that readers of the poem seem reluctant to acknowledge.

Additionally, that resonance ought to inform the other aspects of the poem. For example, the speaker's attitude toward other women, represented by the beekeeper's relationship to the queen and the drudges, is not at all condescending or competitive. Though she makes the important disclaimer, "I am no drudge," she clearly has been acting the part of one for years. She is sympathetic with the "women who only scurry" and worries that they will hate her for refusing to continue scurrying herself. Virtually every critic who discusses the speaker's relationship to the drudges quotes the paradoxical line that describes them but invariably misses the paradox (or avoids it by eliding part of the line). The speaker says, "I stand in a column // Of winged, unmiraculous women." At least half the quotations of this passage omit the word "winged"; the rest treat the line as though it read "wing*less* unmiraculous women." "Winged, unmiraculous women" is paradoxical because a woman with wings would be miraculous; "winged" suggests flight, transcendence, loftiness. The drudges, then, are not inherently ordinary; rather they represent women whose strangeness has evaporated in the service of others, here of the hive and the queen, elsewhere of husbands and children, women whose energies have been "pour[ed] . . . through the direction and force" of others. Their attack on the scapegoat verifies that they are not utterly servile. The speaker recognizes this.

Even the description of the scapegoat is affected by the tone of the opening. The key word from the first two stanzas, "sweet," unexpectedly appears again here:

He was sweet,
. . . .
The sweat of his efforts a rain
Tugging the world to fruit.

There is an initially negative connotation in the "sweat of his efforts," some sense that he has encouraged the world to fruit (probably best read as having fathered her children or more generally having made her blossom) and then left it in a state of vulnerability to suffer. Yet "sweet" and "sweat" associate themselves through sound for a much more positive effect and reveal that the speaker recalls him with tenderness.

Further, she alludes to the Cinderella story in her description of his disappearance:

Here is his slipper, here is another,
And here is the square of white linen
He wore instead of a hat.

These lines acknowledge his vulnerability by feminizing him; he is Cinderella who leaves behind her slipper or the coy woman who drops her hankie in an attention-seeking gesture. It is not surprising that such descriptions are followed by the conciliatory phrase, "He was sweet." It appears that she delegates revenge to the bees— "Molding onto his lips like lies, / Complicating his features"—yet this simile hints that his own evils are his undoing. The bees merely dramatize his crimes. His deceptions have complicated his features, have made him seem altered. However, even his change is qualified by the Cinderella allusion, another tale of personal transformation. Further confusing the purpose of the allusion is the speaker's own implication in it; she, too, is a Cinderella figure: "for years I have eaten dust / And dried plates with my dense hair." (These lines are laden with other allusions as well. The serpent's punishment for tempting Eve was to eat dust; Mary Magdalene washed Christ's feet with her tears and dried them with her hair.) Finally, calling him "a great scapegoat" overtly acknowledges that she is transferring her own guilt to him. When he is chased off by the bees, he carries away her sins as well as his (we recall from "The Bee Meeting" that her black veil "mold[ed] to her face" like the bees here have molded to his); this is perhaps the source of the feminine imagery.[25]

Though some of these lines seem to establish a connection between the speaker and the scapegoat, the passage is framed by the speaker's detachment. First she says, "A third person is watching. / He has nothing to do with the bee-seller or with me." After the bees sting him, an act that assures their death, she asserts, "They thought death was worth it, but I / Have a self to recover, a queen." Her detachment is clearly a much more significant victory for her than revenge would have been. If "Stings" is a vengeful poem, it is only ambiguously so.

The drafts of "Stings," however, disclose a much more brutal treatment of the scapegoat. The speaker's self-possession in the final version is shown to be hard-won as the scapegoat enters the poem a stanza earlier and cuts a quite different figure:

> He was sweet,
>
> The sweat of his efforts a rain
> [On the world that grew under his belly]
> Tugging the world to fruit.
> Now he peers through a warped silver rain drop;
> Seven lumps on his head
> And a [great] big boss on his forehead,
>
> Black as the devil, and vengeful.
>
> *(Original Drafts 14)*

In this version, he begins to look more like the ominous male figure in "Daddy," a later poem that indulges its speaker's resentment. That resentment surfaces here in the evidence that the scapegoat has been recently beaten; he has bumps on his head. The drafts confirm that Plath edited out a more vicious caricature of the scapegoat. Likewise, she deleted many elements from the drafts that added tension and hostility to the poem—gagging repetitions, the idea of desertion, and the specters of dead men. Noticeably, these are the kinds of elements that she emphasized in "The Bee Meeting." "Stings," then, is a poem that self-consciously suppresses excess; yet it is still a poem of tremendous energy and "terribleness."

Here the speaker, like the queen, is "more terrible than she ever was" because she confronts tenderness, loss, anger, resignation, and release bare-handed—as the first word of the poem asserts. And despite the way we generally read it, "Stings" is neither obsessed with maiming the male figure nor with the violence of the queen's flight. She is, after all, a "red / Scar," not a bleeding gash; thus, she embodies a wound that has already begun to heal. And even the "red comet" that leaves such a fierce impression is nevertheless ambiguous— potentially (and historically) a sign of good luck. (Like the red meteor in *The Scarlet Letter,* this comet is susceptible to multiple readings, an intertextual resonance that Plath's poem exploits.)

It would be foolish to deny that the lion-red queen is the precursor of a group of terrifying female images that Plath will create in the next few weeks and days. As the material miseries of her solitary life bear down on her, her anger justifiably explodes. In "Fever 103°" (231–32) the woman is the lantern "going up" as "The beads of hot metal fly, . . . a pure acetylene / Virgin / Attended by roses"; in "Ariel" (239–40) she is "the arrow, / The dew that flies / Suicidal, at one with the drive / Into the red / Eye, the cauldron of morning"; in "Purdah" (242–44) she is "The lioness, / The shriek in the bath, / The cloak of holes"; and, most famously, in "Lady Lazarus" (244–47) she is the phoenix figure who rises "with [her] red hair / And . . . eat[s] men like air." Though these poems postdate the Bee sequence and may articulate Plath's final emotional perspective, they cannot be considered her concluding *poetic* statement. Around Christmas 1962, after all the *Ariel* poems were written, Plath carefully arranged them for the book, placing the Bee poems last. "Stings," with its contradictory emotional swings, is therefore a crucial part of her culminating poetic vision.

Finally, it is the sweetness that causes the sharpest pain in "Stings." Remembering lost tenderness and "excessive love," catching a glimpse of the man who "tugg[ed] the world to fruit," putting the hives in perfect order with another man, even standing with the honey-drudges, watching the honey-machine, and witnessing the queen's ascension—each of these has an element of sweetness that she cannot ignore.

The breakthrough of "Stings" is that it is intensely personal in its themes yet not excessive in its final style. This new relationship between subject and style enables the poem to articulate complex and ambivalent emotions without attempting to depict them as monolithic and overwhelming. In this, it anticipates "Wintering," where the speaker adds resignation and hope to the emotional range she has been developing throughout the sequence. In "Wintering," the speaker faces the most difficult confrontation of all—that with herself. At this point, however, having assessed her relationship to the community in "The Bee Meeting"; to her art in "The Arrival of the Bee Box"; to her husband, children, other women, and her own contradictory fictional selves in "Stings"; she next addresses her relation to history in "The Swarm."

The sense of anonymity that opens "The Swarm" (215–17)— "Somebody is shooting at something in our town"—has the opposite effect of the atmosphere of anonymity in "The Bee Meeting." In the earlier poem, the speaker's inability to distinguish the identities of others serves to heighten her own extreme subjectivity. Here, however, the speaker is not concerned with determining who the particular actors are; on the contrary, the poem will argue that "somebody" is ultimately "everybody."[26]

In "The Swarm" the speaker parallels her own personal story with world history; however, unlike a later poem such as "Daddy" (222–24) that makes historical facts a questionable image for private feelings ("Dachau, Auschwitz, Belsen. . . . / I think I may well be a Jew"), "The Swarm" extends its interest outward to others. Only in the first stanza does the speaker briefly account for the shooting in terms of her own experience: "Jealousy can open the blood, / It can make black roses." Her first impulse when she hears the shooting is to think what would motivate her to violence—jealousy. She indulges her imagination in one vivid metaphor—that visualizes blood-saturated gunshot wounds as "black roses"[27]—but then immediately turns to the larger question: "Who are they shooting at?"

The voice that emerges in the second stanza to answer this question is powerfully accusatory, marshaling a variety of rhetorical resources to the task of declaring an important truth about history. It begins, "It is you the knives are out for / At Waterloo, Waterloo, Napoleon"; the long, repeated *u*-sound of "Waterloo" echoes the direct indictment, "It is you," and insistently recalls the place name of his crushing defeat. The image of the throats is used again in this poem to suggest victimization and vulnerability—the facts about the masses that "somebody" like Napoleon would deny:

> *Shh! These are chess people you play with,*
> *Still figures of ivory.*
> *The mud squirms with throats,*

Stepping stones for French bootsoles.
The gilt and pink domes of Russia melt and float off

In the furnace of greed.

The narrative of Napoleonic aggression is interwoven with that of the swarm. The bees have swarmed into the top of a tree; the sound of the gun shots is supposed to draw them down (it is not the case, as some readers suggest, that the man is actually shooting into the hive). The bees, like "everybody," have learned that the lesson of history is violence:

So the swarm balls and deserts
Seventy feet up, in a black pine tree.
It must be shot down. Pom! Pom!
So dumb it thinks bullets are thunder.

It thinks they are the voice of God
Condoning the beak, the claw, the grin of the dog
Yellow-haunched, a pack-dog,
Grinning over its bone of ivory
Like the pack, the pack, like everybody.

The bees "argu[ing], in their black ball," the "yellow-haunched" pack-dog, Napoleon with "The hump of Elba on [his] short back, the "man with the gray hands" (whose hands turn out not to be human hands at all but "asbestos receptacles") all appear stooped and deformed by violence. Each has learned hostility at the hands of the other and chooses to return it, believing that the sound of aggression is "the voice of God." In fact, the gunman's excuse for shooting at the swarm is that "They would have killed *me*."

The pervasiveness of violence is what allows Napoleon to be "pleased" at the end of the poem, even despite his own defeat at Waterloo. The weapons of the bees, "Stings big as drawing pins!" (their version of the "knives" and "cutlery" and possibly an image suggesting map pins used by military strategists to pinpoint battle sites), prove to him that the "bees have a notion of honor / A black intractable mind." Like the swarming drudges in "Stings" who attack the scapegoat in an act of self-sacrifice for the hive, the bees in "The Swarm" also lay down their lives for the pack. "Napoleon is pleased, he is pleased with everything" because he recognizes that "everyone," indeed "everything," condones the beak and the claw.

The speaker, however, knows from witnessing the self-destruction of the bees in "Stings" that violent retribution is not "worth it"; she comes to "The Swarm" from "Stings" able to confront the abuses of history because she is not susceptible to the lesson they teach. Yet the task of confronting such a history is strenuous. Not surprisingly, the poem employs excess as if to steel itself against its own revelations. The stylistics of excess can be heard in "The Swarm" in the alliteration ("Somebody is shooting at something" and at every repetition), the assonance ("The man with gray hands stands," "marshals, admirals, generals," "black intractable mind,"), the frequent repetitions ("pom, pom" [repeated eight times], "Waterloo, Waterloo," "Mass after mass," "Shh! // Shh!" "Clouds, Clouds," "The pack, the pack," "Elba, Elba," "Napoleon is pleased, he is pleased with everything"), the buckling anagram ("Elba, Elba, bleb on the sea!"), and the onomatopoeic "pom, pom." Additionally, the poem ricochets from metaphor to simile as the parallel between Napoleon's army and the bees provides constant opportunity for analogy. Thus, the speaker, who has been striving throughout the sequence to relinquish verbal excesses, discovers in "The Swarm" the efficacy of such a style once more. The poetic excess that characterizes the poem is, I think, necessitated by the speaker's attempt to square off against history. What she confronts in the poem is the same oppression she experiences in her private life—played out on a world scale. Understandably, then, the tactics that enabled her to withstand her own hardships permit her to address the suffering of others as well.

In "Wintering" (217–19), the final poem of the sequence, the speaker has come to her last and most important confrontation—that with herself. With her work completed, and with no demands upon her from others, she is able to give herself to the natural rhythms that the seasons decree. "This is the easy time, there is nothing doing," she says in the first line of the poem in a colloquial manner that expresses her own ease and patience. A similar line later confirms that she views her wintering as a distinct phase, a certain kind of *time:* "This is the time of hanging on for the bees." Her recognition that wintering is one part of a larger cycle of time is important because it qualifies the images of hibernation—elements that lead many readers to assume this is a poem about passivity and death.

She shares the experience of wintering with her bees, and she will learn a great deal from them. Like them, she has put up her winter stores: "I have my honey, / Six jars of it, / Six cat's eyes in the wine cellar." These jars of honey are clearly more than just pantry supplies, however. It is as though she has gathered that overwhelming "sweetness" of the earlier poems and stored it where it is available but also contained. In fact, the number of jars supports the notion that they serve a symbolic purpose: Plath was married for six years, and they may represent that period of memories and emotions that now must be put away. Moreover, "cat's-eye" is the name of a semiprecious gem distinctive for its band of reflected light that shifts position as the stone is turned. Thus the jars contain treasures that have great value to her and great beauty. And finally, in their similarity to actual cats' eyes, the jars suggest the power of their vision, especially the ability to see in the darkness she is facing.[28]

Though she considers her stores precious, she also understands that she cannot survive on memories (or past emotions or former accomplishments) alone. Proof of this comes when she sees that what is preserved in the jars now is not permanent; they may seem so at the moment, but others have been here before and discovered the transience of such things. She places her jars of honey "Next to the last tenant's rancid jam / And the bottles of empty glitters— / Sir So-and-so's gin," evidence that even these domestic treasures spoil and evaporate.

The symbolic importance of the setting is further established through sound, repetition, and metaphors of the unconscious. The cellar parallels the core of the self, where normal perception fails her because she has never before been there.

> Wintering in a dark without window
> At the heart of the house . . .
>
> This is the room I have never been in.
> This is the room I could never breathe in.

The soft alliteration of *w*'s and *h*'s creates a tone of silent, solitary reflection, yet the sense of calm that these sounds convey does not completely offset the agitation she feels in such surroundings. The repeated "This is the room" suggests how difficult it is for her to accept where she is. The gothic imagery, accompanied by the alliteration of the explosive *b*'s, incites her nervous dread: "The black bunched in there like a bat."

She enters the room with "No light / But the torch," a primitive, or again, gothic, source of illumination that is consistent with the atmosphere of imminent revelation. It is significant that she must supply her own light. Further, she is in another sense "carrying a torch" for her lost love, and that aspect of the light may contribute to the distortion of her vision. More important, though, is that she is looking into the room for the first time in "a dark" that receives no other illumination, and therefore she has trouble seeing. At first she distinguishes only "appalling objects"; but gradually her vision adjusts and she sees, in turn, "appalling objects," "Black asininity," "Decay," and finally "Possession." This may constitute a list of things she sees in the room (a psychological hoard of mementos from the past that she has relegated to her emotional "cellar") or shifting views of the same object, perceptual superimpositions, each one more accurate in perceiving the actual thing.

In either case, she describes a progression from lack of control (appalling objects) to control (possession). At the word "possession" the poem seems to pivot in another direction, away from the past and its emotional keepsakes that have previously "owned her," toward a present that distances itself from that past, paradoxically, by accepting it. The word "possession" triggers an ambiguous statement, "It is they who own me," a recognition of (or "owning up to") this new relation of present and past. Like the beekeeper, who possesses the bees and yet is possessed by them (because she must fulfill her responsibilities to them in order for them to survive), the speaker is possessed by the memories that she herself possesses. Thus, in acknowledging her reciprocal relation to the bees, she turns from the appalling objects of memory with a tacit understanding that they too are her possessions in this double sense: "This is the time of hanging on for the bees." The easy, accommodating tone of the line suggests an even deeper acceptance and understanding.

It is significant that this decisive line echoes the opening statement ("This is the easy time") since it signals the shift toward optimism in the poem. Turning her attention, now, away from the appalling objects, she considers the bees.

At first glance, these bees appear similar to those in "The Swarm." Both are compared to soldiers. In "The Swarm" they are clearly doomed, "Walking the plank . . . / Into a new mausoleum"; in "Wintering," however, they are survivors, "Filing like soldiers / To the syrup tin." And in both poems, the bees form a ball, yet the fisted hive in the earlier poem and the huddled hive in this one again have little in common. In the first poem "the swarm balls and deserts," the "bees argue in their black ball." On the other hand, the "Wintering" bees "ball in a mass" in order to concentrate their vitality against the cold and snow. Their unity is necessary for survival (and is proven efficacious in the last line where all the bees fly, not just the queen). No doubt there is something awesome about their wintering, "Black / Mind against all that white." The season of hibernation is clearly stark and extreme, black and white, and it requires stolid obstinacy ("black asininity" even) rather than the emotional self-indulgence of "The Bee Meeting."

The key to the survival of the bees is their willingness to accommodate their circumstances. As the speaker consents to their claims on her, they accept hers on them. She gives them Tate and Lyle syrup "To make up for the honey" she has harvested, and "They take it." It is no surprise to learn that

> The bees are all women,
> Maids and the long royal lady.
> They have got rid of the men,
> . . . .
> The blunt, clumsy stumblers, the boors.

The sense of alliance and cooperation that the speaker and her bees share simply has no parallel in the world of gender difference glimpsed in the other poems (with the exception of the bee seller in "Stings," where the business relationships of the apiary are apparently modeled on the social practices of the bees). Some readers make an effort to extract from this passage a vindictive spirit toward men, but the tone is so obviously detached and humorous (the onomatopoeic "stumblers" playing on "bumble-bees," the idea that men are merely boors and not tyrants or attackers) that such an interpretation is unconvincing. Furthermore, the lovely, unperturbed portrait of the mother over the cradle immediately detracts attention away from the men who are not there and refocuses it on this female community:

The woman, still at her knitting,
At the cradle of Spanish walnut,
Her body a bulb in the cold and too dumb to think.

The alliteration of *w*'s (winter, women, woman, walnut) recalls the opening tone where that sound has already been associated with forbearance and equanimity.

The poem has retreated inward, arriving at the image in the penultimate stanza of the woman's body as "a bulb in the cold." That she is at the moment "too dumb to think" need not suggest stupefaction and passivity; rather, it represents the period of silence that is necessary to still the incessant questions of "The Bee Meeting" or the maniac metaphor-making of "The Arrival of the Bee Box." Plath's drafts of "Wintering" reveal that this wordless, unthinking confidence in the renewal of spring is a difficult achievement:

What will they taste [like] of the Christmas roses?
Snow water? Corpses? [Thin, sweet Spring.]
  [A sweet Spring?] Spring?
  [Impossible spring?]
  [What sort of spring?]
  [O God, let them taste of spring.]
                    (Van Dyne, "Manuscripts" 169)

Van Dyne observes that "her final revision, when it comes, moves in the opposite direction from her changes in 'The Bee Meeting.' . . . she wills herself to assert a compelling prophecy, continuing to hope, as she has throughout the rest of the sequence, that saying would make it so" (169). Thus, the image of the woman as bulb is unquestionably one of renewal both in its similarity to the (implied) baby in the cradle and, of course, in the realization of the image in the final stanza, where the questions, at last, resolve:

Will the hive survive, will the gladiolas
Succeed in banking their fires
To enter another year?
What will they taste of, the Christmas roses?
The bees are flying. They taste of spring.

It is the lyric beauty of this passage that convinces—the long *i*'s once again suggesting the unity of the hive, the emotional, anticipatory line breaks, the promising "glad" in "gladiolas," the marvelous image of the bulb's vitality as fire (bringing both warmth and color to the ending) and the rounded shape of the bulb redoubled in the verb "banking," the perfectly timed forthrightness of the third line, the Christmas roses that are themselves a symbol of renewal, and the three questions that blend into declarative affirmation in the last line.

The speaker learns from the bees in "Wintering" that spring will follow this time of introspection and stillness, of uniting resources and waiting. The answer to her questions comes in the form of an act rather than in words and thus embodies certainty through enacting it. Only then is she certain that they actually "taste the spring" and have not been deceived by the early blossoms of the Christmas roses. She concludes *Ariel* on this rather simple and understated note of hope; its subtlety is a measure of its sureness. "Wintering" achieves a perspective Plath had advanced years before in her journals: there she promises to herself to write "without any moral other than growth is good. Faith *too* is good" (169). Here, at last, she seems to have listened to herself—a development only made possible by first recovering that self.

Plath's *Ariel* culminates in the Bee sequence because these five poems record her most important vision and embody the farthest development of her poetics. The Bee poems reveal Plath shaping a new aesthetics that is vitalized by the style of excess she had cultivated for so long—but one that is also discovering other energies. The manuscripts show her revising in favor of excess in "The Bee Meeting" and, to some extent, in "The Arrival of the Bee Box"; by "Stings," the third poem in the sequence, however, they document an effort to minimize stylistic excesses. In the final poem, "Wintering," we hear an entirely new poetic voice and confront a subtle new poetics.

The fact that the Bee sequence contradicts our received notion of Plath's poetry accounts for its failure to "make [her] name." As every modern poetry anthology attests, her reputation rests on her most excessive poems, "Daddy," "Ariel," and "Lady Lazarus." It is an interesting paradox that the most frequent charge leveled against her work—that it envisions only violence and self-destruction—remains untroubled by the final ease and hopefulness of the Bee sequence. Critics bemoan Plath's single-mindedness but limit their reading to the poems that confirm it. There are several reasons that the Bee poems remain relatively obscure in the Plath canon.

First, as I have already mentioned, when Hughes published his version of *Ariel,* he imbedded them in the middle of the volume where their significance would naturally be diminished. Further, he deleted "The Swarm" from the English edition and, in doing so, initiated a critical tradition of failing to consider it part of the sequence. By the time "The Swarm" was restored to its place in the volume, readers had already established their interpretations of the Bee poems, and many were reluctant to accommodate another, and in some ways, more problematic poem. The assertion that "'The Swarm' is quite unrelated to the other bee poems" is not uncommon (Uroff 152). Consequently, until the acquisition of the Plath collection by Smith College, scholars and readers had no way of knowing that "The Swarm" was an essential part of the sequence or, in fact, that the Bee poems constituted a sequence at all.

Further, without realizing that the five poems Plath had composed in a week and titled "Bees" was a discrete unit, many readers clustered either four or all five of the poems with one from *The Colossus,* "The Beekeeper's Daughter." While the earlier poem certainly enriches a reading of the Bee sequence, it is not in dialogue with the poems of "Bees" as they are with each other. As Van Dyne discovered in comparing the drafts, "The manuscripts from this single week show evidence of considerable cross-fertilization. These texts refer to each other repeatedly during their period of gestation. An emotionally laden word or image from one poem will reappear in the drafts for several others suggesting a network of symbolic relationships" ("Manuscripts" 155). Thus, while the Bee poems have been denied their own context, they have also been mistakenly transplanted into another.

But the tampering with Plath's *Ariel* is not the sole reason for slighting the sequence. The myth that the poet was governed by a "sensibility . . . deeply captive to the idea of suicide" (Howe 235) makes the Bee poems appear anomalous in her canon. Instead of permitting the works of the poet to characterize her sensibility, Plath criticism too often allows her sensational biography to determine the importance of her works. This causes readers to overlook some poems and to misread others. For instance, "Stings" is considered to be the strongest of the Bee sequence because its ending—the queen bee's terrible bride flight—is consistent with the imagery in the "typical" poems. Consequently, some cognate of the word "central" finds its way into almost every discussion of the poem; Van Dyne calls it the "stunning centerpiece" (160), McCann says it is "central and most optimistic" (31), and Broe, too, considers it "central to the developing drama of the bee sequence" (150), as though the four other poems are not. And these critics rarely mean simply that it falls at the center of the five poems; Broe, for example, includes "The Beekeeper's Daughter" in the sequence of what she calls "six poems about bee-keeping" (150); she clearly means "Stings" is centrally important, not centrally located.

Likewise, the optimistic "Wintering" is frequently faulted for being unconvincing in its hopefulness. McCann insists that "the conclud-ing 'taste of spring' contradicts the rest of the poem" (34), but this can be true only insofar as the season of spring could be thought to "contradict" winter, a notion that would ignore seasonal processes. To employ seasonal imagery is to invoke the notion of movement and change. But this is a vision that readers are loathe to grant to Sylvia Plath. McCann argues that the tone of the poem undermines its promising words, yet she fails to consider that the tone she responds to originates outside the poem in the Plath lore.

Hughes is certainly the person most responsible for consolidating this view of Plath. What he didn't outright destroy of her literary legacy, he sequestered, sealed, suppressed, and rearranged.[29] What he has allowed into print is frequently accompanied by unconscionable reading directives.[30] What has been most influential in defining Plath, however, is his version of *Ariel* where he deleted eleven of the poems she had included and replaced them with nine of his own selections. While Plath's *Ariel* ended with the word "spring" (and all that represented), Hughes' volume ends with two poems that contribute to the idea that *Ariel* was a lyric suicide note, that her life had to close after the creative outburst was over. The two poems, "Edge" (84) and "Words" (85), are ideal for the task. "Edge" kills off Plath the woman:

> *The woman is perfected.*
> *Her dead*
>
> *Body wears the smile of accomplishment,*
> *The illusion of a Greek necessity*

Flows in the scrolls of her toga,
Her bare

Feet seem to be saying:
We have come so far, it is over.

And in the closing poem of the book, "Words dry and riderless" put an end to Plath the poet by intimating her language has lost its vitality.[31] Admittedly, the poems Plath wrote the last days of her life support the connection between the work and the biography. It is not surprising that a poet who dwelled in her "own worded world" (*Journals* 179) and who believed in a "dialogue between [her] Writing and [her] Life" (99) would continue composing poetry right up to the end. However, there need be no connection between her last writings and her final poetic vision. The deletions from and additions to *Ariel* throw a shroud over that vision that remained in place for nearly thirty years. Only with the information available in the *Collected Poems* and in the Smith Collection have we been able to begin lifting it.

Despite the fact that Plath wrote many poems after the Bee sequence, it nevertheless represents the full measure of her poetic achievement. That the later poems exploit the specific resources of stylistic excess once more only confirms the relationship between a poetics of excess and difficulties and pressures the woman poet faces. In the Bee sequence she had not, after all, "outgrown" excess but rather had achieved a wider range of poetic possibilities. The circumstances of Plath's last months—isolation, illness, extreme physical hardship, solitary responsibility for her children, professional rejection, and severe depression—were such that required excess in order for her to be able to write at all.

CHAPTER *5*

The Black Arts Movement

We Survive in Patches . . . Scraps

"A nigger is a nigger is a nigger"

*E*arly in the 1980s, a decade that would see African-American women's writing rise to dominance in American letters, Ntozake Shange responded to criticisms that her writing was "too self-conscious" and "involved with the destruction of the English language" by insisting upon the need for these excesses:

> i cant count the number of times i have viscerally wanted to attack deform n maim the language that i waz taught to hate myself in/ the language that perpetuates the notions that cause pain to every black child as he/ she learns to speak of the world & the "self." yes/ being an afro-american writer is something to be self-conscious abt/ & yes/ in order to think n communicate the thoughts n feelings i want to think n communicate/ i haveta fix my tool to my needs/ i have to take it apart to the bone/ so that the malignancies/ fall away/ leaving us space to literally create our own image. ("Unrecovered Losses" 21)

The renewal of language that would facilitate the creation of these transforming images entailed for some black women writers the appropriation of literary tools that had been problematic to them only a decade before. The history of black feminist excess is preceded by two other black literary histories, the Harlem Renaissance of the 1920s and the Black Arts movement of the 1960s and 70s, when the struggle to write in a hostile literary environment involved, as it did for Dickinson, Stein, and Plath, a battle between decorum and excess. Yet that struggle has been much more complicated in African-American poetics, as pressures to conform have come from inside and outside the community, and individual poets have committed their work to communal and political goals. This chapter will trace the historical specificity of African-American poetic excess by outlining the aesthetic goals of the Harlem Renaissance, the revision of those goals by the Black Arts movement, and the complications a politicized poetics created for black women writers during that period and after.

The Black Arts movement inspired an aesthetic project that would employ excess to promote its collective goals as surely as excess had served the more isolated projects of Dickinson, Stein, and Plath, and because of the movement's emphasis on collective identity and its articulation of a public program for art, I will be discussing a group of writers rather than a single poet. This is not to pit "individual genius" against a communal art or white writers against African-American writers. On the contrary, it is to take the accounts of excess in the preceding chapters to a political level, to make even more explicit what has been true all along, that "writing itself is a form of action" (Silliman 4). The Black Arts movement is thus the fulfillment of an urge to excess in American poetry that can be traced from Whitman and Dickinson, in different ways, through the Beats and Plath. The Black Arts movement stands as the culmination of this study, rather than merely a conclusion to it, because it provides a political analysis of an aesthetic choice that has enabled disenfranchised poets to write when the dominant culture encouraged their silence. Indeed, the complications introduced in this chapter—which studies a poetic movement rather than a single poet, gendered uses of excess as a context for women's excess, racial and sexual conflicts, political imperatives in addition to aesthetic ones—offer a compelling reminder of how a poetic paradigm changes and adjusts in different historical circumstances. By 1965 poetic excess was clearly available in the cultural arsenal, but it would be reinvented by the Black Arts aestheticians for new social and political needs.

According to activist writer Amiri Baraka (formerly LeRoi Jones), the Black Arts movement took shape in response to the assassination of Malcolm X on February 21, 1965.[1] Within a few days of the shooting, Baraka moved away from the white culture of the Village to the black culture of Harlem: "When we came up out of the subway, March 1965, cold and clear, Harlem all around us staring us down, we felt like pioneers of the new order. Back in the homeland to help raise the race" (Jones, *Autobiography* 202). Baraka and other black activists bought a brownstone building and formed the Black Arts Repertoire Theatre School, producing militant black plays, conducting a series of poetry readings and concerts, and organizing a parade, all with the purpose of "rais[ing] the question of art and politics and revolution, black revolution!" (205).

The notion that art could raise the race was not new. Cultural intervention had been the ideal of the Harlem Renaissance during the 1920s when Alain Locke, Claude McKay, Countee Cullen, and others anticipated that artistic achievement on the part of the "New Negroes" would win them acceptance, understanding, and equality in white America.

In 1921, James Weldon Johnson edited *The Book of American Negro Poetry,* with the purpose of uplifting the race by documenting its artistic achievements. The modesty with which he explained his goals suggests how confident he was in the transforming power of art. He wanted, first, to correct the misconception that there was no black poetry—"The public, generally speaking, does not know that there are American Negro poets—to supply this lack of information is, alone, a work worthy of somebody's efforts" (9)—and second, to offer evidence of racial equality—"nothing will do more to change that [white racist] mental attitude and raise [Negroes'] status than a demonstration of intellectual parity by the Negro through the production of literature and the arts" (9). Five years later, Countee Cullen produced another anthology, *Caroling Dusk: An Anthology of Verse by Negro Poets,* to give a hearing to poetry written since Johnson's collection. Like Johnson, Cullen was certain that making black poetry available to white readers would improve social relations between the races. Indeed, he expected that African-American poets would eventually "find inclusion in any discriminatingly ordered anthology of American verse" (xii) and that his own anthology would then be superfluous: "This anthology, by no means offered as *the* anthology of verse by Negro poets, is but a prelude, we hope, to that fuller symphony which Negro poets will in time contribute to the national literature, and we shall be sadly disappointed if the next few years do not find this collection entirely outmoded" (xiv).

Both influential editors and most of the Harlem Renaissance writers imagined African-American poets joining the ranks of "simply" American writers by displaying the artistic wares and values of the dominant culture. Cullen was adamant that there were only "negro poets," there was not "negro poetry" (xi), rejecting the idea of a Black Aesthetic: "the attempt to corral the outbursts of the ebony muse into some definite mold to which all poetry by Negroes will conform seems altogether futile and aside from the facts" (xi). Though Johnson and Cullen recognized that black poetry would be inflected by the experience of black authors, they nevertheless insisted that the poetic capacity itself transcended such racial barriers, and they looked forward to a time when the experiences of black authors were more American and less Negro—and to a time when the poetry of black authors would be more American as well. Both editors expected their anthologies to help the race achieve social parity through documentation of its creative parity. Johnson held an unquestioned trust in the efficacy of art for social reformation: "The final measure of the greatness of all peoples is the amount and standard of the literature and art they have produced. . . . No people that has produced great literature and art has ever been looked upon by the world as distinctly inferior" (9). Behind this confidence in the attainment of artistic equality—conceived of by both Johnson and Cullen as the demonstration of similarity between black and white literary works— was their assumption that both groups of writers shared artistic "standards," as Johnson put it here; in the revised preface to the second edition, written ten years later, he would insist still more adamantly that the Negro writer "strives to fashion something that rises above mere race and reaches out to the universal in truth and beauty" (7). Cullen, less grandly but no less idealistically, asserted that the writers in his anthology tried to "maintain the higher traditions of English verse" (xii).

In their commitment to Anglo-European aesthetics and their belief in the universality of truth and beauty, Johnson, Cullen, and other

Harlem Renaissance writers addressed themselves to a white reader-ship. This was necessary partly because of economic circumstances: white patrons supported much of this work and white readers pur-chased it. Yet even beyond that necessity, these anthologies accepted the dominant aesthetic values, expressed faith in the universal appeal of great art, and anticipated the transformation in human relations that such art would effect. Their views were quickly challenged by "younger Negro artists" like Langston Hughes, Zora Neale Hurston, Bruce Nugent, Gwendolyn Bennett, and Wallace Thurman, who re-jected the aesthetics and values of their New Negro elders. In Novem-ber 1926, they published a journal called *Fire!! A Quarterly Devoted to the Younger Negro Artists,* which recast aesthetic and political differences as generational ones. Though many of the *Fire!!* con-tributors were contemporaries of Cullen and Johnson—and, indeed, though many of them appeared in those earlier anthologies (as Cullen appeared in the pages of *Fire!!*)—they considered themselves younger and newer than Cullen, Johnson, or Locke in their rebellion against white cultural values in general and black middle-class taste in par-ticular. In the foreword of the first and only issue, the journal de-clared its mission to be "melting steel and iron bars, poking livid tongues between stone apertures and burning wooden opposition with a cackling chuckle of contempt" (n.p.).[2] The imagery of this poetic foreword—bursting out of prison, speaking through the mask, destroying rigid opposition, and taking pleasure in expressing con-tempt—indicates the irreverence and even militancy of the *Fire!!* artists. Unlike Cullen and Johnson, they wanted to create a Black Aesthetic by inventing new poetic forms, treating unpopular subjects, and reviving the very folk forms (dialect, ballads, blues) the New Negroes had eschewed. Hughes was the most outspoken of these renegades. In 1925, just months before the publication of *Fire!!,* he declared artistic independence from white readers as well as from conservative black audiences: "We younger Negro artists who create now intend to express our individual, dark-skinned selves without fear or shame. If white people are pleased we are glad. If they are not, it doesn't matter. We know we are beautiful. And ugly too. The tom-tom cries and the tom-tom laughs. If colored people are pleased we are glad. If they are not, their displeasure doesn't matter either. We build our temples for tomorrow, strong as we know how, and we stand on top of the mountain, free within ourselves" (181). Hughes could not have guessed, in 1925 at the height of the Harlem Renaissance, how far away the "tomorrow" of racial equality and artistic freedom would be.

By the 1950s, however, it was painfully obvious to Hughes that tomorrow was a lot like yesterday. His poem "Harlem," part of the book-length poem *Montage of a Dream Deferred,* is one of many reflections on the continuing problem of social injustice in America. It warns that postponing equality will be dangerous:

> *What happens to a dream deferred?*
>
> *Does it dry up*
> *like a raisin in the sun?*
> *Or fester like a sore—*
> *And then run?*
> *Does it stink like rotten meat?*
> *Or crust and sugar over—*
> *like a syrupy sweet?*
>
> *Maybe it just sags*
> *like a heavy load.*
>
> Or does it explode?
> *(Collected Poems 426)*

The final italicized line indicates the answer in a poem that remains rhetorically interrogative: a dream deferred explodes. Forty years after the Harlem Renaissance had attempted to raise the race through artistic achievements, the Black Arts movement organizers declared it a failure and determined to produce an *explosion* of art rather than just a renaissance. The most volatile component of their explosion would be poetic excess.

The Black Arts movement (appropriately nicknamed BAM) categorically rejected the assumptions of the Harlem Renaissance. In "Some Observations on a Black Aesthetic," Adam David Miller attacked the artistic and social ideals of the earlier movement by repudiating the notion of universal values:

> Were someone to say to Johnson, "A nigger is a nigger is a nigger," he would probably be questioned about his sanity. But this same man could say, " 'Beauty is truth, truth beauty,—that is all/Ye know on earth, and all ye need to know,' " and Johnson would probably say, "How profound!" Now neither statement says any more about experience than the other,

yet because of his cultural conditioning, Johnson imagines "universal in truth and beauty" says something about a standard of aesthetics, when in reality he is talking about cultural judgments, and ultimately the way power is exercised in our society. (402)

Miller's last point indicates another crucial difference between the 20s and the 60s: the Harlem Renaissance, so the later theorists would claim, was merely a literary movement, while the Black Arts movement had a political mission and, in fact, was the cultural arm of the Black Power movement. Lacking an adequate political analysis and ignoring the need for political action, the Harlem Renaissance had done more harm than good: "The Black Arts Movement represents the flowering of a cultural nationalism that has been suppressed since the 1920s. I mean the 'Harlem Renaissance'—which was essentially a failure. It did not address itself to the mythology and the life-styles of the Black community. It failed to take roots, to link itself concretely to the struggles of that community, to become its voice and spirit" (Neal 290). Today, African-American scholars have, of course, revised this negative assessment of the Harlem Renaissance; indeed, it is impossible to think of a contemporary critic who underestimates and devalues the cultural achievement of the period. Among many scholarly works that have transformed our understanding of the Harlem Renaissance, Houston A. Baker Jr.'s contributions are seminal: *A Many-Colored Coat of Dreams: The Poetry of Countee Cullen* provided an important defense of Cullen by explaining his historical context as early as 1974, and *Modernism and the Harlem Renaissance* (1987) offered one of the first theoretical accounts of artistic resistance during the period. But Henry Louis Gates Jr.'s *Figures in Black: Words, Signs, and the "Racial" Self* (1987) also brought a new kind of attention to the workings of language in black texts that enabled a rereading of the whole tradition. Maureen Honey's *Shadowed Dreams: Women's Poetry of the Harlem Renaissance* (1989) recovered literary works that altered and enriched our impression of the period.

Without the benefits of this reforming work, however, the founders of the Black Arts movement perceived the Harlem Renaissance as an artistic movement that had misplaced its cultural commitments. "Cultural nationalism" instead called for the artistic productions of a nation (in this case, the black "*nation* within the belly of white America" [Neal 290]) to serve and promote the political revolution.

In "Black Cultural Nationalism" Ron Karenga, one of the movement's most influential leaders, distinguishes between "art for art's sake" (amoral, even immoral, decadent art attentive only to conventional aesthetics) and "art for all our sake" (ethical art concerned with artistic *and* social levels) (34): "For all art must reflect and support the Black Revolution, and any art that does not discuss and contribute to the revolution is invalid, no matter how many lines and spaces are produced in proportion and symmetry" (33). Following the teachings of the Senegalese poet and president Leopold Senghor, Karenga says revolutionary black art must be functional, collective, and committing.

First, to be functional art must be useful, it must "expose the enemy, praise the people, and support the revolution" (33–34). Exposing the enemy would involve, for obvious reasons, attacks upon whites and other nonblacks, conservative blacks, the United States government and its leaders, Christianity, and, for more complicated reasons, Jews, women, and homosexuals. Praising the people would entail celebrating black historical and contemporary heroes, affirming African roots, appreciating aspects of a distinctly African-American culture, and asserting that "black is beautiful." To support the revolution, black art would incite readers to violence, inspire feelings of nationalism, and envision a postrevolutionary world that was possible to attain and clearly worth struggling for.

Second, to be collective, art "must be from the people and must be returned to the people" since "no one is any more than the context to which he owes his existence" (34). Collective art is accountable to the people in four ways: "Number one, the question of popularization versus elevation; two, personality versus individuality; three, diversity in unity; and four, freedom *to* versus freedom *from*" (35). First, says Karenga, the old debate about whether art should be lowered to the level of the people or people raised to the level of art is misguided: "Our contention is that if art is from the people, and for the people, there is no question of raising people to art or lowering art to the people, for they are one and the same thing" (35). He proposes a dialogue between artists and their audience, in which the people teach the artists and the artists teach them. Moreover, "art and people must develop at the same time and for the same reason" (35), or art will soon find itself irrelevant. Second, since "individualism is a luxury we cannot afford," black art must emphasize a collective rather than an individual identity. A particular artist's work will nevertheless be distinctive because it will be marked by personality instead of being marred by individuality: "Individuality by definition is 'me' in spite of everyone, and personality is 'me' in relation to everyone" (35). Third, Karenga argues that unity will not preclude diversity; however, unity will provide a framework within which black artists can work successfully (avoiding the failures of an unguided European tradition). Finally, the revolution will give black artists freedom *from* the restrictions and prohibitions they experience in a white racist society and thus the freedom *to* create legitimate black art, but these freedoms must not be mistaken for freedom from communal responsibilities or freedom to express an isolated or idiosyncratic vision. Though Karenga assures black artists that collective art will not result in "a standardization of every move or creation" (36), the artist's obligations to the people take precedence over any other artistic consideration. An artist's freedom, then, is qualified by the people's freedoms: "And an artist may have any freedom to do what he wishes as long as it does not take the freedom from the people to be protected from those images, words and sounds that are negative to their life and development. The people give us the freedom from isolation and alienation and random searching for subject matter[,] and artists, in view of this, must not ask for freedom to deny this, but on the contrary must praise the people for this" (37).

Karenga's third criterion for black art is that "it must commit us to revolution and change" (37). Though aesthetically vague, Karenga and other revolutionary leaders succeeded in staking out a position for black art that was in crucial ways functional, collective, and committing.[3] Despite being termed the "black *aesthetic,*" however, the cultural program dictated the purposes of art rather than its forms. Its revolutionary goals, nevertheless, promoted revolutionary stylistics. The inaugural poems by the movement's leaders introduced a rebellious, extremist style, and most of the poems that followed took up the charge. The Black Arts theorists demanded in only the most general terms that poems be useful for the revolution; the formal particulars of such a decree were delineated and adopted in the poetry itself.

Black Arts excesses—obscenity, thematic and formal violence, repetition, unorthodox spelling and syntax, typographical tricks, nonverbal noise, signifying, cacophony, and polyrhythms—registered a complete rejection of white American culture and of previous "Negro writing" that had been submissive to Anglo-European literary values.[4] Both male and female African-American writers participated in a poetic and political movement that advocated the use of excess. Like women writers in a masculinist culture, black writers in a white racist culture resisted literary ideals and values that tended to exclude, ignore, demean, or dismiss their works and to conceptualize blacks as incompetent users of the language. I have argued that women writers turned to excess in part because it paradoxically reproduced the dominant male culture's assumptions about the gabby, repetitive, incoherent, inaccurate, inconsequential and yet infuriating discourse of women. Similarly, white American culture depicted blacks as childish, clumsy and clownish speakers, who blubbered incoherently, could not get their tongues around English words, or else used them incorrectly. A stereotype that developed from these racist assumptions was the loquacious, florid, pretentious, and ignorant black speaker who made a fool of himself and provided a humorous distraction for whites.

The minstrel shows in vogue in the nineteenth and early twentieth centuries were just one forum that popularized such figures. The white performers in burnt cork who played the parts of blacks "were expected to cultivate an eccentric vocabulary, full of bad grammar, faulty pronunciation and a kind of bombastic ignorance" (Wittke 142). In a typical skit entitled "Bursting Into Poetry," for example, the black character, Tambo, says he believes he's "the *carnation* of Shakespeare" and insists on reciting a poem. His performance proves, of course, that he's no Shakespeare:

The boy stood on the burning deck,
  Thinking of days gone by;
And he stood and stood and stood and stood,
  But, alas, I know not why.

But he did and did and did and did,
  So he did, so he did, so he did.
An he just kept standing on the deck,
  So nobody else could bid.

When suddenly right before him stood
  The pretty maiden all forlorn,

> Who milked the cow with the crumpled horn,
> That tossed the dog that worried the cat.

> And from his side a dagger drew,
> And jabbed it in an oyster stew . . .
>   *(Clifford 31)*

Tambo confuses poems (Felicia Hemans's "Casabianca") with nursery rhymes ("The House That Jack Built"), repeats phrases mindlessly, produces nonsense, and tediously refuses to quit speaking. While much of the excess of Black Arts stylistics conveys the deadly seriousness of "offing whitey," an aspect of exposing the enemy, they also parody the stereotype of the ludicrous black speaker and appropriate that figure for their own revisionary purposes. Ntozake Shange, for instance, will appropriate the minstrel figure in *spell #7* precisely because she finds his excesses so potent: "in *spell #7* i included a prologue of a minstrel show/ which made me cry the first times i danced in it/ for the same reasons i had included it. the minstrel may be 'banned' as racist/ but the minstrel is more powerful in his deformities than our alleged rejection of him" ("Unrecovered Losses" 22).

African-American poets found recourse in an aesthetics of excess, which enabled them to appropriate the degrading stereotype of the verbally excessive black speaker, to fashion a poetic program that resisted white literary conventions, and to create a literary spectacle with a style of poetry that was threatening to the oppressor, expressive of the people, and committed to artistic and political revolution.

Though men and women participated in the Black Arts movement, the excesses of its cultural program served them differently. The usefulness of the Black Aesthetic was limited for women by its dependence on the trope of masculinity. Black Arts poems tended to present an exclusively masculine persona who thematized homophobia, anti-Semitism, and misogyny. The ideal black revolutionary, and therefore the quintessential black revolutionary poet, was defined in contrast to homosexual men, Jewish men, and women—that is, in contrast to people whose "masculinity" was viewed by the persona as inadequate. Second, while women were excluded as revolutionary agents, they were nevertheless exploited as icons of black pride and solidarity. In many of the poems, women symbolized a black femininity that procreated, nurtured, and inspired but did not write revolutionary poetry.

All of these complexities are at work in the acknowledged *ars poetica* of the period, LeRoi Jones's "Black Art." First published in the *Liberator* in 1966, it appeared in the influential and definitive collection of essays, poetry, and drama *Black Fire: An Anthology of Afro-American Writing,* edited by Jones and Larry Neal, in 1968. The title of the volume recalls *Fire!!* and that earlier period of black art. *Black Fire* recognizes its genealogy but insists on its progress toward a militant black artistic movement. If *Fire!!* burned with creative energies, then *Black Fire* explodes with revolutionary power. "Black Art" (302–03) epitomizes this:

> Poems are bullshit unless they are
> teeth or trees or lemons piled
> on a step. Or black ladies dying
> of men leaving nickel hearts
> beating them down.

The opening phrase announces that the traditions and standards of English verse, so important to Cullen and Johnson, are irrelevant. Here poetry's aesthetic function is utilitarian, in accord with the tenets of cultural nationalism. Though the revolutionary function of teeth, trees, and lemons is not immediately apparent, these objects share an unequivocal concreteness and indicate that anything "real" might prove useful. "Teeth" suggests that poems ought to have a bite (another kind of bite, sourness, is registered in the figure of the lemons), while the image of "lemons piled / on a step" argues that traditional objects of decadent art—say, the luminous lemons in a still life—must be appropriated and deployed like rotten eggs, rocks, or grenades as weapons in the fight against white art and the dominant cultural values. Karenga makes a similar point: "we do not need pictures of oranges in a bowl or trees standing inno-cently in the midst of a wasteland. If we must paint oranges and trees, let our guerrillas be eating those oranges for strength and us-ing those trees for cover" (34). These lemons, then, are not merely aesthetic objects in a bowl but potential missiles that can be lobbed at approaching enemies; they represent the belligerent energies of the poem. Like these real objects that open the poem, the "black ladies dying / of men leaving nickel hearts / beating them down" are real experiences in people's lives that must be acknowledged and corrected.

In an enjambment that introduces the conflation of violence and sexuality central to Black Arts poetry, the poem makes its next crucial move: "Fuck poems / and they are useful, they shoot / come at you." Aggressive, even cheerful, sexually explicit language signals an escalation of the violence only hinted at in the opening lines. We must "fuck poems" for them to be useful. We do this, first, by rejecting (saying "fuck off" to) the traditions of English verse. Once those standards are dispatched, we can give our attention to poems that themselves are capable of "fucking"—that is, poems that reject conventional style and taste and that register a creative force akin to raw sexual energy. These poems not only "shoot" and "come" *at* you—as we'll see later in the poem—but first they "shoot / *come* at you": their "matter" is potent creative material, delivered forcefully. In an instance of syntactic tripling, the phrase "fuck poems" is a command to us to reject traditional poems, an invitation to engage in aggressively direct ways with revolutionary poems, and a descriptive category of the kind of poem that will revolutionize us: Fuck Poems are part of an insurrectionary aesthetics that rhetorically positions violence in the poetry.

Though the poem pauses briefly to survey the meaning of its violent images ("We want live / words of the hip world live flesh & / coursing blood. Hearts Brains / Souls splintering fire"), the physical aggression returns:

> *We want poems*
> *like fists beating niggers out of Jocks*
> *or dagger poems in the slimy bellies*
> *of the owner-jews. Black poems to*
> *smear on girdlemamma mulatto bitches*
> *whose brains are red jelly stuck*
> *between 'lizabeth taylor's toes. Stinking*
> *Whores! We want "poems that kill."*
> *Assassin poems, Poems that shoot*
> *guns. Poems that wrestle cops into alleys*
> *and take their weapons leaving them dead*
> *with tongues pulled out and sent to Ireland.*

Here the aggression finds its victims: blacks who have internalized racism ("niggers," "mulatto bitches"), Jews, who are accused of controlling money and therefore lives ("owner-jews"), white people (as icons, " 'lizabeth taylor," and authorities, the Irish "cops"), and women ("mulatto bitches," "'lizabeth taylor," "Whores"). The speaker longs to beat the self-hatred out of other blacks and kill the nonblacks outright; thus, he now wants "poems that kill" and "Poems that shoot / guns" rather than merely poems that "shoot / come at you." And death is not enough: the speaker fantasizes killing the cops and then pulling out their tongues, an image that suggests the inordinate potency of white speech. Like the white racist lynchers who kill *and* castrate black men who are thought to possess extraordinary sexual powers, the persona of "Black Art" senses that killing the white cops will not diminish the cultural authority of white people. We suspect that the issue of verbal authority raised by "tongues" is central to the poem when the speaker spews nonverbal noise almost immediately after having imagined pulling out the cops' tongues:

rrrrrrrrrrrrrrrrrrrr
rrrrrrrrrrrrrrr . . . tuhtuhtuhtuhtuhtuhtuhtuhtuhtuh
. . . . rrrrrrrrrrrrrrr . . . . Setting fire and death to
whities ass.

This eruption begins with the phrase "Airplane poems" and is obviously the sound of an air raid and machine gun fire; yet, it also constitutes an interruption of speech and a loss of control as the speaker appears tongue-tied with fury and resorts to fierce vocal effects.

Such combative sounds translate racial struggle into a contest of masculinity. Manhood, the speaker's and his opponent's, is constantly under assault. Thus "whities ass" is not merely a degrading metonymy for white people but also a metaphor for male homosexuality through a reference to sodomy. Like Eldridge Cleaver "practicing [rape] on black girls in the ghetto" (26) in preparation for raping the real enemy, the speaker here has been working his way to his most infuriating object of contempt and violence. The ineffectiveness and betrayal of mainstream civil rights leaders are figured forth in the poem as homosexual men compromising their masculinity (by performing fellatio) as they compromise racial equality:

Look at the Liberal
Spokesman for the jews clutch at his throat
& puke himself into eternity . . . . rrrrrrrr
There's a negroleader pinned to
a bar stool in Sardi's eyeballs melting

in hot flame. Another negroleader
on the steps of the white house one
kneeling between the sheriff's thighs
negotiating cooly for his people.
Aggh . . . stumbles across the room.

White sheriffs, we see, can also "shoot come at you," and the poem literally gags ("Aggh" is not only onomatopoeic but also an anagram for "gag") on the idea of civil rights leaders "sucking up" to white authorities and the disturbing similarities between sexual weaponry and sexual betrayal. These confusions become explicit when the poem attempts to exorcise the images of homosexuality in yet another act of sexual aggression—"Put it on him, poem. Strip him naked / to the world!"—that figures the male poem raping the homosexual man. As if to master these unruly terms once and for all, the poem retreats to an easier target, women, and a more final solution, the extermination of the Jews:

Another bad poem cracking
steel knuckles in a jewlady's mouth
Poem scream poison gas on beasts in green berets.

The rhetoric of ethnic cleansing inevitably follows the reference to the Holocaust, as the poem culminates in a utopian vision of a purified "Black World":

Clean out the world for virtue and love,
Let there be no love poems written
until love can exist freely and
cleanly. Let Black People understand
that they are the lovers and the sons
of lovers and warriors and sons
of warriors Are poems & poets &
all the loveliness here in the world.

In lines reminiscent of Johnson's or Cullen's idealistic confidence in the power of art to transform the world, the poem draws to its conclusion:

We want a black poem. And a
Black World.
Let the world be a Black Poem
And Let All Black People Speak This Poem
Silently

or LOUD.

"Black Art" speaks both silently and loudly, moving through thematic and stylistic violence in order, as it argues here at the end, to clean out the world for nonviolence. The poem's "virtue and love" are, understandably, reserved for black people and so are held off until these last lines in which a direct address to African-American people is remarkably reasonable, hopeful, and even tender after the excesses of the rest of the poem. The structure of the poem reproduces its argument; violence and cleansing must precede virtue and love. The deferral of a measured tone until the end eloquently conveys the poem's willingness to sacrifice poetic beauty to political necessity. Those closing lines express a yearning for a time when love poems will be appropriate and imaginable; but in a world of racism and inequality, love poems are irrelevant, and perhaps even dangerous, for they distract readers from the real world where love cannot flourish.

"Black Art" embodies the poetics of excess that would soon be termed the Black Aesthetic. It also establishes two norms that most other Black Arts poets would follow: first, a stylistics of excess and, second, a hypermasculine persona to deploy them. The revolutionary persona and his revisionary poetics would eradicate the artistic conventions and values of the dominant culture and erect new ones in their places. Like the other practitioners of excess I have discussed, the Black Arts poets formed their aesthetics in revolt against the conventions that excluded them, but they did so by appropriating the stereotype that depicted them as unpoetic. Those stylistics, as we see in "Black Art," involve colloquialism, slang, phonetic spellings, and ethnic speech patterns (that is, involve features of nineteenth-century dialect poetry that Johnson and Cullen had rejected in the 1920s),[5] profanity; violence; and racial slur—and derive from the stereotype of the uncouth, macho, dangerous black man. Though this poetic program was relatively short-lived, it was enormously influential and effective.[6]

The ubiquitousness of this macho persona and sensibility is easily demonstrated in *Black Fire,* in which less than 10 percent of the contributors are women. Most of the pieces in the volume reveal a masculinist bias that would discourage thematic and formal heterogeneity. For instance, non-nationalist blacks are depicted as castrated; nationalists as uniformly virile. One poem asks, "America, why are you afraid of the phallus!" (207) and others depict the sterilizing ("We are ejaculating stone" [211]) and emasculating effects of assimilation ("You who swallowed your balls for a piece / Of gold" [228], "You too / Deballed grin you who forever tell your masters / I have a glorious past" [229], "the icy ride of her touch up toward / the place where your penis once was" [309], "[you have] let machines crawl up your cock / rammed your penis into garbage disposals" [286]). In contrast, developing a revolutionary consciousness is equated with the recovery of castrated genitals and the resurgence of sexual potency. One poem "retriev[es] Black balls" through nationalism, which also enthralls the speaker "like the cataract of a cosmic orgasm" (226) and another urges that "our creativity . . . / Must spurt forth again like a thousand coming hardons" (259). In a politics of sexual bravado, such figures are effectively disturbing and potent; however, this hypermasculine persona and the emphasis on a rhetoric of sexual aggressiveness would prove to be limiting to the poets of the Blacks Arts movement, and the female poets would recognize and resist those limitations with particular urgency.

Before turning to the women's poetry and its explicit disagreements with the assumptions about gender in the Black Arts movement, I would like to demonstrate the enormous political and aesthetic potential of Black Arts poetry by looking at Welton Smith's elegy "malcolm," which appeared in *Black Fire* (283–91). Smith's powerful poem fulfills the aspirations of Black Arts excesses and yet also registers deep ambivalence about that rhetorical strategy. "malcolm" apprehends the possibilities and limitations of excess and is structured by these complexities. As in classical elegies, "malcolm" gestures toward lamentation, memorial, transcendence, and reconciliation in its five distinct sections, attempting to treat the death of Malcolm X in a worthy manner. That is, "malcolm" is a poem that recognizes the traditional genre for mourning and recurs to it despite the Black Arts strictures against Anglo-European conventions. However, "malcolm" employs familiar Black Arts excesses in order to reveal the inadequacies of the white tradition for a black poet who grieves for his assassinated black hero. The poem uses excess to reject Anglo-European aesthetics, express the violence of the speaker's grief, and point toward the inexpressible aspects of that grief; but further it casts excess into dialogue with decorum achieving a dialogic voice that carries tremendous political force.

The poem has six sections, the first, a prelude that falls under the general title, "malcolm," the other five designated "The Nigga Section," "interlude," "Special Section for the Niggas on the Lower Eastside or: Invert the Divisor and Multiply," a second "interlude," and finally "The Beast Section." The divisions attest that complicated, even contradictory, emotions require multiple resources and approaches. The two "nigga" sections implicate African Americans themselves in Malcolm X's murder; the "beast" section indicts whites and also studies their role in the speaker's recovery and revenge. The two "interludes" address aspects of grief that are beyond the reach of conventional discourse. They interrupt the logic of the rest of the poem, first with fantasy and then with rage. Excess informs much of the poem, but each section employs it differently. One result of this structural and tonal diversity is to demonstrate the need for excess, while another result is to demonstrate its limits. The poem succeeds in elegizing Malcolm X by mixing flamboyant Black Arts excesses with a subtler rhetorical register.

The first section of "malcolm" is uncharacteristically understated for a Black Arts poem, especially for so incendiary a subject. Even though the stock targets of contempt are here—the "slobbering emaciated man" who "pisses on himself" and is ambivalent about his ethnic heritage and the "fat / jewess" who pretends to support the revolution only to gain sexual access to Malcolm X—they are treated with detachment. In fact, the drunken man and the Jewish woman are part of an impressionistic blur of American culture that includes Malcolm X and his wife Betty in a safe, intimate moment ("in the quiet / after midnight. your hand / soft on her back. you kiss / her neck softly") and the perilous public sphere where children are killed in church bombings ("in birmingham 'get a move / on you, girl. you bet'not / be late for sunday school.' / not this morning—"). The speaker sees all this with an eerie detachment that comes of shock not yet assimilated to grief. Though his remoteness has an almost mystical quality that he associates with Malcolm X's spirituality (in a reference to Mecca), it is too dreamy and "fantastic" to carry him through the stages of grief that the poem—as elegy and as political tract—will require. These social vignettes constitute "a design," a complicated and deadly pattern of personal love and communal commitment, that is reproduced internally in a pattern of psychological contradictions:

"the men / inside you fought. / fighting men inside you / made a frenzy / smelling like shit." What Malcolm X taught was how those inner contradictions, the fractured selves of internalized racism, can be gathered up and purged: "you reached into yourself— / deep—and scooped your frenzy / and rolled it to a slimy ball / and stretched your arm back / to throw." Though the speaker acknowledges his own self-hatred and conflicting selves, he maintains restraint in section one, attending first to his private grief over the loss of Malcolm X:

> now you pace the regions
> of my heart. you know
> my blood and see
> where my tears are made.
> I see the beast and hold my frenzy;
> you are not lonely—
> in my heart there are many
> unmarked graves.

These lines end section one without recourse to excess. Still stunned by grief for the loss of Malcolm X, still feeling the personal heartache of that loss, the speaker adopts a quiet, deliberate, mournful tone and an austere style.

The carefully modulated tone of the first section of "malcolm" reflects not only the gravity of the speaker's mood after the assassination but also the formality of the elegiac mode. The speaker holds his frenzy in the opening part while he absorbs the shock of Malcolm X's death, but the frenzy is nevertheless gathering force. In part two, "The Nigga Section," the first blast of his rage is directed at the blacks who helped murder Malcolm X:

> slimy obscene creatures. . . .
> [you] have [murdered Malcolm X] with precision
> like the way you stand green
> in the dark sucking pus
> and slicing your penis
> into quarters—stuffing
> shit through your noses.
> you rotten motherfuckin' bastards
> . . . you have made
> your black mother to spread
> her legs   wide
> you have crawled in mucous
> smeared snot in your hair

> *let machines crawl up your cock*
> *rammed your penis into garbage disposals*
> *spread your gigantic ass from*
> *one end of america to the other . . .*
> *and called the beasts*
> *to fuck you hard in the ass*
> *you have fucked your fat black mothers*
> *you have murdered malcolm.*

The excesses (name calling, mutilated or severed genitals, bodily grossness, scornful references to homosexuality, emasculated men and castrating women) accrue and escalate, yet they "culminate" in a plain-spoken last line, "you have murdered malcolm." The poem seems to recognize the limitations of such excesses even as it is compelled, by convention and by desperation, to invoke them. Slicing up penises, stuffing excrement in noses, smearing mucous in hair—these are desperate acts delivered in phrases straining to be outrageous. Likewise, "fuck you hard in the ass" is amplified to "fuck your fat black mothers" to intensify an affront that is already losing its force to familiarity. Such rhetorical accretion and aggravation is reminiscent of the "dozens" and other insult games; however, there is only one speaker here, and though in some sense he is in competition with the speakers of contemporary poems, his primary verbal contest is between words and their meanings. The more outrageous his words are, the more ineffective they sound. When this string of abuses concludes simply with "you have murdered malcolm," it is obvious that no amount of rhetorical excess can approximate the blunt fact of Malcolm X's death. "The Nigga Section" concludes with a wish that the blacks involved in Malcolm X's murder will be "smothered / in the fall of a huge yellow moon," an apocalyptic image that suggests how ineffective mere language has been in smothering them. Cultural self-betrayal, self-destruction, and regret mingle ambivalently with accusation and outrage in these lines.

Section three, the first "interlude," makes another abrupt shift in tone, abandoning the obscenities and vulgarities lobbed at the "niggas" in favor of a refined, intimate address to Malcolm X, which repeatedly calls him "Friend." The "interlude" aspect of section three is not merely a pause in the aggressive language of the previous section but also an interruption of setting. Relocating itself to the pastoral scene of classical elegies, the poem attempts to retreat from the "punks," "rodents," and "cockroaches" of contemporary Harlem where Malcolm X was killed. But the natural world is not the place where *this* poem can go to reconcile itself to the passing of Malcolm X, as in the elegiac convention, where nature and natural cycles offer hope and renewal against the finality of death; instead, it is a place to where the speaker and Malcolm X, as black men in the urban industrial north, could *not* retreat: "we never spent time in the mountains," never "spent long mornings fishing or laughed / laughed falling all down into the dirt." He and Malcolm X were not even able to enjoy a city park, an urban substitute for the pastoral scene, "we never danced together as men / in a public park," nor were they able to meander in the affluent parts of the city, "we never walked together / down Fillmore or Fifth Avenue / down Main Street together."

The interlude can envision friendship between the speaker and Malcolm X, and can situate it in congenial settings, but cannot deny the fact that they never actually met. Though the speaker loves Malcolm X (we know he has "loaned / [his] heart in exchange / for [Malcolm X's] voice"), he cannot recall or preserve him in personal memories. The four incantations of "Friend" almost effect an intimacy with Malcolm X, but the six repetitions of the phrase "we never" insistently work against that dream of concord and escape. The cadenced recurrence of "Friend" conveys the speaker's capacity to love the hero he never knew personally. The first interlude offers a lull in the violence of the speaker's anger, but it is a paradoxical "interlude" that also demonstrates the impossibility of escape from either the reality of Malcolm X's death or from the corrupt world where such a thing could happen.

Black intellectuals are the target in the fourth part of the poem, "Special Section for the Niggas on the Lower Eastside or: Invert the Divisor and Multiply." These "jive revolutionaries" have undermined the real revolution, and thus contributed to Malcolm X's death, by selling out to white liberals, "selling black," the poem chants, "for a part in a play," "for a ride in a rolls," "for a quick fuck," "for two lines on page 6,000 in the new york times." Again the speaker employs hyperbole in a diatribe against the Lower Eastside "niggas," and again even the most vile words seem inadequate to the task:

> you are gluttons devouring
> every cunt in every garbage can on avenue b

> *you hope to find*
> *an eighty ton white woman*
> *with a cock big enough*
> *to crawl inside*
> *you don't just want a white woman*
> *you want to be a white woman*
> *you are concubines of a beast*
> *you want to be lois lane, audrey hepburn, ma perkins, lana turner,*
> *jean harlow, kim stanley, may west, marilyn monroe, sophie tucker,*
> *betty crocker, tallulah bankhead, judy canova, shirley temple, and*
> *trigger.*

This litany of famous white women scours the dominant culture randomly from Marilyn Monroe to Betty Crocker to Roy Rogers's horse Trigger; however, its very range reveals the broad spectrum of American culture that entices and excludes black men. Jean Harlow and Marilyn Monroe are sexy, blonde beauties who inspire both lust and loathing. Betty Crocker represents the American dream of domestic order, plenitude, and bliss. And Trigger, the horse of the white cowboy, concludes the list with an absurdity that indicates exasperation with black men who don't understand that wanting those women is the same as wanting to *be* a white woman (that is, desiring whiteness is ultimately to put oneself in servitude to white men) and that to be the "concubine of the beast" is to be his beast of burden—his horse or even his slave.

The section concludes with "turn white you jive motherfucker [white space] and ram the bomb up your ass," but the predictable reference to sodomy as the ultimate insult, even magnified to the global level with the substitution of the nuclear bomb for the phallus, conveys an exhaustion (the white space in the middle of the line seems to be looking for something to say) with these formulas.[7] While the rhetorical violence of excess has served to identify and excoriate the black bohemians who are implicated in Malcolm X's death, it has not succeeded in eradicating them from the external or internal "design" that killed Malcolm X and that Malcolm X himself recognized.

The next "interlude" registers the need for some fuller expression and points up the inadequacy of conventional language for the tasks of elegy, catharsis, recovery, and action, by simply transcribing, as it were, the speaker's inarticulate frenzy:

screams
screams
malcolm
does not hear my screams
screams . . .
screams scraping my eyes
screams from guns
screams
screams
the witches ecstasy . . .
ecstasy king ecstasy salazar rowan ecstasy
screams
screams . . .
screams in my head screams
screams six feet deep.

The speaker gives full vent to his anguish, using the repeated word "screams" to simulate nonverbal shrieking, and purges the "shit" inside him (by expelling the names of the shapers of culture: Ochs, Sulzberger, Oppenheimer, Galbraith, Kennedy, Johnson, Franco, Bunche, King, and others). The screams reverberate everywhere, spreading, like the "gigantic ass" in section two, "from one end of america to the other," replacing the betrayal that encompassed the country in that earlier line with genuine anguish from "st. louis" to "the laughter of children" to "black faces." Though Malcolm X is beyond the reach of these screams, the speaker can hear the screams that emanate from Malcolm X's grave ("screams six feet deep") and can take them up as his own.

The excesses of the second "interlude" carry an emotional force that is not articulated to intellectual concerns. The flood of noise that dislodges Kennedy, Johnson, King, and Schlesinger exorcises them without analysis or other engagement, without, that is, the sort of intellectual entanglements that the jive revolutionaries succumb to.

After this purgation, the speaker can address the worst enemy, whites, with a rhetorical equilibrium and argumentative sureness that are more ominous than excess. In "The Beast Section" he refuses to quibble over who killed Malcolm X—not because he exonerates whites but because he knows that they control everything. He even gives whites their due for being dominant,

> *your civilization*
> *compares favorably with any known*
> *your power is incomparable*
> *i understand why you would destroy*
> *the world rather than pass it to lesser*
> *people. i agree completely[.]*

but he will also take what's due from them by mastering their culture and destroying them. We know he is already well schooled in the dominant culture when he cites Aristotle ("aristotle tells us in the physics / that power and existence are one")—even if we did not already sense his authority in the studied tone and diction of this final section.

At the end of the poem he offers whites a taste of their own medicine, so to speak:

> *i've made you a fantastic dish*
> *you must try it, if not now*
> *very soon.*

And we realize that he has the subtle skills of refinement, articulateness, learning, flattery, and self-control that will eventually entice whites to taste his deadly concoction.[8] Unlike the jive revolutionaries "who will never tear this house down," our speaker will succeed in dismantling the dominant culture from inside: "i am comfortable in your house." In the most threatening line of the poem, he says something even more to the point, "i am comfortable in your language," a fact to which this final section attests. Indeed, it is this mastery of the master's language—and its dialogic relation to Black Arts linguistic excesses—that makes the end of the poem ominous and powerful. The rhetorical frenzies of "malcolm" remain an absolutely necessary part of the radical, revolutionary, uncompromising rejection of the dominant culture—a deliberately unseemly assertion from below—but, in the end, they are not sufficient for a widespread and effective cultural movement. Other kinds of discourses need to be brought in, and they eventually are. These are the complexities of "the design" that Malcolm X "knew" in the opening of the poem, complexities that the speaker now understands. His elegy to Malcolm X succeeds not only because it laments and memorializes its subject but because the speaker has become a person in whom the meaning of Malcolm

X's life can live and flourish. He is no longer paralyzed by grief or contorted with rage; he is comfortable in the language, as Malcolm X was, and prepared for another kind of battle.

Though Welton Smith's "malcolm" utilizes the Black Arts movement excess in quite formulaic ways, it also questions and qualifies the usefulness of those aesthetics. The poem's polyvocality suggests the necessity of expanding the movement's rhetorical range. In doing so, it anticipates the stylistic diversity that would follow the Black Arts aesthetics, yet that development was prepared for by the very excesses it would supersede. A seemingly unmediated poetic excess was historically necessary; it was the only way to clear the ground and open a confident, defensible space for the next generation to do its work. Black Arts excess would remain an empowering part of the rhetoric, but it would be put into relation with other discourses as well. Smith's poem achieves a complicating dialogue, and, in doing so, it anticipates the poetics of later black writers. For now, however, in 1968, those excesses continued to dominate African-American poetry. And the virulent masculinity of the movement's poetry continued to curtail the contributions of women writers.

A variety of factors made the poetry inhospitable to female poets. Most obvious, perhaps, is the fact that women were frequent targets of physical violence and verbal abuse in the writing. If rape constituted revolutionary action, then women could be victims of such programmatic violence but not perpetrators of it. Even though in practice many of the sexual attacks in the poems were directed toward men who were insufficiently radical (manly) and therefore figuratively homosexual (unmanly), women were inevitably the objects of these sexist energies as well. The aggressively heterosexual masculine persona emerged in response to a long history of white racist assaults on black manhood, evidenced by the physical, economic, and political castration of African-American men. Understandably, the militarism of the Black Power movement encouraged a reified view of masculinity since conventional "manhood" was a ready and vital source of power to recover. Wearing uniforms, carrying rifles, and imposing a rigid hierarchy on supporters were just some of the more visible ways that the Black Panther party and other militant organizations asserted a notion of masculinity that was potent and threatening to white people but also exclusive of black women. Likewise, the Nation of Islam, the black Muslim religious organization that many African Americans joined during the period, delineated separate spheres for men and women and dictated stereotypically masculine roles for men and feminine roles for women.

In addition to defending an embattled masculinity, the reification of gender roles during the black liberation movement was partly an antidote to the perceived dominance of African-American women in black culture. In her controversial 1978 study, *Black Macho and the Myth of the Superwoman,* Michele Wallace explains that as the century wore on, the continuing lack of opportunity for social and economic advancement instigated antagonisms between black men and women.[9] There was a general, though unspoken sense that black women had met with greater success in the marketplace than had black men. In 1965 Daniel P. Moynihan published a policy planning and research report for the Department of Labor, *The Negro Family: The Case for National Action,* which asserted that the "matriarchal structure" of the black family "seriously retards the progress of the group as a whole, and imposes a crushing burden on the Negro male" (29). Wallace argues that the Moynihan report exacerbated tensions between black men and women, giving expression to a complaint that many already held: "Moynihan bared the black man's awful secret for all to see—that he had never been able to make his woman get down on her knees" (Wallace 31). Wallace contends that black liberation constituted not the advancement of the race but "the pursuit of manhood" (33): "Come 1966, the black man had two pressing tasks before him: a white woman in every bed and a black woman under every heel. Out of his sense of urgency came a struggle called the Black Movement, which was nothing more nor less than the black man's struggle to attain his presumably lost 'manhood'" (31–32). The fact that African Americans had been thwarted for centuries by racism was modified by some into the narrower charge that African-American *men* in particular had been diminished by white America and even by African-American women. Wallace and other women reacted to the notion that they were too strong by trying to prove their allegiance to black men through demonstrations of submissiveness and femininity (95). Women writers must have felt the contradictions of their position acutely. Many of the male leaders proposed outright silence for women, an idea that issues from the suspicion of women and their talk that Malcolm X recorded in his influential autobiography and that was prevalent in the culture at large.[10] Indicative of this suspicion is the assertion, in a 1971 survey of contemporary black poetry, that "women seem to dominate the movement" (A. Russell Brooks 8), a movement that categorically dominated *them.* Women writers in the Black Arts movement were faced with the impossible task of being revolutionary poets, who were aggressive, irreverent, and menacing, while being supportive black women, who were submissive, reverent to black men, and feminine. The two personae could not comfortably inhabit the same poem, and their contradictions would trouble African-American women's poetry for the next decade.

While the philosophical misogyny of the Black Arts movement was certainly enough to restrict the contributions of African-American women writers, aesthetic considerations also militated against them. Excessive literalism, in figurative language and in the conception of the persona, made adopting the stylistics of the movement problematic for women writers. Technically, women ought to have been able to construct a male persona in their poems; even in confessional poetry, and certainly in most poetry, the persona is distinct from the writer of the poem. However, the literary authenticity dictated by the Black Arts program tended to result in poems delivered in the spontaneous, urgent, autobiographical voice of their authors. Though those authors engaged in exaggeration and boasting, contrived speakers, like other conventional literary effects, were looked upon with suspicion.

Moreover, the strict delineations of gender differences would have rendered a woman writing in the voice of a man unlikely—and, again, questionable and even antirevolutionary—since women contributed to liberation in "womanly" rather than "manly" ways. Prescriptions for proper female behavior proliferated in the countless poems dedicated to black women during the early days of the Black Arts movement. Two poems in *Black Fire,* for instance, suggest the received view of sexual difference. "For Our Women" (310–11), by editor Larry Neal, celebrates "these women wrapped / in the magic of birth" who "wordlessly know" that maternal love shapes the world despite the dominance of hatred and evil. The maternal function is especially valorized since the race is literally regenerated through reproduction:

> the breath of your life
> sustains us
> . . . the female in the middle passage,
> you endured.
> we endured through you.

Similarly, in "Earth" (327–28) by Rolland Snellings, the "Mother of the World" is invoked and the distinctions between the roles of men and women are taken for granted: "Where are the warriors, the young men? / Who guards the women's quarters." Black men are "broken . . . babble . . . lift their bloody genitals" on the battlefields of history, while women, once again, endure because of their reproductive capacity: "They are gone . . . and . . . *only you remain! / You whose Womb has warmed the European hills and made the Pale Snows tawny.*" The generative function of women casts them in a predictably complementary relationship to men, but this is envisioned as compensatory rather than equal. For example, "BLACKWOMAN" (*Don't Cry, Scream* 55) by Don L. Lee conceives of the woman as reflecting "her" man:

> blackwoman:
> is an
> in and out
> rightsideup
> action-image
> of her man.

And though he insists in nearly all his early writings that a black poet is first and foremost a *black* man—"*Black. Poet. Black poet am I. This should leave little doubt in the minds of anyone which is first*" (*Think Black!* 6)[11]—he nevertheless inverts the formula for women:

> first.
> a woman should be
> a woman first,
> if she's anything.
> but
> if she's black, *really* black
> and a woman
> that's special, that's
> realspecial.
> > (New World 39)

Baraka's "Beautiful Black Women . . ." (*Selected Poetry* 118) entreats women to help men by being a physical and emotional repository for them: "will you help us, will you open your bodysouls." There are hundreds, perhaps thousands, of poems that depict African-American women in these terms, and I include this survey not to exhaust the point but to give a sense of the unrelenting conformity of the poetry.

And, finally, the poems sought to exert a brute force that was only partially figurative, as I have shown—and was, in any case, inconsistent with the feminine role accorded black women in the movement.

At first, many women poets responded to the revolutionary program by imitating the masculinist poems that had quickly defined the times. Nikki Giovanni's "The True Import of Present Dialogue: Black vs. Negro" (*Black Feeling Black Talk* 11–12) is a well-known example:

> *Nigger*
> *Can you kill*
> *Can you kill*
> *Can a nigger kill*
> *Can a nigger kill a honkie . . .*
> *Can you stab-a-jew . . .*
> *Can you piss on a blond head*
> *Can you cut it off.*

Written in 1968, "The Present Dialogue" participates fully in the aesthetic program of the Black Arts movement. When Giovanni published it in her first volume of poetry, the incitement to violence, anti-Semitism, incantatory vulgarity, and even the depiction of aggressive urinating had become commonplaces of the Black Aesthetic. Most of the male poets and many of the women wrote such poems; yet, because of the rigid gender roles and strict aesthetic rules within the movement, women poets could only ventriloquize the hypermasculine expostulations of their male comrades. The pronoun "you" in Giovanni's poem, "Nigger / Can you kill," uneasily tries to address both African-American men (as the only viable revolutionary *agents*) and the speaker herself (as a woman who wants to participate in the revolution through language). When the poem asks "Can you piss on a blond head / Can you cut it off," it invokes Bigger Thomas (who cut off the head of a white woman in *Native Son*), a literary precursor of the black liberation writers,[12] invoking a masculine figure as a model. While the call to violence in the poem is directed at men, the speaker attempts to include herself in the "dialogue." "*We* ain't got to prove *we* can die," she says, "*We* got to prove *we* can kill" (emphasis added). Yet each instance of the first-person plural pronoun cites something that only black men have done: fighting in World War II, occupying Europe after the war, fighting in Viet Nam, performing military duties for the United Nations and other world organizations. The final line of the poem acknowledges its only intelligible subject when it asks if "we" can "Learn to be Black men," not black men and women, not black people. Indeed, there is no generic masculine in the Black Arts poetry; the poems unambiguously address men and women in severely limited contexts. When black *people* are addressed, they are called just that. The speaker in "The True Import" has only two choices; she can mimic the male persona who embodies the Black Arts movement program, and risk sounding ridiculous, or she can call him to action, and accept her own inaction and subordination.

The *true* import, then, of the contemporary debate about whether African Americans should refer to themselves as "blacks" or "Negroes" is that words don't matter. The right question for the revolution is not "what do you call yourself?" but "can you kill?" The right tools for the revolution are not words but actions. In dismissing the significance of language, the poem inevitably disqualifies the authority of its speaker—and the final line reveals that the speaker's irrelevance is related to her gender. As a woman, she cannot replace talk with action.

Giovanni's career exemplifies the difficulties the Black Aesthetic imposed on women writers of the Black Arts movement. She was heralded as the "poet of the Black revolution" (McDowell 144) and the "princess of Black poetry" (Bonner 29) for poems like "The True Import" and then vilified as a sentimental individualist when she tried to find a more suitable voice.[13] As early as 1969, she had been critical of the masculinist character of the Black Arts movement. In a *Negro Digest* article, "Black Poems, *Poseurs* and Power," she criticizes the militarism of the movement in general and Karenga and Jones in particular. Citing her own radical credentials, she insists that violence and separatism are not enough to create a revolution: "I mean, I wrote a poem asking, 'Nigger, can you kill?,' 'cause to want to live under president-elect no-Dick Nixon is certainly to become a killer. Yet, in listening to Smokey and The Miracles sing their Greatest Hits recently, I became aware again of the revolutionary quality of 'You Can Depend On Me.' And if you ask, 'Who's Loving You,' just because I say he's not a honkie you should still want to know if I'm well laid. There is a tendency to look at the Black experience too narrowly" (30). Giovanni's independence of thought and courage of conviction in rejecting the sexism of the Black Arts movement are striking in a period that required artists to conform to the revolutionary program. However, her resistance to the misogyny of the movement is complicated because she accepts the terms of its logic. She attacks Richard Nixon's masculinity and reduces women's concerns to the purely (and conventionally) sexual when she insists that having sex with black men is only revolutionary if they are good lovers.

Giovanni concludes the piece astutely—"it will take more than a Black poem or your Black seed in me to rid the country of [racism]" (34)—and seems to reject the equation of political action with sexual activity. Indeed, the essay itself offers an analysis of the ways that sexism, militarism, internal conflict, and male posturing have restricted the movement. Yet it does not finally dismantle the structures of masculinity and femininity that undergird these problems. The opening gesture of the essay attracts the reader's attention by engaging in just the sort of posturing and bragging for which the revolutionary men are criticized. "Black Poems, *Poseurs* and Power" introduces a rhetorical machismo that distracts from—and finally undermines— its analysis of such behavior.

In this same passage, Giovanni contrasts militant poetry with the love lyrics of popular songs by black performers and suggests that the revolution needs the latter. Indeed, she insists that the "latent militarism of the artistic community is . . . despicable—art and the military have always been traditionally opposed" (32). In setting up a contrast between militant poetry and love lyrics, she anticipates the opposition that will structure the careers of several women in the Black Arts movement. Having first attempted to imitate the model hypermasculine revolutionary poet, some female poets retreated from its vulgarity and violence into a hyperfeminine mode that provided relief from certain stereotypes even as it imposed others.

Though the founding father of the Black Arts movement had de-creed there should "be no love poems written" until the world was safe for black people, many of the Black Arts women turned from poetry of rage to poetry of love—a genre they often conceived of as supporting the revolution. While each poet made the turn in a distinctive way, Love became the project of black women writers who began their poetic careers in a more combative mode. Poems addressing black men as lovers, honoring the black family, paying homage to ancestors, and especially celebrating and educating children dominated their books. For several of these poets, books written exclusively *for* children outnumbered the volumes of adult verse.

As Margaret B. McDowell has documented, this shift in Giovanni's work had already occurred by 1969, when she published the "Black *Poseurs*" essay. By 1970, readers noticed the change, and several black reviewers attacked her work for betraying the revolution.[14] Yet Giovanni's dissatisfaction with the revolutionary mentality surfaces even in her first book, *Black Feeling Black Talk* (1968), the same volume that contains "The True Import" and other militant poems. "Seduction" (25) warns that one day the black man is going to come home to a black woman who wants to share a private life with him. The poem concentrates on sex and borrows its tone from the sexual bravado of the revolutionary speaker; however, this is not the physical aggression depicted in so many of the period's poems but physical intimacy:

> you'll sit down and say "The Black . . ."
> and i'm gonna take one arm out [of my African gown]
> then you—not noticing me at all—will say "What about this brother . . ."
> and i'm going to be slipping it over my head
> and you'll rap on about "The revolution . . ."
> while i rest your hand against my stomach
> . . . .
> then you'll say "What we really need . . ."
> and i'll be licking your arm
> and "The way I see it we ought to . . ."
> and unbuckling your pants
> "And what about the situation . . ."
> and taking your shorts off

Love is not deferred until the world is a safer place for black people; the speaker seduces the man addressed one of *these* days, during the revolution he's talking about. While "The True Import" argues that talk must be preempted in favor of violent acts, in "Seduction," revolutionary activity is preempted in favor of intimate acts. When the man in the poem finally notices he's naked, he asks: "Nikki / isn't this counterrevolutionary . . . ?" The poem ends there without an answer. In 1968, Giovanni let the question ride. Yet "Seduction" wants something more than the movement is providing—but here again, as in the "Black *Poseurs*" essay, Giovanni limits herself to the movement's terms.

Many of Giovanni's early poems struggle with the opposition between revolution and love as Jones had formulated it in "Black Art." "Love Poem (For Real)" (*Black Feeling Black Talk* 21–22), signaling its defensiveness on the subject with a parenthetical assurance in the title, laments that

> *it's so hard to love*
> *people*
> *who will die soon*
>
> *the sixties have been one*
> *long funeral day[;]*

"For Saundra" (*Black Judgement* 30) tries to recover conventional love poetry (responding to "my neighbor / who thinks i hate") but concludes that

> *perhaps these are not poetic*
> *times*
> *at all.*

By 1970, with the publication of her third book, *Re:Creation,* and the birth of her son, Giovanni had settled these questions for herself. "Revolutionary Dreams" (20) claims to redefine what it means to be revolutionary.[15] Having formerly had "militant / dreams of taking / over america" and "radical dreams / of blowing everyone away with my perceptive powers," she now has "natural dreams":

> *. . . if i dreamed natural*
> *dreams of being a natural*
> *woman doing what a woman*
> *does when she's natural*
> *i would have a revolution.*

Her natural dreams, however, place women in exactly the position accorded them by the militant movement, as the book's dedication to Giovanni's son makes clear:

> *to tommy who:* . . .
> *defined my nature*
> *and gave me a new name (mommy)*
> *which supersedes all others*
> *controls my life.*
>
> *(3)*

This is the book's re-creation: renewing the self by giving birth to another. Taken together, the dedication and this poem argue that the experience of motherhood allows a woman to discover her true, or "natural," self. But this is precisely what hundreds of poems by men "to beautiful black women" had offered. In "Revolutionary Dreams" the speaker merely gives up the dream of being one of the men and accepts being one of the women. The problem in her formulation is that it only admits of these two stereotypes: the warrior man and the maternal woman. Like many of her contemporaries, Giovanni rejected the excessive masculinity of the black liberation movement but sought refuge in an excessive femininity that left the oppressive categories of gender securely in place.

By 1979, the "poet of the Black revolution" had mellowed into "a kind of nationalistic Rod McKuen" (Wallace 166) and was now known for a romantic vacuousness that seemed to be the antithesis of her early militant declamations. The titles of her books of verse from the sixties and seventies indicate the move from political to personal poetry: *Black Feeling Black Talk* (1968), *Black Judgement* (1968), *Re-Creation* (1970), *Spin a Soft Black Song: Poems for Children,* (1971), *My House: Poems* (1972), *Ego-Tripping and Other Poems for Young People* (1973), *The Women and the Men* (1975), *Cotton Candy on a Rainy Day* (1978), and *Vacation Time: Poems for Children* (1980). Though all of Giovanni's books treat personal subjects, readers have rightly acknowledged a shift from a nationalistic to an individualistic scope. Giovanni's own explanation for the change is simply the inevitability of change: "Sure the militant posture has left contemporary writing. First of all, it was boring. . . . You want me to rewrite 'Nigger can you kill/Can you kill/Nigger can you kill?' I wrote it. It's not just that it's written, but I wrote it. And I wasn't even the first person to write it. Nor will I be the last. But I did it *my* time. Now it's time for me to do something else" (Tate 62). In describing the militant poetry as boring and dismissing it as something she needn't repeat, Giovanni acknowledges the limitations of such writing.

Nikki Giovanni came of age artistically during the Black Arts movement and succeeded briefly in imitating the revolutionary persona the movement had invented and valorized. But when she became dissatisfied with that persona and attempted to move beyond him, she took with her his misconceptions about gender—and, more important, about the gender of writing. Other women writers of the Black Arts movement followed a similar path, beginning their careers with black macho poems and retreating to various forms of "feminine" writing in reaction to a masculinist aesthetic ideal that they could only mimic. The variety of ways that conventional femininity asserted itself in the poetry accounts for the distinctiveness of each writer's canon. Giovanni chose a personal, romantic mode that was not likely to challenge the gender norms of the culture, while other women joined the Nation of Islam or embraced Christianity, two alternatives to the militant liberation movement that did not, however, offer alternative roles to women.

Sonia Sanchez's move from the militant poetry of her early books to a more feminine verse reads quite differently from Giovanni's. This is owing in part to Sanchez's wide-ranging thematic and technical interests. She began writing poetry as a young girl and was influenced by reading Dunbar, Hughes, Brooks, and Pushkin in college (Tate 138, 147). She studied writing with Louise Bogan, who encouraged young writers to read their poems aloud and to work in closed forms, practices that Sanchez has consistently relied upon (Liebowitz 362–63). She also cites Neruda, Lorca, Margaret Walker, DuBois, McKay, Hurston, Atwood, Piercy, Dickinson, and Bogan as significant literary models (Liebowitz 363).

Another important difference between Giovanni's and Sanchez's early militant poetry is that Giovanni seemed to want to speak as a revolutionary man while Sanchez wanted to be his woman. While she sometimes employed the Black Arts excesses like the male poets to condemn institutionalized racism, she more frequently used it to demonstrate solidarity with the very revolutionaries whom she simultaneously criticized for ignoring black women. In "blk / wooooomen / chant" (45), from her second book, *We a BaddDDD*

People (1970), Sanchez challenges black men to love and protect black women; the poem's stylistic excesses suggest a speaker who is bursting with frustration and contradictions:

> yo blk/bitches/queens/
> nigger wooooomen
> waaaiten for yo
> sign that u be
> see/en us.
> we walk rite up
> to u and turn yo corner
> of beauty
> blk/mennnnnNN
> do u SEEEEEEE us? HEARRRRRR us? KNOWWWW us?

Referring to herself as a bitch, queen, and nigger, the speaker traverses the range of female stereotypes current in the culture. She is idealized as a queen in Black Aesthetic poetry but accused of being a bitch if she asserts herself in language or in life. These contradictions frequently emerge in Sanchez's most excessive poetry. "Short Poem" (*Home Coming* 17) invokes machismo excess in order to sound out its ironies:

> my old man
> tells me i'm
> so full of sweet
> pussy he can
> smell me coming.
> maybe
> i
> shd
> bottle
> it
>   and
> sell it
> when he goes.

"Coming" obviously puns on the speaker's arrival and on her sexual orgasm; more important, it stands in contrast to the man's "going" away, which the speaker senses is inevitable. While he praises her sexual availability, she recognizes that emotional availability is harder to achieve, and especially with men.[16] Though Sanchez was able to register such nuances of meaning even in the classical Black Arts style, she quickly exhausted its usefulness. *Home Coming* (1969) and *We A BaddDDD People* (1970) employ the familiar excesses: typographical violence, "screaming," vulgarity, slang, sex, and a menacing posture. By 1971, however, she had published a children's book (*It's a New Day*) and by 1973 a book about women (*A Blues Book for Blue Black Magical Women*) and a volume of *Love Poems,* three volumes that signal her change of direction, thematically and stylistically.

Like Giovanni, Sanchez decided that the masculine posturings of the Black Arts movement were not revolutionary; however, she did not, like Giovanni, retreat to a private world of love and family. Even once she acknowledged the conceptual and formal shortcomings of the Black Aesthetic, she was able to resituate herself within the rich and diverse traditions of African-American, American, and world poetries. Writing free-verse poems and African chants, blues, sonnets, haikus, tankas, and prose poems, Sanchez trained her writing to achieve a poetic statement that differs markedly from the "blk/ rhetoric" Sanchez identifies in the poem of that title, from *We A BaddDDD People* (15–16), a fairly typical Black Arts movement volume. There, Sanchez calls for more than "catch / phrases" and "fucks in the hall / way":[17]

> who's gonna make all
> that beautiful blk / rhetoric
> mean something.
> > like
> i mean
> > who's gonna take
> the words
> > blk / is / beautiful
> and make more of it
> than blk / capitalism.
> > . . .
> like this. is an S O S
> > me. calling. . . . .
> > > calling. . . . .
> > > > some / one
> pleasereplysoon.

Haki Madhubuti (Don L. Lee), a Black Aesthetic poet himself, chides her for the "overuse of the page and the seemingly confusing punctuation" ("Sonia Sanchez" 426), yet the exploding and colliding words—

like the vulgarity—are clearly clamoring to grab the attention of readers in a literary context that has inured them to formal aggression. In the same book, she challenges empty Black Arts rhetoric even more directly in "TCB" (59), an abbreviation for "taking care of business." The poem repeats the phrase "wite/motha/fucker" in three-line stanzas, each one punctuated at the end with a single derogatory word for white people: whitey, ofay, devil, pig, cracker, and honkey. But it concludes: "now. that it's all sed. // let's get to work." Sanchez's poems do not dismiss the revolutionary power of language, by opposing *words* and *work,* but they do insist that the macho rhetoric of the militant movement is not an effective language for change.

Partly in response to her dissatisfactions with the militant movement, Sanchez joined the Nation of Islam in 1972 in order to "be around people who had a sense of nationhood, a sense of righteousness and morality" (Tate 139). Yet the Nation offered an even more rigid model of sexual difference, describing separate spheres for men and women and curtailing women's speech, activities, and even dress. Though Sanchez wore the Muslim garb (full-length dress and head covering) and accepted the maternal role it prescribed for women, she would not give up her right to speak in public and compose poems: "I would be reading my poetry some place, and men would get up to leave, and I'd say, 'Look, my words are equally important.' So I got into trouble. . . . One dude said to me once that the solution for Sonia Sanchez was for her to have some babies, and I wrote a long satirical poem called 'Solution to Sonia Sanchez,' which was my response" (Tate 139). The fact that Sanchez responded to the notion that she should not write poetry by writing a satirical poem indicates how intellectually unsuited she was to an organization that demanded not merely conventional but archaic femininity. She left the Nation in 1976 because of these disputes but wrote one of her most important volumes of poetry while still a member. It is significant that she wrote *A Blues Book for Blue Black Magical Women* and *Love Poems* while in the Nation—that is, poetry that concerned itself with "women's" subjects. And while *Blues Book*'s invocation, "Introduction (Queens of the Universe)" (11–20), employs familiar excesses (vulgarity and typographical tricks), it presents them in order to dismiss them:

> *We Black/woooomen have been called many*
> *things: foxes, matriarchs, whores,*
> *bougies, sweet mommas, gals,*
> *sapphires, sisters and recently Queens. . . .*
> > *but today, in spite*
> *of much vulgarity splattering us, there are*
> *many roles we can discard. . . .*

Blues Book wants black women to discard black and white American stereotypes for them in favor of the Nation's:

> WE ARE MUSLIM WOMEN
>
> *wearing the garments of the righteous*
>
> *recipients of eternal wisdom*
>
> *followers of a Divine man and Message*
> *listen to us*
> > ("WE ARE MUSLIM WOMEN" 57–58)

Sanchez wrote the book to guide other black women through the treacherous and uncharted journey to adulthood in a sexist, racist world: "*Blues Book* is about my motions and observations as a child, as a young black woman, and about how society does not prepare young black women, or women period, to be women" (Tate 140).

The volume chronicles the speaker's development from girlhood to womanhood in four parts that follow the invocation titled "PAST," "PRESENT," "REBIRTH," and "FUTURE." The first two sections employ thematic excess in order to depict the corrupt and perilous environment where black women struggle to survive. The black female body is under constant assault in these sections. In "young/black/girl" (26–29), the speaker hides and stutters in order to avoid being physically abused by her stepmother and recognizes she will have to continue hiding when she's older in order to avoid being groped and taunted by "corner store jews." Despite these early resistances, she absorbs the culture of her oppressors in "young womanhood" (30–37), when the desire for love leads her to efface herself in order to appeal to the dominant culture:

> *and i dressed myself*
>
> *in foreign words*
>
> *became a proper painted*
>
> *european Black faced american.*

However, "young womanhood" ends with a violent rejection of that world, again depicted as a bodily trauma:

> and i vomited up the past.
> the frivolous years and i
> threw up the smiles and bowings
> . . . .
> and i vomited up the stench
> of the good ship Jesus
> sailing to the new world
> with Black gold
> i vomited up the cries of
> newborn babies thrown
> overboard
> . . . .
> and i vomited out names like beasts
> and death. and pigs and death.
> and devil and death
> and the vomiting ceased.
> and i was alone.

Like Welton Smith's speaker in "malcolm," who must resort to screaming in order to dislodge the cultural evils that have settled in him, Sanchez's speaker must vomit out the poisoning details of slavery and racism. In both poems the stylistic and thematic excesses of screaming and vomiting make a purgation through language possible. The speaker here is solitary when "Part Two: PAST" ends because she has purged herself of everything her family and culture have given her.

Freed of the lies, the corruption, the terrible history, she appears in the first poem (41–44) of "Part Three: PRESENT" wandering the world alone, "vomiting her // hunger over the world." Though she laments that

> there is no place
>
> for a soft/black/woman.
>
> there is no smile green enough or
>
> summertime words warm enough to allow my growth[,]

she herself creates such a world through her own words and memory:

> this woman, wet with wandering,
>
> reviving the beauty of the forests and winds
>
> is telling you secrets.

Creating a lush, fertile world as she goes, the speaker moves to the
end of the poem on a journey that has become a pilgrimage. The holy
place she seeks is, first, the sacredness of the self:

> and my singing
> becomes the only sound of a
> blue/black/magical/woman. walking.
> womb ripe. walking. loud with mornings. walking.
> making pilgrimage to herself. walking.

Though she seems to be giving birth to herself (in phrases like "womb
ripe" and "loud with morning") and to be discovering her*self* ("making a pilgrimage to herself"), the next poem finds her with a different
purpose. In the second poem (43–44) of "PRESENT," the pilgrimage
takes her past herself, as it were, to the Nation of Islam and its leader,
Elijah Muhammad: "We are in the sun age // the age of Elijah." The
"I" of the woman who has been the subject of the book until now is
subsumed in the "we" of Elijah's followers: "we will put the universe
again into // righteous hands. Black hands."

"Part Four: REBIRTH" (45–49) envisions the speaker returning to her
homeland, where she is reborn after nine months of gestation in the
purifying ocean there: "nine months i wandered amid waves // that
washed away thirty years of denial." The section ends with a chant
to Allah; though the speaker again refers to herself as "i," it is the
lower case "i" of someone who has effaced herself in order to merge
her identity with something greater:

> i have become like a temple
>
> i have made my form from
>
> HIS form and i am
>
> trying to be worthy.

She is now a black "goddess" who submits to the "FATHER"; that is,
the specific woman of "PAST" and "PRESENT" is reborn and enters the
"FUTURE" not as a woman at all but as a goddess. The self-effacement
of the real woman and her apotheosis into religious myth are accompanied by an effaced poetic style that registers the unperturbed
certainty of religious attainment.

"Part Five: FUTURE" (51–62) depicts the apocalypse, judgment, and
paradise with the equanimity of one who is saved. The penultimate

poem of the volume, "WE ARE MUSLIM WOMEN" (57–58), gives voice to a chorus of goddesses chanting their submission to Allah:

> And we speak only what we know
> And do not curse God
> And we keep our minds open to light
> And do not curse God
> And we chant Alhamdullilah
> And do not curse God.

Though they claim to be "giving birth to [themselves]," these "new women created from the limbs of Allah" represent a female principle so abstract and idealized that it can have little force in actual women's lives. Indeed, the only thing identifiably female about them is that their speech is curtailed. The final poem, "in the beginning" (59–62), continues the abstraction and erasure of distinctions until the women are subsumed under "Original Man" and then both genders subsumed under "Blackness." Like time, which is negated in favor of a perpetual beginning ("in the beginning // there was no end"), women are negated in the effort to retrieve an originary, glorious race ("we were Original Man"). The final vision of the book, in its closing lines, embraces all black Muslims, welcoming them into a mythic world where there is neither beginning nor end, neither man nor woman:

> let us begin again the
> circle of Blackness
> > me and you
> > me and you
> > you and me
> > me and you
> > you and me
> > me, me, meeeeEEE
> > you, you, YOUUUUU
> & have no beginning
> > or endddDDDDD!

The eruption of capital letters suggests a poetry that is trying to give typographical vitality to lines that are otherwise devoid of thematic substance and formal interest. As *Blues Book* approaches the Nation's vision, it loses its force and purpose. Begun as a guide to black women, it ends without reference to women at all. The Nation of Islam may have provided a temporary haven for Sanchez, but one could predict from this poetry that the answers attained there would quickly become unsatisfactory for a woman who hoped to lead other black women to a better future.

Like Giovanni, Sanchez rejected the masculinist vision of the black liberation movement only to replace it with another masculinist vision: the teachings of the Nation of Islam. Her account of the struggle to become a woman in *A Blues Book for Blue Black Magical Women* is still the *blues* because women remain limited and submissive to male authority: "the job of Black/woooomen is to deal with [racism] // under the direction of Black men" and "Black/woooomen must embrace // Blackness as religion/husband" ("Queens of the Universe" 12).

And again like Giovanni, the shift away from militant subject matter was attended by a shift away from Black Arts excesses. *Love Poems,* another volume published while Sanchez was a member of the Nation of Islam, collects poems written from 1964 to 1973; in it one can trace this movement away from formal excess. One of the many poems titled "Haiku" (83) in the volume associates excess with the passions:

> *simplicity you*
> *said. no excess. these tears exceed*
> *their worth. i'll cry no more.*

The poem is dated 1971, the year her writing took the turn toward conventionally female concerns. A love poem, it equates simplicity with self-control and excess with self-indulgence, simplicity with the curtailment of feelings and excess with the expression of them. In an interview that same year, Sanchez explained the appeal of the haiku form: "I think it had a lot to do with a movement in my life, how I felt I had to compress a lot of emotion . . . to stay sane. . . . Haiku seemingly was a form that allowed me to put a lot of emotion into three lines, and allowed it to be finished in a sense. It allowed me also to reflect on it, smile and gain some insight" (Harris and Davis 303). Though "Haiku" opposes simplicity and excess in an emotional context, its equation of excess with extremity and simplicity with equanimity is instructive for understanding the stylistic change from excess to simplicity. Sanchez's speculation about the usefulness of the short, simple haiku form indicates that she sought order, control, and an opportunity for reflection after the disorder, anarchy, and impetuousness of the Black Arts movement.

Carolyn Rodgers, a Chicago poet who first learned her trade in the Organization of Black American Culture (OBAC) Writer's Workshop meetings and Gwendolyn Brooks's Writers Workshops, was distinctive as a new black woman poet in the late 1960s, when she published her first two books, for her vehement adherence to the Black Arts program. Noted for her vulgarity and other excesses, Rodgers was quickly criticized by other Black Aesthetic practitioners for her unladylike uses of the very rhetorical excesses they had promoted. In his introduction (7–8) to Rodgers' second volume of poetry, *Songs of a Black Bird* (1969), David Llorens hinted at the tensions caused by her appropriation of the masculinist style: "Some 'revolutionary' brothers had put the 'bad mouth' on her, and had run down something as old as . . . and far more insidious than 'nigger bitches ain't shit.' And they had me check the sister out, looking for a badge that ain't never been there as far as I know or think" (8). Llorens wrote the introduction because he found no evidence of such treachery (the "badge" of bitchiness that he says never existed), viewing her rhetorical vigor as "new energy" (8) that would aid rather than undermine the revolution.

Still, near the end of that same volume, Rodgers responds to critics who dictate a more conventionally feminine role for black women. In "The Last M.F." (37–38), she promises to stop employing vulgar language in her poems; like Dickinson's excessive compliance when her brother asks her to write more simply ("As *simple* as you please, the *simplest* sort of simple"), Rodgers vows never again to use obscenities like "mother fucker," but she does so in lines that obviously savor this last opportunity for such expressiveness:

> *they say,*
> *that i should not use the word*
> *muthafucka anymo*
> *in my poetry or in any speech i give.*
> *they say,*
> *that i must and can only say it to myself*
> *as the new Black Womanhood suggests*
> *a softer self*
> *a more reserved speaking self. they say,*
> *that respect is hard won by a woman*
> *who throws a word like muthafucka around*
> *and so they say because we love you*
> *throw that word away, Black Woman . . .*

i say,
  that i only call muthafuckas, muthafuckas
  so no one should be insulted.

Once again, the charge against the revolutionary female speaker is that she is a contradiction: if revolutionary aesthetics are aggressive and menacing, then simply by speaking, she is unwomanly. Her role in the revolution is to be soft and feminine. In fact, as the poem indicates, black women are admonished to cultivate a "reserved speaking self"—a demand that risks discouraging them from speaking at all.

Typically, then, the woman who chooses to speak must prove her femininity. The speaker of the poem parodies this necessity:

i say,
that i am soft, and you can subpoena my man, put him
on trial, and he will testify that i am
soft in the right places at the right times
and often we are so reserved, i have nothing to say.

The speaker recognizes exactly the equation required to vindicate herself: she's demonstrably feminine because she's sexy. She is physically feminine ("soft in the right places") and so focused on love-making ("reserved") that she is sometimes speechless. Yet the hush of sexual intimacy is not the same as enforced silence, and the poem records the debate between what "they say" and what "i say" in the structure of alternating arguments about women speaking. Finally, she accedes to being a listener rather than a talker—"but they say that this new day / creates a new dawn woman, / one who will listen to Black Men"—yet still hates to give up her point. As she complies with their demands, she registers her scorn for black men who censor women, her delight in deploying obscenities against them, and the futility of censoring the truth that obscenities can convey:

and so i say
this is the last poem i will write calling
all manner of wites, card-carrying muthafuckas
and all manner of Blacks (negroes too) sweet
muthafuckas, crazy muthafuckas, lowdown muthafuckas
cool muthafuckas, mad and revolutionary muthafuckas,
But anyhow you all know just like I do (whether I say
it or not), there's plenty of MEAN *muthafuckas out*
here trying to do the struggle in.

The parenthetical remark, "(whether I say / it or not)," uses punctuation like hands cupped over ears—the parentheses simultaneously muffle the sound of her utterance and channel it toward our attention. The eloquent line break after "I say" and the solitary instance of the capital "I" lend authority to the speaker's voice even as the parentheses appear to take it away. The words of those we ignore continue to nag us: they say that censorship hides the truths that ought to be revealed, silences the people we need to hear from, and ultimately undermines the revolution.

Songs of a Black Bird represents Rodgers's Black Arts period; however, amid the expected paeans to black men and the revolution, "Black Woman! / let yr man (ev'ry Black Man) / be yr Hero," are hints of dissatisfaction with the Black Arts program ("Now Let's Be Real" 18). In "Breakthrough" (31–33), for example, the speaker admits that "my mouth has been open / most of the time, but / I ain't been saying nuthin." Yet, the two poems that open *Black Bird* say a great deal about the direction Rodgers will eventually take. "Jesus Was Crucified, or, It Must Be Deep" (9–11) and "It Is Deep" (12–13) relate the tensions between the speaker, a black liberation radical, and her mother, a middle-class Christian. Over the telephone, the speaker disagrees with her mother's worldview: that there is a God, that some white people are good, that all revolutionaries are Communists, and that her daughter shouldn't curse in public. To her mother's insistence that "deep deep down" in her heart the daughter knows that the Bible is true, the speaker sarcastically responds "it must be d / eeeep," meaning that any faith she has is buried so deep—in the past— that it's no longer accessible. Her response also resonates with the sixties' sense of "deep" as something complicated and ponderous: the speaker can't fathom religious belief.

In the next poem, however, the edge of sarcasm is gone as the speaker restates the phrase but this time to assert its accuracy. "It Is Deep" rehearses a similar conversation; this time, though, the mother has arrived unexpectedly at her sick daughter's apartment to give her some money and make certain she's all right. Though her mother doesn't "recognize the poster of the / grand le roi" or her own daughter's "book of / Black poems," she most certainly acknowledges her relationship to her daughter: she

> *pressed fifty*
> *bills in my hand saying "pay the [telephone] bill and buy*
> *some food; you got people who care about you."*

The speaker is moved by her mother's demonstration of love and solidarity and realizes her mother is "a sturdy Black bridge that I / crossed over on."

The idea of crossing over to a new way of life provides the substance that Rodgers explicitly longed for in several poems of self-doubt about her writing. Her third book takes its title from this concern: *How I Got Ovah* (1975) collects new and selected poems in a volume that marks a turning point in Rodgers's career. Like Giovanni and Sanchez, Rodgers rejects the official hatred of the liberation movement and embraces love. "Some of Me Beauty" (53) recalls and dismisses her revolutionary persona:

> *the fact is*
> *that i don't hate any body any more*
> *i went through my mean period.*

Now, however, she awakes to find herself

> *carolyn*
> *not imani man jua or soul sister poetess of*
> *the moment*
> *i saw more than a "sister" . . .*
> *i saw a Woman. human.*
> *and black.*
> *i felt a spiritual transformation*
> *a root revival of love.*

The correlation between a spiritual transformation and the revival of love is critical. Two of the new poems, "how i got ovah" (5) and "how i got ovah II/ It Is Deep II" (77–78), record the poet's conversion to her mother's Christianity. As the titles suggest (in their allusions to the titles and last line of the poems about her mother's love and faith in *Black Bird*) Rodgers "got over" hatred and self-doubt by getting over the militant movement and the Black Aesthetic—and by getting over *to* Christianity and a new style.[18]

The "Author's Note" (xi) that introduces the volume hints at the changes in the book proper by hinting at the change in the author:

> When a book is finally published, an author is very likely to have changed his style and his mind. About many things. . . .

> Still, a person does not wish to offer apologies for where she or he was. For certainly where one has been makes where one is more meaningful. Many of you will recognize some of these poems. You will not recognize quite a few others. . . .
>
> I want my work to interest as many people as possible; therefore, some words have been either altered or eliminated completely.

As that last statement suggests, there will be no "MF"s here. These new poems suggest "a softer self," "a more reserved speaking self." Now, however, the softness and reserve are consistent with the Christian notion of femininity rather than the black militant one, though, in practice, the two models of proper female behavior are indistinguishable.

The crudeness, recklessness, and ineffectiveness of the revolutionaries are explicitly contrasted with the civility, patience, and effectiveness of the "church folk" in "and when the revolutionaries came" (65–67) just as her former poetry is explicitly repudiated in "Living Water" (79–81):

> i keep feeling my mouth with my tongue
> afraid that something has slipped loose
> dropped out all the time i was opening and closing
> saying nothing nothing nothing.

Here "nothing nothing nothing" dismisses those former poems (by saying they amounted to nothing) at the same time it recalls them (by mimicking the characteristic repetitions of Black Arts verbal aggression). If she's going to write now, she'll have to write a new kind of poetry. Yet the speaker in "Living Water" feels an inward spiritual fullness that she isn't sure she can tap for her writing. The final section of the poem resolves this worry by relinquishing verbal authority to God:

> I think sometimes
> when i write
> God has his hand on me
> i am his little black slim ink pen.

This obviously female pen is slight, diminutive, merely an instrument of masculine authority: she embodies exactly the sort of femininity that Carolyn Rodgers had once aggressively rejected.

In Christianity, Rodgers found an alternative to the Black Power movement that, like the Nation of Islam, did not provide an alternative to conventional femininity. "For Women" (*Ovah* 72–75), for example, celebrates the long-suffering, silent woman, who endures her abusive marriage because she is strengthened by God's "amazing grace":

> she is mostly silent taking his abuses
> when she can.
> as he cuts her with words that
>   wisely know her
> human weaknesses.

In the face of his ridicule, name calling, physical aggression, drinking, gambling, and faithlessness, she

> goes on
> singing
> singing
> singing
> amazing
> grace.

Indeed, unbeknownst to him,

> he is alive
> somewhat saved
> somehow sanctified

because of her faith and prayer. She receives grace from God, and her husband, in turn, "saps a strength from her."

The poem is clearly not just about this one woman; she represents the poem's conception of womankind, as the epigraph suggests: "(women are the fruit of the earth)." Yet in what sense can "For Women" be considered *for* women when it glorifies silent suffering and deferred spiritual rewards? The amazing grace that sustains the woman in the poem, or even the poet herself, might provide solace to any particular woman, but it did not offer a more generally efficacious response to the misogyny of the liberation movement.

However well their thematic and formal developments suited the individual careers of Nikki Giovanni, Sonia Sanchez, and Carolyn Rodgers, the retreat from Black Arts excesses to a more moderate style associated with a more feminine project rendered their poetry less "useful," to borrow Karenga's term, for other women poets. This is not to fault the poetry; indeed, Sanchez's and Rodgers's work grows more beautiful and compelling as it finds its uniqueness. But if excess can be described as a writing strategy peculiarly suited to the expression of marginalized voices, then their poetry became less revolutionary as it became less excessive, shifting the weight of its political work from style to subject. While Black Arts movement excesses had established a public aesthetic program that enabled a community of voices to express themselves, its fundamental misogyny ultimately disabled most black women writers within that community. Though they recovered their individual women's voices in developing their own poetry, they no longer participated in or promoted a public artistic program. Yet the sexism of the black liberation movement would eventually have to be resisted, like that movement had resisted the dominant culture's racism, in a more public utterance. And, not surprisingly, the later black feminists who succeeded in challenging the misogyny in their culture turned to excess once again in *their* struggle to be heard.

It is true, of course, that not all black women poets writing in the late 1960s and early 1970s followed the trajectory from hypermasculinity to hyperfemininity that I have outlined in the careers of Giovanni, Sanchez, and Rodgers. Gwendolyn Brooks was an established, award-winning poet, who had already developed her poetic voice, by the time she embraced the Black Arts movement values in 1967.[19] Her earlier poetry—with its eccentric diction and ornate structures—changed dramatically under the influence of the Black Aesthetic. While her poems retain their penchant for the word choice that is as precise as it is unusual, they abandon closed forms for free verse, register anger and outrage directly, employ colloquial language, strive for formal and thematic clarity as a political ideal, and reiterate the cultural program. Even so, as a mature woman and poet, a wife and mother, a published writer, Brooks quickly became the mentor of the movement that had recently been mentor to her. She began teaching and running workshops for black gang members and other youngsters, established literary prizes for aspiring writers, and published their works in numerous anthologies. Yet even as she devoted her time, resources, prestige, and her writing to black liberation, she did not embrace the aesthetics of excess dictated by the Black Arts movement.[20]

Though Lucille Clifton published her first volume of poetry in 1969 at the height of the Black Arts movement, her native independence, family-centered experiences and values, and religious optimism inclined her away from participation in a militant movement. A few of her early poems celebrate black leaders, but even when her writing is informed by black liberation, it is not shaped by the Black Aesthetic.[21] In 1984 Haki Madhubuti praised Clifton for her treatment of black men, contrasting her work to that of explicitly feminist writers: "Much of today's writing, especially much of that being published by Black women writers, seems to invalidate Black men or make small of them, often relegating them to the position of white sexual renegades in black faces. No such cop-out for Clifton. There is no misrepresentation of the men or women" ("Lucille Clifton" 151). Ironically, however, the intellectual and artistic independence that kept Clifton from becoming programmatic in her feminism also kept her from becoming programmatic in her nationalism. Though Madhubuti authoritatively claimed Clifton for the revolution nearly twenty years after the fact ("Clifton is a Black cultural poet" [153]), at no time in her career did she accept the persona of the black cultural poet as it was defined during the Black Arts movement.

Audre Lorde was dedicated to black liberation from the beginning of her career, but her concerns as a lesbian and feminist precluded her acceptance of the Black Arts misogyny and machismo. In her fourth book of poetry, *New York Head Shop and Museum* (1974), Lorde uncharacteristically expresses an aggressive edge, though even here she does not employ Black Arts excesses. In "Naturally" (35) she seems to mock the emphasis on physical appearance in the black liberation movement:

> *Since Naturally Black is Naturally Beautiful*
> *I must be proud*
> *and, naturally,*
> *Black*
> *Beautiful.*

The speaker gives up the "pomades" of an earlier era's physical ideal and now spends all summer sunbathing to darken her skin. Yet as she submits her body to the new ideal, she recognizes the ironies of seeking liberation through looks: "if I die of skin / cancer / oh well— one less / black and beautiful me." These external ideals of beauty, especially female beauty, are not only physically self-destructive, but they also distract attention from the real work of liberation. To counteract the misogyny in the Black Power movement, from which such standards of beauty come, Lorde insistently combines black nationalism and feminism. In "Now" (20), a poem whose title overlays the single word "now" that urges change and the acronym for the National Organization of Women, she tries to break down the gender barriers in the Black Power movement by bringing it into relation with the feminist movement:

Woman power
is
Black power
is
Human power.

Lorde's great regard for all humanity, her recognition of the complexities of social life (she was married to a white man with whom she had two children; she lived most of her life with a white lesbian lover; she raised a daughter and a son), did not dispose her toward the machismo and separatism of the Black Arts movement.

But for most of the women who came of age artistically during the Black Arts movement and who were tutored in the Black Aesthetic, the struggle to create a place for themselves in the literary environment was arduous. Giovanni, Sanchez, Rodgers, Evans, Amini (Latimore), and countless others, who published one or two bombastic poems and were never heard from again, frequently retreated to some form of conventional femininity that was almost as disabling as the overbearing masculinity they sought to escape.

An exception to this pattern and a harbinger of future developments in African-American women's poetry is Jayne Cortez. She published her first volume of poetry in 1969 and produced a book every few years until 1984. In 1976, when the Black Arts movement was past its prime, Stanley Crouch singled out Cortez for praise in an otherwise negative assessment of the period:

> During the nationalist promenade and the charade of ineptitude, the very shoddiness of which was supposed to breach a "revolutionary" standard, only one female poet was consistently interesting to me, and that one was Jayne Cortez. . . . [In her work] there was a passion and an *ear* for melody and the manipulation of sounds and rhythm units that smoked away the other contenders for the crown, revealing their entrapment in a militant self-pity and adolescent rage more akin to tantrums than the chilling fire and evil of someone like Bessie Smith, the super bitchiness and dignity

of a Billie Holiday or a Dinah Washington . . . . Jayne Cortez is, then, the *real* thing. (99)

Crouch not only reappropriates "fire" from the Black Arts movement in order to redefine it (the "chilling fire" of the blues queens is superior to the "adolescent rage" of the militants) but also reestablishes the vital link between contemporary black poetry and the older tradition of the blues. Crouch rejects the militant claim to have superseded the blues and instead recognizes the revolutionary potential of the blues singers' bitchiness and dignity.

Indeed, Cortez herself will make much of these traits. Dinah Washington speaks in "Dinah's Back In Town" (*Pisstained Stairs,* n.p.) and asserts the dignity of bitchiness:

> *I wanna be bitchy*
> *I said I wanna be a bitch*
> *cause when you nice*
> *true love don't come*
> *into your life.*

In "Phraseology" (*Scarifications* 23), she makes bitchiness a formal principle of her poetry:

> *I say things to myself*
> *in a bitch of a syllable . . .*
> *completely savage to the passing of silence.*

Savaging silence—violently expressing her concerns in an environment that discourages female expressivity—is certainly the result of Cortez's use of excess.

In her first book, *Pisstained Stairs and the Monkey Man's Wares* (1969), Cortez's excess appears to be in service of Black Arts values. In "Race," for example, she vilifies gay black men for betraying the race in betraying their "manhood":

> *[His] tongue hangs low*
> *with loose diseased pink*
> *pale dying flesh*
> *between his gums*
> *suffocating in farts*
> *& howling like a coyote in the wind*
> *his bent over dedication to*
> *the grunting demons that madly*
> *ride upon his back*

> *flying high his ass tonight*
> *swallowing sperms of fantasy.*

The poem blames internalized racism for this "lost tribe of whimpering sons" who can only create "A Race called Faggot." These confused sons, who have repudiated their mothers in turning away from women, must be slaughtered in order to "bring a revolution on." The pitch of desperation, both thematic and formal, reaches a peak in the closing couplet, where the speaker calls out to black fathers (who, by virtue of having "fathered" these sons, have demonstrated their masculinity) for help: "Oh black man quick please the laxative / so our sons can shit the White Shit of Fear out and Live." The association of heterosexuality with liberation, the homophobia, the sexual bluntness, and the excremental imagery all signal adherence to the program of the Black Arts movement in 1969.

However, while Black Arts excesses continued to inform her style, Cortez increasingly brought these stylistics to bear on a wider range of concerns. By 1982, well after the heyday of the new black poetry, Cortez was deploying such excesses against misogynist men, that is, against the very sort of man whom these excesses formerly valorized. In "Rape" (*Firespitter* 31), the style is the same, but the names have been changed to expose the guilty:

> *What was Inez supposed to do for*
> *the man who declared war on her body*
> *the man who carved a combat zone between her breasts*
> *Was she supposed to lick crabs from his hairy ass*
> *kiss every pimple on his butt*
> *blow hot breath on his big toe*
> *draw back the corners of her vagina and*
> *hee haw like a Calif. burro.*

The poem answers these questions for us by allowing Inez to shoot her rapist; then Joanne, another rape victim, stabs her rapist with an ice pick. The poem celebrates the "day of the dead rapist punk"—a far cry from poems that had urged militants to "Rape the white girls. . . . / Cut the mothers' throats" (Jones, "Black Dada Nihilismus" 41).

In 1971 a Cortez poem, "Watch Out" (*Festivals and Funerals,* n.p.), had warned about the "bitter," "neglected" woman, "her tongue working out like a machete." By 1982, in a poem like "Rape," we begin to get a sense of this warning, of what it will mean for women to use their tongues in their own defense. Cortez never retreated from the excesses of the Black Arts period, but she trained them on an entirely new subject matter. She did not accept the misogyny of the movement; rather, she turned those aggressive stylistics back on the culture that had glorified violence against women and others as a means of exerting its limited power. Cortez was able to discern the continuing relevance of Black Arts excesses because she was able to distinguish the potent stylistics from the paralyzing subject matter. The other Black Arts women writers abandoned formal excess when they became dissatisfied with the militant posture; Cortez, however, found new and important uses for excess. Not all of her poetry employs these excesses; in fact, her strength lies in her range of poetic resources. But Jayne Cortez provides a literary link between the dignity and bitchiness of the earlier blues queens and the empowered voices of the later black feminist poets because she was able to deploy excess without being silenced by it.

Perhaps the reason Cortez escaped censure even though she used excess to expose the oppression of women, as in "Rape," is that the men targeted by her excess were white. Inez's rapist is compared to a "giant hog," suggesting pink skin, and Joanne's rapist is explicitly called a "racist." But in the mid-seventies, with the women's liberation movement giving expression to concerns that had previously been unspeakable, African-American women writers began to include black men in their analysis of gender problems. To do this, they would employ the very excesses that had troubled black female poets a decade before. Ntozake Shange would be the most prominent writer to reappropriate Black Arts excesses and deploy them against black men, but she would not be alone.

Shange's "choreopoem" *for colored girls who have considered suicide when the rainbow is enuf* grew from feminist inklings that began around 1972 to the published volume, "as close to distilled as any of us in all our art forms can make it" (xv), that appeared in 1976. In only two years *for colored girls* journeyed from San Francisco Bay area women's bars, where Shange and others first performed the poems, to Broadway. This swift ascent to prominence suggests the momentum that eager audiences lent to the work. *for colored girls* consists of twenty poems performed by seven women dressed in and designated in the text by different colors. "Lady in brown," "lady in blue," "lady in red," and the others are literally, even emblematically "colored girls." These designations single them out as particular colors (not all colored girls are the same) at the same time that they render the women anonymous. The effect is that each performer is both a particular woman and a representative of women of color, a soloist and a member of the chorus. Each woman is part of the rainbow, the symbol of beauty and transcendence; seeing the rainbow in the sky is just "enuf" to keep these suffering women from committing suicide until they can discover the rainbows in themselves.

The task of the book is to help women recognize their own beauty and divinity, as the final lines, spoken significantly by the lady in brown (the most racially explicit color since it is not a hue of the rainbow) assert:

> & this is for colored girls who have considered
>
> suicide/ but are movin to the ends of their own
>
> rainbows.
>
> (64)[22]

To achieve this, the women must be brought into light and visibility from darkness and invisibility, and their voices must be retrieved from silence:

> dark phrases of womanhood
> of never havin been a girl
> half-notes scattered
> without rhythm/ no tune . . .
> another song with no singers
> lyrics/ no voices
> & interrupted solos
> unseen performances.
>
> (3–4)

The repeated warning "don't tell nobody don't tell a soul" hints at the strictures against black women speaking out about their lives that have left these colored girls silent and invisible. This is the same threat that inaugurates Alice Walker's novel, *The Color Purple,* when the protagonist Celie's stepfather warns her not to speak about the fact that he regularly rapes her: "*You better not never tell nobody but God*" (11). The similarity between Shange's and Walker's lines is not coincidental; African-American women writing for the first time about their own concerns as women were accused of betraying African-American men.[23] The lady in brown insists that black women cannot begin to live until they begin to express themselves:

> somebody/ anybody
> sing a black girl's song
> bring her out
> to know herself . . .
> sing her song of life
> she's been dead so long
> closed in silence so long
> she doesn't know the sound
> of her own voice.
> (2–3)

The black girl's "song" is not just a trope for her experience; the song unites words and music in a form that calls upon the rich and powerful African-American oral tradition and the ritual beginnings of poetry. It provides a structure for women's voices that can be adapted to the solo or the chorus, as the needs of the individual are juxtaposed with the resources of the group. Moreover, the melody of the music buoys up not only the lyrics but the actual bodies of the colored girls. For this is not merely a poem but a choreopoem: words choreographed with bodies. Shange explains the significance of this new genre: "With the acceptance of the ethnicity of my thighs & backside, came a clearer understanding of my voice as a woman & as a poet. . . . Just as Women's Studies had rooted me to an articulated female heritage & imperative, so dance . . . insisted that everything African, everything halfway colloquial, a grimace, a strut, an arched back over a yawn, waz mine. I moved what waz my unconscious knowledge of being in a colored woman's body to my known every-dayness" (xi). The choreopoem renders black women's lives not only audible but visible. This is crucial, for words often fail these women:

> i can't i can't
>
> talk witchu no more
>
> . . . we gotta dance to keep from cryin
>
> we gotta dance to keep from dyin.
> (15)

Everywhere in *for colored girls* we meet women who don't know how to speak, are afraid to speak, are interrupted when they speak, or who suffer tremendously for speaking. In "now I love somebody more than" (11–13), the lady in blue pretends to be Puerto Rican so she can dance rather than talk; in "abortion cycle #1" (22–23), the lady in blue faces a pregnancy and abortion alone because she is too ashamed to tell anyone about it; throughout the book, stage directions indicate light and sound interruptions ("*The lights change, and the ladies are all hit by an imaginary slap*" [21]), and the seven voices frequently preempt and interrupt each other; in "a nite with beau willie brown" (55–60), Crystal's two children are killed by Beau Willie because she can only whisper when he demands she give verbal assent to marrying him.

Dance and music constitute extraliterary excess in *for colored girls;* even more drastic than Sanchez's blaring capitals and agitated dispersal of letters on the page, Rodgers's vulgarity, or Cortez's descriptive violence, Shange's choreopoem must rely on physical movement, musical accompaniment, and the immediacy of performance to give substance and force to a weakened language and expressiveness to silenced speakers.

Another of the book's excesses is talking back: Shange's speakers appropriate Black Arts excesses to challenge Black Arts ideas. In response to the dictum "let there be no love poems written," Shange sarcastically writes a *numbered* sequence of "*no more* love poems," which offers an analysis of why love is embattled that differs significantly from the one proposed in Jones's "Black Art." In "no more love poems #1" (42–43), the lady in orange describes trying to "deserve" love from black men by being submissive and loving:

> ever since i realized there waz someone callt
> a colored girl an evil woman a bitch or a nag
> i been tryin not to be that & leave bitterness
> in somebody else's cup.

When her lover mistreats her anyway, she is left with only "a real dead // lovin." Love poetry is not possible because women's love is not reciprocated by men. In "no more love poems #2" (43–44), the lady in purple begs to be loved by one of the revolutionary men, "the niggah/ . . . the baddest muthafuckah // out there," but he, too, fails to recognize her authenticity and value. In the third poem (44–45) the lady in blue associates the denial of love with the emotional poverty of white people—

we deal wit emotion too much

so why don't we go on ahead & be white then/

& make everythin dry & abstract wit no rhythm.

She needs to be loved, she says, but she can't say "where are you," nor does she know whom "to say it to." The fourth poem (45) insists that abandoning love (by repudiating love poetry) is not an acceptable solution: "my love is too delicate to have thrown // back on my face." Taken together, the four poems reveal that white racism is not the only evil that makes the world unsafe for love; when black men mistreat black women, love, and therefore conventional love poetry, is rendered impossible.

Finally, Shange translates Black Arts thematic violence into melodrama, resituating it in an excessively "feminine" genre. In "a nite with beau willie brown" (55–60), Crystal supports a drug addict who beats and verbally abuses her, breaks into her apartment, and kills their children. In an almost preposterous staging of masculine aggressiveness and feminine passivity, Beau Willie holds the children out of a fifth-story window, insisting that Crystal "say to alla the neighbors/ // you gonna marry me." When Crystal can only whisper her assent, he lets the babies drop to their deaths.

By the late 1970s Shange's *for colored girls* and Michele Wallace's *Black Macho and the Myth of the Superwoman,* two books that had appropriated excess for women, were both wildly popular and causing a furor.[24] In the printed reviews and debates about these groundbreaking works of black feminism, it was clear that many readers were not yet ready to hear the African-American woman's uninterrupted solo. Shange alludes to these critical readers and reviewers in her 1981 booklet of poetry called *Some Men.*[25] "Some Men" is a sequence in ten parts; the first part introduces the problem:

some/ men
have no language that doesn't hurt
a language that doesn't reduce what's whole
to some part of nothing.

(37)

Here Shange employs verbal excess once again, but this time it is the damaging speech of men that the poems record. The "pretty man," who uses and abuses women like his other pretty things, "thought of the most beautiful thing he cd say": "SUCK MY DICK & MAKE SOME COFFEE" (39). In the third poem, a woman receives obscene phone calls from a man who enjoys tyrannizing women. The caller, it turns out, is a friend of hers; after frightening her a few times, he calls as though by coincidence and comforts her when she thinks she hears "a man she cd trust in the middle of the night" (40). Another man is jealous that his baby nurses at his wife's breasts, and he bites her breasts trying to get some milk for himself (42), while another "pull[s] his dick out" in front of a terrified woman who's trying to unlock her front door. Finally, as a woman abandons herself to lovemaking, she is brutalized by yet another crass and violent man:

> she felt him coming
> & let go of all her powers
> when without warning
> he shot all his semen up her ass
>   she kept screaming
> WHAT ARE YOU DOING WHAT ARE YOU DOING to me
> he relaxed/ sighing
>   "i had to put it somewhere, it was
> too good to be some pussy."
>
> (44)

The tenth poem (44) explains the need for these excesses, that is, the need to depict gender relations with unflinching clarity:

> some men would rather see us dead than imagine
> what we think of them/
> if we measure our silence by our pain
> how could all the words
> any word
> ever catch us up
> what is it
> we cd call equal.

The "some men" Shange vilifies in the poem are like those reviewers and readers who excoriated her for singing a black girl's song in the earlier book. We know from *for colored girls* that to be without words is to be without life: "she's been dead so long // closed in silence so long" (4). Those men who want black women to be silent about their concerns impose a death sentence on women. Another reason excess is crucial in "Some Men," we learn in this last poem, is that all the words Shange can muster will never be enough to articulate the pain that black women have silently endured. Moreover, lacking expressive equality (words will never equal experience), how can social equality be achieved? Like her Black Arts movement predecessors, then, Shange employs excess as a means of being heard in a hostile literary environment and as a way to counteract the inadequacies of language itself.

That black feminists of Shange's generation utilized Black Arts excess as a tool to dismantle the master's house attests to the usefulness of excess as a writing strategy for those the dominant culture discourages from print. In "Hands: For Mother's Day" (*Those Who Ride the Night Winds* 16–18), Nikki Giovanni remarks on the African-American woman's capacity to create art with meager resources: "We weave a quilt with dry, rough hands . . . Quilts are the way our lives are lived . . . We survive on patches . . . scraps . . . the leftovers from a materially richer culture . . . We do the far more difficult job of taking that which nobody wants and not only loving it . . . not only seeing its worth . . . but making it lovable . . . and intrinsically worthwhile . . . ." (17; ellipses in the original poem). Though the wealth of contemporary African-American women's poetry abundantly demonstrates that their artistic resources are not scant, Giovanni's poem reminds us that these women created literary works and a tradition out of experiences the dominant culture had dismissed and of materials it had discarded. Just as the Harlem Renaissance poets found new and subversive uses for literary conventions (like the sonnet, the ballad, or idealized representations of nature) that mainstream writers were discarding, black feminist poets found new and subversive uses for Black Arts excesses—long after the Black Arts movement aestheticians abandoned such stylistics themselves. Poetic excess has repeatedly served the needs of marginalized poets, offering them a strategy for transgressing convention, and its rhetorical power is ironically evidenced in the fact that excess continues to function as a *convention for transgression* in contemporary poetry.

Notes

Chapter 1. The Poetics of Excess

1. Johnson, the editor of the three-volume variorum Dickinson and the one-volume *Complete Poems,* prints only stanzas one, four, and five in the one-volume edition, making the choice between the three stanzas appearing before the "Or" and the two appearing after it that Dickinson herself did not make. Moreover, his selection removes the nightingale from the poem in favor of the explicit reference to "Brontë," a decision that seems to cut out Philomela's tongue, which in this case is the complexity of the figure, once again.

2. In *Choosing Not Choosing: Dickinson's Fascicles,* Sharon Cameron argues that "with respect to the variants [alternate word choices that Dickinson places outside the text of the poem proper, typically in the space beneath the poem], Dickinson sets up a situation that seems exclusionary, and that she then refuses choices which she presents as inevitable. Thus in Dickinson's poetry the apparent need to choose is countered by the refusal to choose" (21). Cameron does not discuss poem 148, probably because its signal of an alternate reading, the "Or" after stanza three, is contained within the poem. Cameron would call this an "inclusive or" because the " 'or' does not only not require but positively precludes choice" (23), a situation that is "common in poetic tradition" (21). Dickinson's "not choosing" is exceptional elsewhere, however, because "the words occasioning it appear exported to the margins or interlinear spaces." She continues, "Choice appears to engage words which lie outside the text, at least to lie 'outside' as that text has conventionally been defined" and "results in a heteroglossic situation" (24). Though poem 148 does not seem to meet this criterion, a reading of it benefits from Cameron's notion of "not choosing."

3. In "Vesuvius at Home: The Power of Emily Dickinson," Adrienne Rich writes that "[Dickinson's] niece Martha told of visiting her in her corner bedroom on the second floor at 280 Main Street, Amherst, and of how Emily Dickinson made as if to lock the door with an imaginary key, turned, and said: 'Matty: here's freedom' " (158).

4. The impossibility of reading the "A" as a stable, consistent sign is illustrated repeatedly in the novel. The red meteor "A" that streaks through the sky while Dimmesdale stands on the scaffold at midnight (from his point of view a revelation of his sin) is interpreted by the townsfolk who see it as standing for "Angel"—a heavenly sign that Governor Winthrop, who has just died, has gone to heaven (158). This reading, of course, must suppress the demonic character of the meteor "A," "burning duskily through a veil of cloud" (155). Similarly, when Dimmesdale finally bares his chest in order to reveal *his* sign of guilt, his spectators all "read" it differently (258–59). Most ironic of all, however, is that no one reads the scarlet letter's most obvious reference though it answers the question that consumes and befuddles them: "A" might simply stand for "Arthur," the father of the child and Hester's partner in sin.

5. George Bataille's *Visions of Excess* associates excess with cultural extravagances or obsessions, which he calls "unproductive [or unconditional] expenditures: luxury, mourning, war, cults, the construction of sumptuary monuments, games, spectacles, arts, perverse sexual activity . . . activities which . . . have no end beyond themselves" (118). These unconditional expenditures, and poetry would be one of them (119), exceed the economic principle of balanced accounts ("expenditure regularly compensated for by acquisition" [118]). While this notion of excess is suggestive, especially for reading Dickinson and Stein, Bataille's concept does not inform my discussion.

6. Thomas Kranidas offers an excellent, concise history of decorum in the first chapter ("The Background of Milton's Decorum") of *The Fierce Equation: A Study of Milton's Decorum.* There he shows that the two persistent concerns in almost every discussion of decorum are clarity and propriety, consistently held values that must respond, however, to changing literary environments: "No matter how central decorum is to the work of art, no matter how long the tradition of its importance, it is applied anew to every piece of discourse, it adapts constantly to the environment" (18).

7. A typical formulation of this opposition, rich in its ironic association of sewing and poetry, is Thomas Tickell's from the eighteenth-century magazine *The Spectator:*

> This [needlework] is, methinks, the most proper way wherein a Lady can shew a fine Genius, and I cannot forbear wishing, that several Writers of that Sex had chosen to apply themselves rather to Tapestry than Rhime. Your Pastoral Poetesses may vent their Fancy in Rural Landskips,

and place despairing Shepherds under silken Willows, or drown them in a Stream of Mohair. The Heroick Writers may work up Battels as successfully, and inflame them with Gold or stain them Crimson. Even those who have only a Turn to a Song or an Epigram, may put many valuable Stitches into a Purse, and crowd a thousand Graces into a Pair of Garters. (qtd. in Messenter 128)

In *My Emily Dickinson,* Susan Howe chides feminist critics for making use of the sewing/writing metaphor: "This is poetry not life, and certainly not sewing" (14). However, the analogy between sewing and writing suggests not that women's poetry is merely like sewing but that women's sewing can be poetic—and that the whole range of women's artist production has been dismissed and demeaned as mere craft or superfluous ornament.

Chapter 2. Emily Dickinson

1. Stephen Cushman has recently devoted a chapter in *Fictions of Form in American Poetry* to the subject of Dickinson's theory of poetic form, "The Broken Mathematics of Emily Dickinson." Cushman also refers readers to John Hollander (*Vision and Resonance* 233), Cynthia Griffin Wolff (*Emily Dickinson* 531, 209, 523), and Robert Sherwood (*Circumference and Circumstance: Stages in the Mind and Art of Emily Dickinson* 24).

2. Virtually any discussion of Dickinson's poetics will refer to her correspondence with Higginson. One of many examples is George Perkins's 1972 anthology, *American Poetic Theory,* in which the chapter on Dickinson is composed entirely of "Letters to Thomas Wentworth Higginson." See Martha Nell Smith's *Rowing in Eden: Rereading Emily Dickinson* (1992) for a thorough study of Dickinson's correspondence in relation to her life and art.

3. All Dickinson letters are quoted from Johnson's three-volume edition and will be cited parenthetically in the text by letter number (L) to distinguish short quotations easily from Dickinson's poems. Readers of Dickinson's letters will be familiar with her oddities of spelling and punctuation, in this passage the unnecessary apostrophe in "it's."

4. There is a good deal of debate about which edition of Webster's dictionary Dickinson used. Cushman surveys the options in a thorough note to his chapter on Dickinson (197–98, n. 8). I am using the 1844 Webster's but also consulting other contemporary dictionaries since I agree with Cushman that "an important consideration is not only which edition Dickinson owned but also which edition tells us the most about American English during the years she wrote" (198). Cushman uses the 1847 edition.

5. Austin's efforts to discourage Dickinson's literary aspirations are typical of what Joanna Russ calls "informal prohibitions" against female writers in *How To Suppress Women's Writing.* She points out that a formal prohibition— like keeping women illiterate—"tends to give the game away . . . it will occur

to somebody sooner or later that illiteracy absolutely precludes written liter-ature." However, "in a nominally egalitarian society the ideal situation (so-cially speaking) is one in which the members of the 'wrong' groups have the freedom to engage in literature . . . and yet do not do so, thus proving that they can't. . . . The trick thus becomes to make the freedom as nominal as possible and then . . . develop strategies for ignoring, condemning, or belittling the artistic works that result" (4–5). The strategies for the suppression of women's writing she discusses at length in the chapters of the book are informal prohibitions, denying authorship of a work, belittling the work, isolating the work from its tradition, suggesting that the work reveals the bad character of its author, and simply ignoring the work. Dickinson, one of the most frequently cited authors in the book, is discussed in nearly every chapter.

6. All Dickinson poems are quoted from Johnson's three-volume edition and will be cited parenthetically in the text by poem number (P) to distin-guish them from short quotations from the letters. References to variant words included by Johnson following each poem will be cited by page number.

7. Cristanne Miller's essay on "The Humor of Excess" (Juhasz, Miller, and Smith, *Comic Power in Emily Dickinson*) treats many of the same stylistic traits that I analyze here. As my frequent citations to Miller's work sug-gest, we are interested in similar aspects of Dickinson's poetry, and Miller's scholarship has been particularly relevant to mine. Though she and I discuss different poems, we are in agreement on the formal manifestations of excess (106–7) and on its political implications (105). We differ, though without disagreement, about Dickinson's motivations for employing an excessive style. And I argue, further, that the tensions created by excess reproduce not only the poet's uneasy relationship to her culture but, more immediately, the volatile experience of writing. Sharon Cameron also uses the word "excess" to describe Dickinson's poetry in a chapter section by that title in *Choosing Not Choosing: Dickinson's Fascicles* ("Excess" 30–46). Here, "excess" refers to "too much meaning determined too many ways," which Cameron notes "is not particular to Dickinson's poetry" (43).

8. Tennyson's "The Lotos-Eaters" first appeared in 1830; Rossetti's *Goblin Market and Other Poems* was published in April of 1862, several months before Dickinson's letter employing the goblin figure, to great critical acclaim. In her study of Dickinson's and Rossetti's poetic language, Sharon Leder indicates that "it is likely Dickinson knew Rossetti's poetry" (6).

9. In addition to the letter to Higginson I have already discussed (L 271), Dickinson mentions Barrett Browning in letters 174, 179, 210, and 214. Erkkila discusses Dickinson's attitude toward Barrett Browning extensively in chapter 3 of *Wicked Sisters,* "Dickinson, Women Writers, and the Market-place."

10. This poem occurs in packet 14 as well as in the letter to Higginson, with slight variations (L 271). I have reproduced the poem here as she sent it to Higginson.

11. Being at odds with her father about an appropriate writing manner is only one part of a wider ranging contest of their worldviews. In a letter to Austin from 1851 she remarks, "we do not have much poetry [now that Austin is no longer living at home], father having made up his mind that its pretty much all *real life*. Father's real life and *mine* sometimes come into collision, but as yet, escape unhurt!" (L 65).

12. For Erkkila's excellent discussions of Dickinson's relationship to her women friends and to famous women writers, see chapters 2 and 3 of *Wicked Sisters*, "Emily Dickinson and the Wicked Sisters" (17–54) and "Dickinson, Women Writers, and the Marketplace" (54–98).

13. Cristanne Miller associates Dickinson's notion of difference with Derrida's: "Dickinson use of 'Difference' [in P 1068] and in 'There's a certain Slant of light' uncannily anticipates Jacques Derrida's idea of *difference* and of negative or deconstructive interpretation. Using Derrida's language, one might say of Dickinson's poems generally and of these poems in particular that they do not acknowledge a center of meaning" (*A Poet's Grammar* 102).

14. Cris Miller makes a similar point in her discussion of "terms" and "golden words" in the poetry: " 'Terms,' then become language that is *used* reductively, not a type of vocabulary or grammatical form" ("Terms and Golden Words" 51).

15. Other senses of "deal" inform the stanza: dealing out justice in the biblical sense; dealing a word may be as forceful as dealing a blow; dealing, in addition to suggesting distributing, may refer to dividing, as in dividing riches; and, although not grammatically obvious, "deal" may connote the process of negotiation or enduring something that is not negotiable.

16. The 1844 Webster's dictionary defines "goblin" as "1. An evil spirit; a walking spirit; a frightful phantom. 2. A fairy; an elf" (381). In "Words within Words: Dickinson's Use of the Dictionary," Richard Benvenuto makes a convincing case for consulting Dickinson's dictionary as an aid to explication. He says,

> One can assume that she did not refer to the dictionary cursorily, to check spelling or syllabication, but that she read it as one does who loves words. She would learn all that she could about a particular word, including words similar to it in spelling or sound, and collateral words related to it in meaning or origin. She drew especially upon the etymologies of words; and though Webster's etymologies have been long discredited by linguists, there is no evidence that Dickinson questioned them. She would have accepted the etymons in Webster as the roots of the words she was using, as their buried past meanings, and hence as integral parts of those words and legitimate for poetic use. In fact, the etymons of a words, as well as collateral words and *different connotations or definitions of a word,* often function in her poems as a word or words within the original word, with meanings that add to, enrich, and clarify the more apparent meaning. (47; emphasis added)

17. The idea that imaginative realms are peopled ("tenanted") by her own poetic power is expressed even more directly in poem 1677, one of several poems representing poetic power with the figure of the volcano: "How red the Fire rocks below— / How insecure the sod / Did I disclose / Would populate with awe my solitude."

18. For a persuasive reading of a point of view opposing mine, see Cris Miller, "Terms and Golden Words," where Miller views the Wilderness as the loss of language, or "broken words" (59).

19. The 1855 Webster's dictionary gives the following etymology for "brocade": "so. Fr. *brochure,* a pamphlet or stitched book" (150).

20. The 1844 Webster's dictionary gives this definition of "brocade" (108).

21. In "Appendix D: Sales of Dickinson Volumes in the Nineties," Willis J. Buckingham provides evidence of Dickinson's immediate popularity. The *Poems* First Series went through twenty printings in eight years; the Second Series through ten printings in six years; the *Letters* through two printings, 1,000 and 1,500 copies each, in two months; and the Third Series of *Poems* through two printings of 1,000 copies each in six months. By the end of the decade, when insistent and virulently negative reviews had "nearly obliterate[d] Dickinson's fame" (Buckingham 47), 19,860 copies of Dickinson's poems and letters had been sold in America and Britain. All quotations from these reviews are taken from Buckingham's *Emily Dickinson's Reception in the 1890s: A Documentary History* and cited by page number parenthetically in my text.

22. Russ covers this sort of denial, that a woman's poetry *is* poetry in chapter 8, "Anomalousness": "*She wrote it, but 'she' isn't really an artist and 'it' isn't really serious, of the right genre—i.e., really art*" (76).

23. Buckingham makes just such a connection in introducing an article from the *Springfield Republican* for July 25, 1878, which Dickinson probably read. In it, the author tries to solve the "Saxe Holm" mystery—that is, who wrote the popular, sentimental stories and poems published under the pseudonym Saxe Holm—by comparing the texts of Saxe Holm unfavorably to those of Helen Hunt Jackson, who was thought to be (and was) Saxe Holm. In his defense of Jackson's "superior" writing, the author of the article details prevailing objections to popular women's writing; his description includes many traits that Dickinson would have recognized in her own work. Buckingham notes, "If Emily Dickinson had read the original *Republican* article, as seems likely, she might have found shadowed forth within it a near mirror image of the critical tone and portraiture that was largely to prevail during her early reception" (88).

24. For Erkkila's provocative discussion of Dickinson's refusal to publish, see chapter 3 of *Wicked Sisters,* "Dickinson, Women Writers, and the Marketplace" (55–98).

25. In one of the most useful books on Dickinson's stylistics, Cristanne Miller treats the poet's "grammar," which consists of compression,

disjunction, repetition, syntax, and speech (*Emily Dickinson: A Poet's Grammar*).

26. When Dickinson encloses a word in quotation marks, she is typically calling conventional uses of it into question or mocking those who would use the word in conventional ways. In "[They shut me up in Prose-]," for instance, the speaker says "They put me in the Closet—/ Because they liked me 'still' "; the next lines seems to explode with contempt for those who would try to keep her still, and this violent rejection of the norm seems to liberate the word from those confining quotation marks that are a typographical equivalent to the closet: "Still! Could themself have peeped—And seen my Brain— go round— / They might as wise have lodged a Bird / For Treason—in the Pound—" (P 613). In "[Rearrange a 'Wife's' affection!]," the quotation marks indicate contempt for the standard meaning of "wife."

27. In fact, Dickinson gives "reach" as an alternative word for "sound" (682).

28. These three connotations of "justify" appear in the 1855 Webster's dictionary.

Chapter 3. Gertrude Stein

1. Wagner-Martin's recent biography treats Stein's relationship with Leo in detail. See *"Favored Strangers": Gertrude Stein and her Family,* especially chapters 5, "The Steins in Paris," for a discussion of Leo's resistance to Stein's writing, and chapter 7, "Portraits," for Leo's tendency to deliver harangues, for his criticisms of Stein's work in particular, and for various perspectives on the rupture between Leo and Gertrude.

2. In formulating her predicament here, Stein anticipates several of Russ's categories for how women's writing is suppressed: to be "renounced" is to have one's work belittled or misread, to be "diminutive" is again to be trivialized, to be "in consequence" is to be labeled unoriginal, to be "with" and "placing it with" is to have one's work attributed to something or someone else, and, finally, to be "delayed" is to be held back or hindered in some way.

3. Many readers would describe this "unique language" as a private language or code. For discussions of lesbian encoding in Stein's work, see Ruddick's "A Rosy Charm," Stimpson's "The Mind, the Body, and Gertrude Stein," Linda Simon's "Appendix: A Word About Caesars and Cows," and Elizabeth Fifer's "Is Flesh Advisable: The Interior Theater of Gertrude Stein." I avoid viewing Stein's hermetic writing as a lesbian code because her writing project seems to me, above all, inclusive rather than exclusive, though she clearly insists that readers engage with her work on *her* terms. Her poetic experiments are meant to teach us how to read and to demonstrate the delights of reading. Moreover, nothing in Stein's work indicates that she felt the need to hide or code her lesbianism. If she invented a new poetics for

writing about her relationship with Toklas, as I argue she did, it is because exhausted literary conventions were not equal to the task. The notion that she invented a hermetic form in order to elude her brother's scrutiny need not assume that she prized elusiveness more generally. As I argue above, the thing that delighted her about hermetic language was that it *simultaneously* confused and engaged and ultimately, then, clarified.

4. Because Stein's poems are frequently extremely long, and because the distinctions between poetry and prose are challenged in many of her works, I give the inclusive page numbers of each piece parenthetically in the text when it is first mentioned; thereafter, page numbers for specific passages will appear parenthetically in the text.

5. Stein was persuaded to this view by Otto Weininger's book *Sex and Character,* which she probably embraced because he "took an enlightened stand on homosexuality" (Mellow 120). However, Mellow points out that the book "is frankly antifeminist and anti-Semitic. Women are denied any possibility of genius simply by their nature, which is 'devoted wholly to sexual matters, that is to say, to the spheres of begetting and of reproduction' " (120). Stein's adherence to Weininger's viewpoint surfaces in the first few pages of her novella *Fernhurst,* which she finished shortly after reading him: "Will different things never be recognized as different. I am for having women learn what they can but not to mistake learning for action nor to believe that a man's work is suited to them because they have mastered a boy's education. In short I would have the few women who must do a piece of the man's work but think that the great mass of the world's women should content themselves with attaining to womanhood" (4–5).

6. It is difficult to know where to begin explicating Stein's experimental poems, but once one has begun, it is often even more difficult to know where to stop. The alliteration in "sudden say separate" provides another paradoxical linguistic account of the simultaneous oneness and separateness of the lovers: the alliterated *s*'s unify them aurally while the word "separate" semantically denotes their difference. One is tempted to excess in reading Stein's poems by the conviction that throwing all ideas into the ring will benefit others. The risk in this is becoming intoxicated with the possibilities of reading the poems and over-reading them to serve a fixed program. Context is one check against flagrant misreadings; intertextual knowledge of Stein's canon is another since she recycles lines and words. Certainly Stein's poems encourage playfulness on the part of the reader; however, one must find a balance between playful and willful readings.

7. Stein herself was capable of trivializing women's talk in practice, even if she valued it in poetry. When the male artists and "geniuses" visited with their wives at 27, rue de Fleurus, Toklas was in charge of occupying the wives with domestic chatter so Stein and the men could talk about philosophy and art without interruption. Mellow recounts that "one afternoon, while [Man Ray] was having an animated discussion with Gertrude, they became aware

of Alice carrying on a lively discussion with one of the women visitors. Gertrude turned toward Alice and 'shouted belligerently for them to lower their voices.' For the rest of the afternoon there was mortified silence in Alice's corner" (254).

8. It is not overstating the importance of the line to say that Stein and others viewed it as a quintessential Steinian utterance. In *The Autobiography of Alice B. Toklas,* Stein recalls that she had the line printed on her note paper to personalize it, like others would have their names and addresses printed on private stationery; and she had the line painted on a plate for Carl Van Vechten (129). Toklas, the book claims, "insisted on putting it as a device on the letter paper, on the table linen and anywhere [Stein] would permit" it (130).

9. Stein herself felt that Roche's criticisms were related to gender prejudice; when Brinnin recounts the exchange between Stein and Roche, he adds his own sexual bias to the story, "she ignored his criticism and took refuge in a feminine . . . reply, telling Roche that he would never have written to a man in such a way" (151).

10. The judgment that Stein's work is too long, repetitive, redundant, diluted, or diverse has had unfortunate critical results. First, it encourages us not to read her works completely and even leads reputable scholars to boast in print that they have never gotten all the way through *The Making of Americans.* Second, it permits a tradition of scholarship that relies on excerpts culled from anthologies, from quotations in previously published scholarship, and, most misleading, from compilations. *Gertrude Stein's America* offers a "gathering" of fragmented, out-of-context tidbits that serves only to document the editor's myth of Stein, yet otherwise scholarly books quote from it. Stein's words are frequently explained away rather than explained. For example, one analysis of "Arthur A Grammar" pivots upon the assertion that it is "a work whose title suggests that grammar belongs to the patriarchy" (Benstock 185) because the grammar is given a man's name, Arthur. Yet such a claim must ignore the opening lines of the piece:

> *Successions of words are so agreeable.*
> *It is about this.*
> *Arthur angelic angelica did spend the time.*
> > *(How To Write 42)*

Here grammar is the succession of words, where a noun and its modifier can transform Arthur into Angelica; consequently, grammar cannot be associated with one gender. The reader further misses the pun arthur/author (even though there is a line that reads "Arthur is an author" [58]), overlooks that Stein often referred to herself as male, and suppresses lines like these: "Daisy a grammar." "Josephine a grammar." "Susan a grammar." "Louisa a grammar." "Francine a grammar." "Mary Rose. A grammar." "Florence a grammar." "Antoinette a grammar." "Alice a grammar." "Winifred a grammar." "Katherine a grammar." and "Mildred a grammar."

11. I am not advocating never quoting from Stein's poetry; that would certainly not serve her work well. But we must proceed with care when quoting from any experimental work. Stimpson, for instance, argues that it is possible to extract any passage from a poem like *Tender Buttons* "because the poem has such a successful decentering device, almost any group of lines, pulled out at random, inflects the 'present sensual' tense" ("The Somagrams of Gertrude Stein" 189). Stimpson's proposal seems justified in the context of the point she is making but should not be taken as a general rule for reading Stein's writing.

12. While many of Stein's works exceed the conventional page lengths for their particular genres (*The Making of Americans* is a thousand-page novel, "Patriarchal Poetry" is a forty-page poem), it was probably the other characteristics (repetition, opaqueness) in connection with length that made publishers take issue with the length of her manuscripts.

13. In "Arthur A Grammar," she substitutes the word "duplicate" for "insistence" but appears to mean the same thing: "I am a grammarian. I believe in duplicates. Duplicate means having it be twice . . . You cannot repeat a duplicate you can duplicate" (*How To Write* 110).

14. Stein tries to put old words to new uses rather than invent new words. In "Poetry and Grammar" she explains why:

> Of course you might say why not invent new names new languages but that cannot be done. It takes a tremendous amount of inner necessity to invent even one word, one can invent imitating movements and emotions in sounds, and in the poetical language of some languages you have that . . . but this has really nothing to do with language. Language as a real thing is not imitation either of sounds or colors or emotions it is an intellectual recreation and there is no possible doubt about it and it is going to go on being that as long as humanity is anything. So everyone must stay with the language their language that has come to be spoken and written and which has in it all the history of its intellectual recreation. (*Lectures in America* 237–38)

15. In an interview that appears as the afterword to *What Are Masterpieces*, Stein discusses the value of reducing words to pieces: "You had to recognize words had lost their value in the nineteenth century particularly towards the end, they had lost much of their variety and I felt that I could not go on, that I had to capture the value of the individual word, find out what it meant and act within it" (100). It is clear from this that breaking words into pieces (capturing "the value of the individual word") was necessary for referential as well as nonreferential language.

16. One unusual piece of punctuation—the equal sign—appears in a late essay, "We Came. A History" (1930); it forces us to read the sentences as

completed equations rather than as progressing points in an exposition, and once again foregrounds the importance and autonomy of each single language event: "How do you like what you have heard.=History must be distinguished.=From mistakes.=History must not be what is=Happening.=History must not be about=Dog and balls in all=The meaning of those=Words history must be=Something unusual and=Nevertheless famous and=Successful" (*Reflection on the Atomic Bomb* 148). The passage, too, seems to assert the importance of language by arguing that history is not events ("what is=Happening") but words ("The meaning of those=Words history must be=").

17. In his headnote to the poem, Thomson links the paragraph structure to Stein's "research into the paragraph both as a literary form and as a carrier of pure emotion" (252).

18. In "On Reading Stein," Michael Davidson identifies the single stumbling block to most Stein scholarship—referential language:

Stein has been haunted by two antithetical criticisms. One proposes that her writing is all play, that it derives strictly out of her early researches with William James and motor automatism and was later invigorated by Cubist formalism. The other proposes that Stein is a kind of hermetic Symbolist who encodes sexual and biographical information in complex little verbal machines which contextualize their own environments. Both views operate on either side of a referential paradigm; one wants her to mean nothing and the other wants her to mean intrinsically. (2–3)

19. A few feminist critics have taken the title at face value, though doing so hasn't provided what DeKoven fears would be a "passkey" to the poem ("by using the title as a passkey, one might *contrive* to interpret some passages" [168; emphasis added]). Introducing the poem in an early anthology of women's poetry, Louise Bernikow splices one line from Stein's poem with her own commentary: " 'Patriarchal Poetry might be what they wanted,' Gertrude Stein wrote in the long poem from which this selection is excerpted, but patriarchal poetry is not what she gave them" (232). Likewise, Shari Benstock acknowledges that the poem is "significantly entitled 'Patriarchal Poetry' " (186). Elyse Blankley offers a fine analysis of the first two stanzas (203) and gives us an inkling of what might be discovered in the other forty pages of the poem. Alicia Ostriker considers "Patriarchal Poetry" significant not only as the title of "the definitive parodic opus on the subject of masculine and feminine voices within culture" but also as "a term she invented" for masculinist literature (49).

20. Chessman's book, *The Public is Invited to Dance: Representation, the Body, and Dialogue in Gertrude Stein,* offers a six-page reading of "Patriarchal Poetry" and thus is the first detailed account of the poem in print. While Chessman and I read several of the same passages and interpret them in strikingly similar ways, her argument concerns the poem's "considerations of

literary origination and ownership" (126)—developing her thesis of "creation as dialogue"—while my argument demonstrates that aesthetic excess is the poem's subject *and* methodology. Thus, Chessman and I both claim that "Patriarchal Poetry" challenges the authority of the dominant culture; however, Chessman's discussion focuses on Stein's revision of the narrative of authority while mine focuses on Stein's aesthetic strategies for challenging and disrupting that authority. Our readings are not only compatible but in concert; in fact, the many points of similarity in our discussions encourage me to think that convincing readings of Stein's experimental poetry are possible.

21. The speaker at the end of Eliot's *The Waste Land* reflects on the poem's cultural collage: "These fragments I have shored against my ruins" (*Complete Poems* 50); in the final fragments to the *Cantos,* Pound says, "I have tried to write Paradise" (*Cantos* 802).

22. In this respect, the entire *Aeneid* is cast as a revision of the *Odyssey:* in the *Aeneid* Troy is destroyed and thus cannot be regained. Odysseus's journey home is replaced by Aeneas's journey of discovery. I am grateful to John Watkins for pointing this out.

23. Though much is at issue here—genre, theme, style—narrative itself is at the core of the problem. In her own fiction and in her essays on narrative, Stein had been working to break the grasp of traditional narrative structure for a long time. Later in this poem she will suggest that the frequency with which patriarchal poetry employs narration reveals something significant about it, "How often do we tell tell tell tale tell tale tell tale might be tell tale" (271).

24. Blankley reads this passage as going back before "spell" where Stein can "be" and "tell": "This is Stein's formula for releasing herself from the burden of the past (including its inherited intellectual and linguistic traditions) by returning language to the free-form primordial melange in which each word vibrates with the energy it possessed before the spell was cast and language fixed" (203). While I generally agree with Blankley's reading, I am convinced that it is the narrative of patriarchal poetry—the tale—that she attempts to elude by setting these words in motion. We might concentrate less on the specific words she precedes with "before" and think more of the way in which "before" as a preposition (the most energetic category of lively words) can move other words.

25. I have already pointed out some allusions to Homer's *Odyssey* and Shakespeare's *Hamlet* in the beginning of the poem. See also phrases like "Once upon a time" (254), "Once" (260, 263, 294), and "by and by" (294), which employ common fairy-tale formulas; "Behold" (255), "Let it be" (261), "In the beginning" (262), and "lily of the valley" (270), which invoke a biblical tone; the phrase "Out out" (255, 273), which recalls *Macbeth*; the nightingale (255), which can only be Keats's; and the "rose" (257), which, as we have seen, is Stein's abbreviation for all of Western literature. Addi-

tionally, the poem is riddled with references to other birds and flowers that are clearly intended as place holders for traditional poetic images, and more important, meant to reveal how mechanical and interchangeable such images have become.

26. I am grateful to my colleague George Rowe for reminding me of this aspect of the sonnet persona, though it must be said that not all sonnet sequences in the tradition are driven by unsatisfied desire in Petrarchan terms. See Spenser, Shakespeare, Barrett Browning, for instance.

27. The elisions are important and could alter the reading of the line. I quote these selections with some reservation having seen many willful readings of excerpts. Certainly I am lifting significant words from one context into another and suppressing surrounding words. This passage, like many Steinian passages, is composed of instrumental and noninstrumental language use. Reading such a stanza is like listening to a conversation in a language with which one is only slightly familiar: individual recognizable words will untether themselves from the blocks of unrecognizable ones, and the listener will begin to make sense out of what she knows by supplying or inventing a syntax and context that she cannot be sure of. Perloff's "word systems" are related to this; in her reading of "Susie Asado," she moves through the poem using certain words as stepping stones or links in a reading. She also shows how a quite different reading can be arrived at by following different word systems. The justification for such readings is that invention is exactly what Stein demands of us in such a passage; in fact, she writes this way to give the reader a sense of foreignness, as I have discussed above. The following is the sentence in which these phrases occur: "I know what it is it is on the one side a to be her to be his to be their to be in an and to be I know what it is it is he who was an known not known was he was at first it was the grandfather then it was not that in that the father not of that grandfather and then she to be to be sure to be sure to be I know to be sure to be I know to be sure to be not as good as that" (272).

28. Not coincidentally, the example from which de Man derives this question concerns a husband who asks the question of his wife; he intends only the figurative level of the question while she answers at the rhetorical or literal level: "asked by his wife whether he wants to have his bowling shoes laced over or laced under, Archie Bunker answers with a question: 'What's the difference?' Being a reader of sublime simplicity, his wife replies by patiently explaining the difference between lacing over and lacing under, whatever this may be, but provokes only ire" (9). It is interesting that de Man considers the wife merely simple, overlooking the possibility that she is lodging a protest against her husband's ill treatment of her by intentionally annoying him with her tedious answer, or even pointing out *his* childishness in not answering her civilly (not to mention, in expecting her to lace his shoes). Except that it provokes humor in him rather than anger, de Man lines up with Archie

Bunker in his analysis of the interaction. Many of Stein's reviewers and critics similarly deem her attempts to restore the literal or elemental properties of language childish.

29. Two of the main recurrent devices in "Patriarchal Poetry" are also central in *How To Write:* the interrogation of metaphor through the question "What is the difference between [A] and [B]" and the constellation of lines based on the formula "When this you see . . ." (remember me; remarkably; you will kiss me; give it to me; you are all to me; will he). Further, both the book and the poem constitute treatises on her theory of language and writing.

30. This contradiction is played out again in her publishing career where she worked vigorously—even maniacally—her whole life for publication and recognition, yet she adamantly refused to compromise her project in order to get it into print—even when the promise of publication for such a compromise was explicit.

31. The grammatical construction of this passage suggests she is "determined [to] re-enter" but also recognizes that in doing so she herself is affected by her association with patriarchal poetry, "entered again and upon" by it.

32. Additionally, "left" appears to connote a political position when she says that she is "left of it Patriarchal Poetry" (275)—that is, more radical than such poetry. Yet, while the poem makes this political distinction, it has already begun to undermine its own claims, for "left of patriarchal poetry" becomes "Patriarchal Poetry left. / Patriarchal Poetry left left. / Patriarchal Poetry left left left right left" (294) as the marching militarism of "left right left" insinuates itself into the lines. She is at once more radical than traditional poetry and deeply suspicious of politicizing innovation—because that can easily become a means of policing it. Certainly several of her male contemporaries would shortly demonstrate the affinities between radical art and fascist politics. Nevertheless, being left of patriarchal poetry is always connected to being left out of it: "They might change it as it can be made to be which is which is the next left out of it in this and this occasionally settled to the same as the left of it to the undertaking of the regular regulation of it" (260). Here again, "left" seems to move along some spectrum of meanings that includes being left out, being politically radical, and being drawn into the militaristic "regular regulation" suggested by the sequence "left right left."

33. In "A Rosy Charm: Gertrude Stein and the Repressed Feminine," Ruddick associates Stein's red colors with the repressed female body, and suggests that menstrual blood is figured as the ink of writing: "Stein in these years not only writes about the body; she also thinks of herself as writing with the body. . . . During the period of *Tender Buttons,* and even somewhat earlier, Stein conceives of her writings as 'secretions.' . . . In 'A PETTICOAT,' . . . 'a white light, a disgrace, an ink spot, a rosy charm'—the third term standing between the two menstrual images of 'a disgrace' and 'a rosy charm' is 'an ink spot.' The association is between the ink spots on Stein's page and the rosy spots on a petticoat" (228).

34. "Let" is, of course, also the imperative refrain of Genesis, and Stein is certainly invoking that ultimate creative power by appropriating the word that signifies it.

35. In a psychoanalytic reading, nonsense passages might represent a feminine prelanguage that existed "before spell," that is, before the authorized language of the grandfathers, fathers, and sons repressed the feminine. I don't pursue such a reading because it is my contention throughout this study that poetic excess is an available feature of ordinary language, especially suited to marginal writers for political and social reasons rather than for strictly psychological ones (except, of course, to the extent that psychology is shaped by political and social forces).

36. In "Canto LXXXI" Pound attributes the birth of modern poetry to the disavowal of conventional metrics: "To break the pentameter, that was the first heave" (518).

Chapter 4. Sylvia Plath

1. For an excellent study of Plath's troubled relationships with her father, mother, husband, and literary precursors, see Steven Gould Axelrod, *Sylvia Plath: The Wound and the Cure of Words.*

2. From very early in her writing career, Plath had identified the *Ladies' Home Journal* and the *New Yorker* as symbolic publishing sites for her divided commitments, domestic and professional. She nevertheless valued publishing in the *New Yorker* more highly. She enjoyed reading the *Ladies' Home Journal* herself, referring to it in a letter to her mother as "my beloved *Journal*" (*Letters Home* 455), but repeatedly disdains its female readership. In her journals she imagines "the unsatisfied ladies" who "scan the stories in *The Ladies' Home Journal*" in order to read about men like her husband; she, on the other hand, is actually married to "the man women read romantic novels for" (201). Similarly, she is self-deprecating about her plans to write a story for the women's magazine, defensively assuring herself, "I don't have to be a bourgeois mother to do it either" (270). To publish in the *Ladies' Home Journal* is merely a "step forward" (270) while publishing in the *New Yorker* is "a minor triumph" (235), a "shot of joy" that "conquers an old dragon and should see me through the next months of writing on the crest of a creative wave" (220). And, once again imagining successful writing in a non-women's magazine as a beauty makeover (an image, ironically, straight out of a women's magazine), she recounts a dream in which publishing in the *New Yorker* gives her "a *New Yorker* glow . . . A pale, affluent nimbus emanating from my generally podgy and dough-colored face" (277).

3. For Plath's own account of this dilemma see *The Journals of Sylvia Plath: 1950–1962* and *Letters Home by Sylvia Plath: Correspondence 1950–1963.* Nearly every study of Plath's life and work proceeds on the assumption that the poet was pulled in these opposing directions. See, for example, Linda

W. Wagner-Martin's *Sylvia Plath: A Biography* or Judith Kroll's *Chapters in a Mythology: The Poetry of Sylvia Plath*. In Kroll's work, the two contradictory pursuits are translated into a mythic system in which the "true self" struggles to overcome the "false self"—with the true and false selves roughly corresponding to the writer/woman opposition:

> The true self (the positive, whole, reborn self) is associated with artistic creativity, and with the autonomy possible only if one is not defined primarily in relation to an other. When the true self has emerged fully, the heroine will not be defined primarily in relation to man—particularly since she considers her attachment to (now-absent) males to be responsible for the origin of the false self. When wifehood, daughterhood, and motherhood appear primarily as male-defined roles . . . , then these roles are negative and may be considered forms of the false self. (10)

Kroll's study encourages us to view Plath's dichotomy in its full complexity; it is not the particular role that oppresses the poet but whether that role has been defined by men or by the poet herself. For more recent efforts to draw these opposing aspects of Plath's life into a more complicated relationship, see Axelrod, *Sylvia Plath: The Wound and the Cure of Words*, Paul Alexander, *Rough Magic: A Biography of Sylvia Plath*, and Jacqueline Rose, *The Haunting of Sylvia Plath*.

4. The text for all of my quotations from Plath's poems is *The Collected Poems*. Since the poems are relatively short, I will give the inclusive page numbers in parentheses in the text the first time the title of the poem is mentioned. Thereafter, I will quote from the poem without supplying page references.

5. See, for example, Kroll (244). Though I think "Words heard" is a substantial poem, Plath herself did not select it for *Ariel;* instead, she chose another poem on the same subject, "The Fearful." This fact may discourage readers from taking the poem more seriously.

6. In *The Telephone Book: Technology—Schizophrenia—Electric Speech,* Avital Ronell, argues just the opposite: that the telephone "destabilizes the identity of self and other" (9). Yet Ronell's larger claim, that because its development and use are historically coincident with the rise of fascism, the telephone represents "the apocalyptic call" ("the call as decisive, verdict, the call as death sentence" [6]), is chillingly consistent with the attitude toward the phone call in "Words Heard." Moreover, this parallel between Ronell's thesis and Plath's poem suggests a way to read the analogy between personal oppression and historical oppression in poems like "Daddy" or "The Swarm."

7. Elizabeth Sigmund, the friend to whom Plath turned for help the night of the discovery, recounts the story of the phone call: "Assia [Gutman] apparently rang Court Green to speak to Ted, but when Sylvia answered Assia pretended to be a man. Sylvia said she knew who it was, but Assia kept up the

charade, asking to speak to Ted" (105). Plath's poem "The Fearful" (256) also employs this detail of the phone call, linking the woman's impersonation of a man to her dubious femininity:

> *This woman on the telephone*
> *Says she is a man, not a woman.*
> . . . .
> *The voice of the woman hollows—*
> *More and more like a dead one,*
> . . . .
> *Worms in the glottal stops.*
> *She hates*
> . . . .
> *The thought of a baby—*
> *Stealer of cells, stealer of beauty—*
> . . . .
> *She would rather be dead than fat.*

The last line of "The Fearful," like the first two stanzas of "Words heard," renders both lovers male in order to suggest that marital infidelity is fundamentally man's crime against woman. The poem concludes with an image of the homosexual sterility of the lovers: "Where the child can never swim, / Where there is only him and him."

8. For discussions of the development of Plath's poetry and the contrasts and similarities between her early and late work, see Robert Lowell, Foreword to *Ariel;* Perloff, "*Angst* and Animism in the Poetry of Sylvia Plath" and "On the Road to *Ariel:* The 'Transitional' Poetry of Sylvia Plath"; Alvarez, "Sylvia Plath"; Howard, "Sylvia Plath: 'And I Have No Face, I Have Wanted to Efface Myself' "; and Nims, "The Poetry of Sylvia Plath: A Technical Analysis."

9. For one of many possible illustrations of this point, see Jo Brans's comparison of Plath's attitude about her March 1961 appendectomy in letters to her mother that "focus on the usual aspects of a hospital stay, the food, the other patients, the good-natured nurses" with her treatment of the same subject in "Tulips," a poem that "shows a patient . . . falling in easily with nothingness and death" (57). Plath's journal entries during the hospital stay provide an even more striking contrast with "Tulips" since in writing for her own journal she did not have to present the optimistic attitude that she would understandably have wanted to convey to a concerned parent in a letter. She chronicles many details and descriptions with incisive humor and narrates making friends with the other patients and entertaining them with her gossip and stories. The mood of the entries can be summarized in just one example: "Three days since my operation and I am myself again: the tough, gossipy, curious enchanting entity I have not been for so long. The life here is made up of details. Petty pleasures and petty annoyances" (305). Such discrepancies

between actual events and the poetic rendering of them ought not to be cause for much remark, but the insistence in much of the Plath criticism that the life and the poetry necessitated each other makes the repetition of this point important.

10. For classic discussions arguing that Plath's actual suicide and the theme of self-destruction in her poetry collaborate to minimize her vision and render her only a minor poet, see Schwartz and Bollas, "The Absence at the Center: Sylvia Plath and Suicide"; Howe, "The Plath Celebration: A Partial Dissent"; Perloff, "On the Road to *Ariel*"; and Oberg, "Sylvia Plath and the New Decadence."

11. *The Collected Poems* provides information—the chronological ordering of poems and a list of the contents of Plath's *Ariel*—that must change the course of Plath scholarship. For powerful and incisive analyses of the fate of Plath's literary remains after her death, see Marjorie Perloff, "The Two Ariels: The (Re)making of the Sylvia Plath Canon" and "Sylvia Plath's *Collected Poems:* A Review Essay" and Steven Gould Axelrod's "The Second Destruction of Sylvia Plath." Perloff had been dubious about how Plath's literary executors had constructed the Plath myth (of "a courageous free spirit who sacrificed her life for her art" [581]) even without the benefit of the information in *The Collected Poems;* see "Extremist Poetry: Some Versions of the Sylvia Plath Myth." Likewise, a handful of prescient scholars recognized the impulse toward rebirth and regeneration even in Hughes's *Ariel;* see Judith Kroll, *Chapters in a Mythology: The Poetry of Sylvia Plath* (for example, 106, 165, 186–87, 199), and Margaret Dickie Uroff, *Sylvia Plath and Ted Hughes* (for example, 146, 155, 166–67). Susan R. Van Dyne has led the way in reassessing Plath's *Ariel* poems in light of the information revealed in the *Collected Poems* and the manuscript collection made available to scholars at Smith College; see " 'More Terrible Than She Ever Was': The Manuscripts of Sylvia Plath's Bee Poems" and *Revising Life: Sylvia Plath's Ariel Poems.*

12. For studies of influences on Plath's work, see for example Nims, "The Poetry of Sylvia Plath: A Technical Analysis"; Gilbert, "In Yeats' House: The Death and Resurrection of Sylvia Plath"; Lane, "Influence and Originality in Plath's Poems"; and Uroff, *Sylvia Plath and Ted Hughes.*

13. Perloff also notices the pun on "Assia" in "The Two Ariels" (11). Plath continues to play with the name in other poems, "Wintering" ([217–19] "Black asininity"), "Medusa" ([224–26] "your wishes / Hiss at my sins"), "Lesbos" ([227–30] "Viciousness in the kitchen! / The potatoes hiss"), "Purdah" ([242–44] "I am his. / Even in his // Absence"), "Lady Lazarus" ([244–47] "Ash, ash"), and probably others. The sound of the name is often associated with a snake's hiss, perhaps because Assia gave Plath "an articulated toy snake of scorch-patterned bamboo joints" as a gift (*Poems* 295).

14. Most readers have assumed that "Medusa" is about Plath's mother; indeed, she had originally titled it "Mum: Medusa." However, it should be obvious from Plath's own statements regarding personal subject matter that

a ritual designed to maintain the status quo. . . . She is covered by the others, like a virgin being prepared for sacrifice or a corpse being shrouded. . . . The townspeople have no identities beyond their roles . . . and they strip her of her individuality" (29).

McCann goes even beyond Perloff in her reading of the long white box; it does not merely prefigure the speaker's death but rather confirms it: "The operation, from the point of view of the townspeople, is a great success: the patient dies" (29). All of these readings put too much confidence in the speaker's point of view.

23. She might also be referring to another circus trick that has some of the same elements as Sawing the Lady, in which the magician's assistant stands against a board (or spins on a revolving disk) unflinchingly while the magician throws knives that outline her body as they pierce the board. In this trick, the assistant would be a "pillar of white," that is, holding as still and straight as a pillar so she won't get hit and appearing white from calmness (or, more likely, fear; and, of course, "white" because her skin is mostly bare in the skimpy costume that makes her look more vulnerable and makes the whole trick more sensational), in a "blackout of knives" as the knives flash and flicker in their flight toward her. If this is the trick the poem has in mind, then the speaker is more justified in her sense of isolation since the Live Target trick depends upon skill rather than optical illusion and thus the assistant's risk is greater. In either case, the speaker feels that her stoical performance has gone unnoticed by those who view her and fears there is some other trick that she isn't in on.

24. Margaret Dickie Uroff also observes this level of meaning: "In the box imagery, with its rampant life, Plath begins to develop a familiar situation in her poetry: inner turmoil and outer form" (148).

25. An unusual discarded line that seems to make the scapegoat pregnant complicates the female imagery even more: "The sweat of his efforts a rain / [On the world that grew under his belly]" (*Original Drafts* 14).

26. The inconsistent pronouns bear this out: the singular "Somebody" is referred to in the fifth line with the plural pronoun "they." The phrase "our town" in the first line may also indicate the urge to generalize.

27. My reading of this phrase is suggested by a similar image of blood stains as a blossoming flower in "Poppies in October" (240) where the heart of "the woman in the ambulance / . . . blooms through her coat so astoundingly."

28. Perloff suggests that the six jars of honey represent the six poems written before the "Terrible Lyrics" of October 1962 that Plath included in her *Ariel* ("The Two Ariels" 12).

29. For an excellent and disturbing account of how Plath's papers have been destroyed, suppressed, edited, sealed, and tampered with, see Axelrod, "The Second Destruction of Sylvia Plath."

30. There are numerous examples of editorial comments that attempt to manipulate the reader. In a note on "Death & Co.," for instance, Hughes first

quotes Plath's account of the subject of the poem and then contradicts it, "The *actual* occasion was a visit by two *well-meaning* men who invited T[ed] H[ughes] to live abroad at a tempting salary, and whom *she therefore resented*" (*Poems* 294; emphasis added). Likewise, in the *Journals* (for which Hughes is the consulting editor), an italicized intrusion from the editor explains that the rage Plath records in the following pages is misdirected toward her husband and young women ("the real source is her father"); further, it characterizes a problem that was significant to Plath as a "small incident": "In the passage that follows it is a rage against her husband in which a small incident takes on enormous proportions, and it is quickly transferred to some girls in a public park" (207). And in *Letters Home,* Aurelia Plath prefaces the letters written during the breakup of Plath's marriage: "These letters were, of course, written under great strain. They were meant, as were her many phone calls to me during this period, to reassure herself as well. They are desperate letters, and their very desperation make[s] it difficult to read them with any objectivity; I could not, at the time. But I must ask the reader to remember the circumstances in which they were written and to remember also that they represent one side of an extremely complex situation" (459). This seems an unnecessary preface to a selection of letters that is so heavily edited it has almost as many ellipses as words. The editing is what makes them difficult to read "with any objectivity."

31. My reading of "Words" differs greatly from others. I think it is arguable that those words that are "dry and riderless" at the end of her life are not her own words at all but the same ones she had "heard over the phone" (or words of that nature). Understood this way, the poem is no longer in "metaphoric shambles" (Stilwell [45]). The metaphoric movement from axes (that strike wood), to echoes (the ring of the ax on the wood), to sap welling at the site of the gash, to tears, to water, to "the bottom of the pool" where "fixed stars / Govern a life" enacts the dissolution of language's power to hurt while it simultaneously acknowledges its continuing power to control. That is, in my reading, the words that she experiences as painful ax strokes at one time eventually lose their power to hurt her; but the results of those words (in Plath's case, abandonment, poverty, isolation, excessive responsibility) continue to determine her days.

Chapter 5. The Black Arts Movement

1. In "The Black Arts Movement," an essay in *The Black Aesthetic,* Larry Neal dates the origin of the movement a year earlier "in the spring of 1964" (277) when "LeRoi Jones, Charles Patterson, William Patterson, Clarence Reed, Johnny Moore, and a number of other Black artists opened the Black Arts Repertoire Theatre School" (277). See "The Black Arts (Harlem, Politics, Search for a New Life)" for Baraka's history of the movement (Jones, *Autobiography* 202–29).

2. The text of the foreword is a poem by Langston Hughes titled "Fire."

3. In one of the most unusual discussions of the black aesthetic, Houston A. Baker Jr. calls the idealistic criticism of Karenga, Neal, Gayle, and others "*conative utterances*" that "attempt to *will* into being a new art and criticism" (134): "Taken as representative discourse, they illustrate the distressingly limited amount of information conveyed by conative utterances. Such speech acts fail as analytical statements because their speakers substitute will for reason, volition for analysis, and desire for systematic observation" ("The Black Spokesman as Critic: Reflections on the Black Aesthetic" 136).

4. For contemporary descriptions and delineations of the particular features of the black aesthetic, see Fuller, "Towards a Black Aesthetic"; Lee, "Towards a Definition: Black Poetry of the Sixties (After LeRoi Jones)"; and Rodgers, "Black Poetry—Where It's At."

5. Though by 1931 Johnson insisted that "the passing of traditional dialect as a medium for Negro poets is complete" ("Preface to the Second Edition" of *The Book of American Negro Poetry* 3), Langston Hughes, Sterling Brown, Zora Neale Hurston, and many others resisted that decree and found new, even radical, uses for African-American dialect writing.

6. Jones (Baraka) himself moved away from cultural nationalism by the early 1970s, though his stylistics did not change then. See Werner Sollers, *Amiri Baraka/LeRoi Jones: The Quest for a Populist Modernism* (especially chapters 8, 9, and 10) for an account of Jones's shifting conceptions of art and politics.

7. That the line is formulaic rather than shocking is further evidenced in its allusion to a poem written nearly a decade earlier. Allen Ginsberg's "America" (1956) had famously urged: "[America,] Go fuck yourself with your atom bomb" (31). The allusion to Ginsberg, the chief Beat poet, is apt in this section, which vilifies black bohemians.

8. The "fantastic dish" also suggests the conventional revenge concoction made from the children of the oppressor; for instance, Tereus eats his son Itys in the Philomela myth.

9. A short bibliography of pertinent commentary on gender relations among African Americans might include Mualana Ron Karenga at one extreme and Michele Wallace at the other. Karenga's views on women are condensed in *The Quotable Karenga,* a collection of epigrammatic sayings, in the section on women titled "House System." Karenga asserts there: "What makes a woman appealing is femininity and she can't be feminine without being submissive," "The role of woman is to inspire her man, educate their children and participate in social development," and "We say Male supremacy is based on three things: tradition, acceptance, and reason" (20–21). I cite Wallace in my discussion because her prose work deploys feminist excess, which parallels such excess in poetry, as the quotations from *Black Macho* should indicate. For a range of studies, see Cleaver, *Soul On Ice;* Hernton, *Sex and Racism in America;* Ladner, *Tomorrow's Tomorrow: The Black Woman.*

Most recently, "Reconstructing Black Masculinity," a chapter in bell hooks's *Black Looks,* is a particularly informative, careful, thorough, and moderate history and analysis of the subject.

10. Though Malcolm X had separated from the Nation of Islam and many of its views at the end of his life, and though these developments are recorded at the end of *The Autobiography of Malcolm X,* the book still promotes a suspicion of women, especially of women's talk, and an acceptance of distinct and traditional roles for the sexes—ideas that were common at the time. For his assertion that "women talked too much," see 225–26.

11. In an article published in 1968, two years before the epigraph I have quoted indicating that black women must be *women* first, Lee appears to include women in his injunction that black poets must be *black* first: "A black poet is not a Negro; he is first and foremost a *black man* (or woman)" ("Toward a Black Aesthetic" 27); however, the later poem indicates that gender is the foremost consideration for women, then race, and perhaps the parenthetical inclusion of women in his 1968 statement reveals an equivocation about the priorities of race and gender for black men and black women.

12. Wallace suggests that "Richard Wright's *Native Son* was the starting point of the black writer's love affair with Black Macho" (55).

13. Kalamu ya Salaam attacked Giovanni for writing nonrevolutionary poems in terms that are unabashedly sexist: "Nikki has gone quietly crazy" and "I betcha Nikki wanted to be married" (150, qtd. in McDowell). Baraka's poem "Niggy the Ho" (*Selected Poetry* 246–47) depicts Giovanni as an opportunist who has prostituted herself (racially: Nikki/Niggy and sexually: ho/whore) to white audiences. For a thorough survey of Giovanni's career and reception, and a discussion of Salaam's review, see Margaret B. McDowell, "Groundwork for a More Comprehensive Criticism of Nikki Giovanni."

14. Two other useful discussions of Giovanni's postmilitant poetry are Paula Giddings, "Nikki Giovanni: Take a Chance on Feeling," and William J. Harris, "Sweet Soft Essence of Possibility: The Poetry of Nikki Giovanni," in Mari Evans, *Black Women Writers (1950–1980).*

15. After 1970 Giovanni's work continues to insist on a redefinition of "revolution" that often reads as a defense of her own postmilitant writing. "When I Die" (*My House* 1972, 36–37) indicts the domineering liberation movement leaders and denies their political authority:

> my rebirth was stifled not by the master
> but the slave

> and . . . i know that touching was and still is and will always be the true
> revolution.

"My House" (67–68) again declares that acts of love, not acts of hate, are revolutionary:

> i'll make fudge and call

it love and touch my lips
to the chocolate warmth
and smile at old men and call
it revolution.

In an interview with Claudia Tate published in 1984, Giovanni is still insisting that acts of love and kindness are more revolutionary than militancy: "I bought three new windows for my mother's basement. Have you ever bought windows for your mother's basement? It's revolutionary! It really is" (Tate 61).

16. Sanchez dramatizes this important distinction between sexual and emotional availability in a play that offers a scathing critique of the revolutionary machismo. See *Uh-Uh; But How Do It Free Us?*

17. Sanchez uses the slash mark as punctuation within the line. In quoting short passages of her poems incorporated into my text, I have used one slash to indicate her usage, two to indicate a line break, and three to indicate a stanza break.

18. For a discussion of the range of meanings in the phrase "how I got ovah," see the opening paragraphs of Estella M. Sales, "Contradictions in Black Life: Recognized and Reconciled in *How I Got Ovah*." For overviews of Rodgers's shift from militant to nonmilitant poetry, see Angelene Jamison and Bettye J. Parker-Smith.

19. Brooks encountered the new black poets at the second Fisk Writers' Conference in 1967. She discusses her transition to their ideals and values in an interview with Claudia Tate in *Black Women Writers at Work* (39–48) and in her autobiography, *Report from Part One* (83–86).

20. In *A Life of Gwendolyn Brooks,* George Kent relates the conflicts Brooks had with some of the younger writers about the use of profanity in the new black poetry: "A walkout issue for Don L. Lee was Gwendolyn's questioning the value of so much profanity in a work of art . . . It was Gwendolyn's view that profanity at some point became trite, detracting from the quality of a work" (209). In the interview with Tate, Brooks insists that her poetry does assume a militant posture, even if it does not employ obscenity and violence (42–43). And in an appendix to her autobiography entitled "Marginalia," Brooks both distinguishes herself from and claims kinship with the younger poets: "My newish voice will not be an imitation of the contemporary young black voice, which I do so admire, but an extending adaptation of today's G.B. voice" (183).

21. During the period under discussion, Clifton produced *Good Times Poems* (1969), *Good News About the Earth: New Poems* (1972), and *An Ordinary Woman* (1974), all published with Random House, a fact that points to her independence. In "A Simple Language" (Evans 137–38), Clifton distinguishes herself from "some of [her] friends" who were bothered that she published with a white, mainstream company: "Sometimes I think that the most anger comes from ones who were late in discovering that when the

world said nigger it meant them too. I grew up knowing that the world meant me too but that was the world's insanity and not mine" (138). Scholarship on this unusual poet is scarce, but one can get a sense of her views in "We Are the Grapevine," an essay Clifton published in *Essence,* and a discussion of her "Christian optimism" in Audrey T. McCluskey, "Tell the Good News: A View of the Works of Lucille Clifton."

22. Since Shange uses the slash mark in her lines, I will designate line breaks with the double slash and stanza breaks with a triple slash.

23. See, for example, Madhubuti regarding Lucille Clifton's loyalty to men; Robert Staples "response to angry black feminists" in the *Black Scholar* (Mar.-Apr. 1979) and the debates about Wallace's and Shange's books that followed (May-June 1979); and Lorde's *Sister Outsider.*

24. See the *Black Scholar* gender debates, above.

25. *Some Men* was first published privately by Shange and the illustrator Wopo Holup. Since that edition is not easily available, I quote from "Some Men" as it appears as a long poem in *A Daughter's Geography.*

Works Cited

Ai. *Cruelty.* Boston: Houghton Mifflin, 1973.

———. *Cruelty/Killing Floor.* Foreword by Caroline Forché. New York: Thunder's Mouth Press, 1987.

———. *Killing Floor.* Boston: Houghton Mifflin, 1979.

———. *Fate.* Boston: Houghton Mifflin, 1991.

———. *Greed.* New York: Norton, 1993.

———. *Sin.* Boston: Houghton Mifflin, 1986.

Alexander, Paul, ed. *Ariel Ascending: Writings About Sylvia Plath.* New York: Harper, 1985.

———. *Rough Magic: A Biography of Sylvia Plath.* New York: Viking, 1991.

Alvarez, A. "Sylvia Plath: A Memoir." In *Ariel Ascending: Writings About Sylvia Plath,* edited by Paul Alexander. New York: Harper, 1985. 188–213.

Axelrod, Steven Gould. "The Second Destruction of Sylvia Plath." *American Poetry Review* 14, no. 2 (Mar./Apr. 1985): 17–18.

———. *Sylvia Plath: The Wound and the Cure of Words.* Baltimore: Johns Hopkins University Press, 1990.

Baker, Houston A., Jr. "The Black Spokesman as Critic: Reflections on the Black Aesthetic." In *The Journey Back: Issues in Black Literature and Criticism.* Chicago: University of Chicago Press, 1980. 132–43.

———. *A Many-Colored Coat of Dreams: The Poetry of Countee Cullen.* Detroit: Broadside Press, 1974.

———. *Modernism and the Harlem Renaissance.* Chicago: Chicago University Press, 1987.

Baraka, Amiri. See also LeRoi Jones.

———, and Amina Baraka, eds. *Confirmation: An Anthology of African American Women.* New York: Quill, 1983.

Barthes, Roland. "Listening." In *The Responsibility of Forms: Critical Essays on Music, Art, and Representation.* Translated by Richard Howard. New York: Hill, 1985. 245–60.

————. "The Third Meaning." In *Image, Music, Text*. Trans. Stephen Heath. New York: Hill, 1977. 52–68.

Benstock, Shari. *Women of the Left Bank: Paris 1900–1940*. Austin: University of Texas Press, 1986.

Benvenuto, Richard. "Words within Words: Dickinson's Use of the Dictionary." *ESQ* 29 (1983): 46–55.

Bernikow, Louise, ed. *The World Split Open: Four Centuries of Women Poets in England and America, 1552–1950*. New York: Vintage, 1974.

Bernstein, Charles. *A Poetics*. Cambridge: Harvard University Press, 1992.

"*The Black Scholar* Reader's Forum on Black Male/Female Relationships." *Black Scholar* 10, nos. 8, 9 (May/June 1979): 14–67.

Blankley, Elyse. "Beyond the 'Talent of Knowing': Gertrude Stein and the New Woman." In *Critical Essays on Gertrude Stein*, edited by Michael J. Hoffman. Boston: Hall, 1986. 196–209.

Bridgman, Richard. *Gertrude Stein in Pieces*. New York: Oxford University Press, 1970.

Brinnin, John Malcolm. *The Third Rose: Gertrude Stein and Her World*. New York: Grove, 1959.

Broe, Mary Lynn. *Protean Poetic: The Poetry of Sylvia Plath*. Columbia: University of Missouri Press, 1980.

Brooks, A. Russell. "The Motif of Dynamic Change in Black Revolutionary Poetry." *CLA Journal* 15, no. 1 (Sept. 1971): 7–17.

Brooks, Gwendolyn. *Report from Part One*. Detroit: Broadside Press, 1972.

Buckingham, Willis J., ed. *Emily Dickinson's Reception in the 1890s: A Documentary History*. Pittsburgh: University of Pittsburgh Press, 1989.

Burns, Robert. "A Red, Red Rose." In *Robert Burns: Selected Poems*, edited by Carol McGuirk. London: Penguin Books, 1993. 178.

Butscher, Edward. "In Search of Sylvia: An Introduction." In *Sylvia Plath: The Woman and the Work*, edited by Edward Butscher. New York: Dodd, 1977. 3–29.

————, ed. *Sylvia Plath: Method and Madness*. New York: Seabury, 1976.

————, ed. *Sylvia Plath: The Woman and the Work*. New York: Dodd, 1977.

Cameron, Sharon. *Choosing Not Choosing: Dickinson's Fascicles*. Chicago: University of Chicago Press, 1992.

Chessman, Harriet Scott. *The Public Is Invited to the Dance: Representation, the Body, and Dialogue in Gertrude Stein*. Stanford: Stanford University Press, 1989.

Cleaver, Eldridge. *Soul On Ice*. 1968. New York: Dell, 1992.

Clifford, Vance. [Arthur LeRoy Kaser.] "Bursting Into Poetry." In *Minstrel Laughs*. Chicago: T.S. Denison and Co., 1927. 29–32.

Clifton, Lucille. *Good News About the Earth: New Poems*. New York: Random House, 1972.

————. *Good Times: Poems*. New York: Random House, 1969.

————. *An Ordinary Woman*. New York: Random House, 1974.

————. "A Simple Language." In *Black Women Writers*, edited by Mari Evans. Garden City, N.Y.: Anchor/Doubleday, 1984. 137–38.

————. "We Are the Grapevine." *Essence* 16, no. 1 (May 1985): 129.

Cortez, Jayne. *Festivals and Funerals*. New York: Phrase Text, 1971.

————. *Firespitter*. New York: Bola Press, 1982.

————. *Pisstained Stairs and the Monkey Man's Wares*. New York: Phrase Text, 1969.

————. *Scarifications*. New York: Bola Press, 1973.

Crane, Hart. *Letters*. Berkeley: University of California Press, 1965.

Crouch, Stanley. "Big Star Calling." *Yardbird Reader* 5 (1976): 99.

Cullen, Countee, ed. Foreword to *Caroling Dusk: An Anthology of Verse by Negro Poets*. New York: Harper, 1927. ix–xiv.

Cushman, Stephen. *Fictions of Form in American Poetry*. Princeton: Princeton University Press, 1993.

Davidson, Michael. "On Reading Stein." *L=A=N=G=U=A=G=E* 1, no. 16 (1978): 2–4.

Davis, Ossie. "On Malcolm X." In *The Autobiography of Malcolm X*, by Alex Haley and Malcolm X. New York: Ballantine Books, 1965. 457–60.

DeKoven, Marianne. *A Different Language: Gertrude Stein's Experimental Language*. Madison: University of Wisconsin Press, 1983.

de Man, Paul. *Allegories of Reading: Figural Language in Rousseau, Nietzsche, Rilke, and Proust*. New Haven: Yale University Press, 1979.

Dickinson, Emily. *The Manuscript Books of Emily Dickinson*, edited by R. W. Franklin. 2 vols. Cambridge, Mass.: The Belknap Press, 1981.

————. *The Poems of Emily Dickinson*. Edited by Thomas H. Johnson. 3 vols. Cambridge: Harvard University Press, 1955.

————. *The Letters of Emily Dickinson*. Edited by Thomas H. Johnson and Theodora Ward. 3 vols. Cambridge: Harvard University Press, 1958.

Eliot, T.S. "The Waste Land." In *Collected Poems: 1909–1962*. New York: Harcourt, 1963. 51–76.

Emerson, Ralph Waldo. "The Poet." In *The Oxford Authors: Ralph Waldo Emerson*, edited by Richard Poirier. Oxford: Oxford University Press, 1990. 197–215.

Erkkila, Betsy. *The Wicked Sisters: Women Poets, Literary History, and Discord*. New York: Oxford University Press, 1992.

Evans, Mari, ed. *Black Women Writers (1950–1980): A Critical Evaluation*. New York: Doubleday, 1984.

Fifer, Elizabeth. "Is Flesh Advisable? The Interior Theater of Gertrude Stein." *Signs* 4, no. 3 (1979): 472–83.

"Foreword." *Fire!! A Quarterly Devoted to the Younger Negro Artists* 1, no. 1. (Nov. 1926): n.p.

Fuller, Hoyt W. "Towards a Black Aesthetic." In *The Black Aesthetic*, edited by Addison Gayle Jr. New York: Doubleday, 1972. 3–15.

Gates, Henry Louis, Jr. *Figures in Black: Words, Signs, and the "Racial" Self*. New York: Oxford University Press, 1987.

Gayle, Addison, Jr., ed. *The Black Aesthetic*. New York: Doubleday, 1972.

Giddings, Paula. "Nikki Giovanni: Taking a Chance on Feeling." In *Black Women Writers (1950–1980): A Critical Evaluation*, edited by Mari Evans. New York: Doubleday, 1984. 211–17.

Gilbert, Sandra M. "In Yeats' House: The Death and Resurrection of Sylvia Plath." In *Critical Essays on Sylvia Plath*, edited by Linda W. Wagner. Boston: Hall, 1984. 204–22.

———, and Susan Gubar. *The Madwoman in the Attic: The Woman Writer and the Nineteenth-Century Literary Imagination.* New Haven: Yale University Press, 1979.

Ginsberg, Allen. "America." In *Howl and Other Poems.* 1956. Reprint, San Francisco: City Lights Books, 1993. 31–34.

Giovanni, Nikki. *Black Feeling Black Talk.* New York: Black Dialogue Press, 1967; Detroit: Broadside Press, 1968.

———. *Black Judgement.* Detroit: Broadside Press, 1968.

———. "Black Poems, *Poseurs* and Power." *Negro Digest* 18, no. 8 (June 1969): 30–34.

———. *Ego-Tripping and Other Poems for Young People.* New York: Lawrence Hill, 1973.

———. "An Interview with Nikki Giovanni." With Bonner Carrington. *Black American Literature Forum* 18.1 (1984): 29–30.

———. *My House: Poems.* New York: Morrow, 1972; New York: Quill, 1983.

———. *Re:Creation.* Detroit: Broadside Press, 1970.

———. *Spin a Soft Black Song: Poems for Children.* New York: Hill and Wang, 1971.

———. *Those Who Ride the Night Winds.* New York: Morrow, 1983.

———. *Vacation Time: Poems for Children.* New York: Morrow, 1980.

———. *The Women and the Men.* New York: Morrow, 1975.

Griffin, Susan. "Red Shoes." In *The Eros of Everyday Life: Essays on Ecology, Gender and Society.* New York: Doubleday, 1995. 161–76.

Haas, Robert Bartlett. *A Primer for the Gradual Understanding of Gertrude Stein.* Los Angeles: Black Sparrow, 1971.

———. Afterword to *What Are Masterpieces,* by Gertrude Stein. 1940. Reprint, New York: Pitman, 1970. 97–104.

Haley, Alex, and Malcolm X. *The Autobiography of Malcolm X.* New York: Ballantine Books, 1965.

Hamilton, Edith. *Mythology: Timeless Tales of Gods and Heroes.* 1940. New York: New American Library, 1969.

Harris, Trudier, and Thadious M. Davis, eds. *Dictionary of Literary Biography.* Vol. 41: *Afro-American Poets Since 1955.* Detroit: Gale Research, 1985.

Harris, William J. "Sweet Soft Essence of Possibility: The Poetry of Nikki Giovanni." In *Black Women Writers (1950–1980): A Critical Evaluation,* edited by Mari Evans. New York: Doubleday, 1984. 218–28.

Harrison, Gilbert A., ed. *Gertrude Stein's America.* New York: Liveright, 1974.

Hawthorne, Nathaniel. *The Scarlet Letter.* 1850. Reprint, Columbus: Ohio State University Press, 1962.

Hernton, Calvin C. *Sex and Racism in America.* 1965. Reprint, New York: Anchor/Doubleday, 1988.

Hoffman, Michael J., ed. *Critical Essays on Gertrude Stein.* Boston: Hall, 1986.

Honey, Maureen, ed. *Shadowed Dreams: Women's Poetry of the Harlem Renaissance.* New Brunswick: Rutgers University Press, 1989.

hooks, bell. "Reconstructing Black Masculinity." In *Black Looks: Race and Representation.* Boston: South End Press, 1992. 87–113.

Howard, Richard. "'And I Have No Face. I Have Wanted to Efface Myself . . .' " In *The Art of Sylvia Plath: A Symposium,* edited by Charles Newman. Bloomington: Indiana University Press, 1970. 77–88.

Howe, Irving. "The Plath Celebration: A Partial Dissent." In *Sylvia Plath: The Woman and the Work,* edited by Edward Butscher. New York: Dodd, 1977. 225–35.

Howe, Susan. *My Emily Dickinson.* Berkeley: North Atlantic, 1985.

Hughes, Langston. *The Collected Poems of Langston Hughes.* Edited by Arnold Rampersad and David Roessel. New York: Knopf, 1994.

———. "The Negro Artist and the Racial Mountain." *Nation* 122 (1926): 692–94.

Jamison, Angelene. "Imagery in the Women Poems: The Art of Carolyn Rodgers." In *Black Women Writers,* edited by Mari Evans. Garden City, N.Y.: Anchor/Doubleday, 1984. 377–92.

Johnson, James Weldon, ed. "Preface to the First Edition." In *The Book of American Negro Poetry.* 1922. Reprint, New York: Harcourt, 1931. 9–48.

———. "Preface to the Second Edition." In *The Book of American Negro Poetry.* 1922. Reprint, New York: Harcourt, 1931. 3–8.

Jones, LeRoi. See also Amiri Baraka.

———. *The Autobiography of LeRoi Jones/Amiri Baraka.* New York: Freundlich Books, 1984.

———. "Black Dada Nihilismus." In *Selected Poems: Amiri Baraka/LeRoi Jones.* New York: William Morrow, 1979. 40–42.

———. *Selected Poetry of Amiri Baraka/LeRoi Jones.* New York: William Morrow, 1979.

Jones, LeRoi, and Larry Neal, eds. *Black Fire: An Anthology of Afro-American Writing.* New York: Morrow, 1968.

Juhasz, Suzanne, Cristanne Miller, and Martha Nell Smith. *Comic Power in Emily Dickinson.* Austin: University of Texas Press, 1993.

Karenga, Ron. "Black Cultural Nationalism." In *The Black Aesthetic,* edited by Addison Gayle Jr. New York: Doubleday, 1972. 32–38.

———. *The Quotable Karenga.* Edited by Clyde Halisi and James Mtume. Los Angeles: US Organization, 1967.

Kent, George E. *A Life of Gwendolyn Brooks.* Lexington: University Press of Kentucky, 1990.

Kranidas, Thomas. *The Fierce Equation: A Study of Milton's Decorum.* London: Mouton, 1965.

Kroll, Judith. *Chapters in a Mythology: The Poetry of Sylvia Plath.* New York: Harper, 1976.

Ladner, Joyce A. *Tomorrow's Tomorrow: The Black Woman.* Garden City, N.Y.: Doubleday, 1971.

Lane, Gary, ed. *Sylvia Plath: New Views on the Poetry.* Baltimore: Johns Hopkins University Press, 1979.

———. "Influence and Originality in Plath's Poems." In *Sylvia Plath: New Views on the Poetry,* edited by Gary Lane. Baltimore: Johns Hopkins University Press, 1979. 116–37.

Lanham, Richard A. *A Handlist of Rhetorical Terms: A Guide for Students of English Literature.* 2nd ed. Berkeley: University of California Press, 1991.

Leder, Sharon, with Andrea Abbott. *The Language of Exclusion: The Poetry* of *Emily Dickinson and Christina Rossetti.* New York: Greenwood Press, 1987.

Lee, Don L. See also Haki Madhubuti.

———. *Don't Cry, Scream.* Detroit: Broadside Press, 1969.

———. *Think Black!* Detroit: Broadside Press, 1969.

———. "Toward a Black Aesthetic." *Negro Digest* 17, nos. 11, 12 (Sept./Oct. 1968): 27–32.

———. "Toward a Definition: Black Poetry of the Sixties (After LeRoi Jones)." In *The Black Aesthetic,* edited by Addison Gayle Jr. New York: Doubleday, 1972. 235–47.

———. *We Walk the Way of the New World.* Detroit: Broadside Press, 1970.

Lewis, Wyndham. "The Prose Song of Gertrude Stein." In *Critical Essays on Gertrude Stein,* edited by Michael Hoffman. Boston: Hall, 1986. 54–55.

Lorde, Audre. *The New York Head Shop and Museum.* Detroit: Broadside Press, 1974.

———. *Sister Outsider: Essays and Speeches.* Trumansburg, N.Y.: Crossing Press, 1984.

Lowell, Robert. Foreword to *Ariel,* by Sylvia Plath. New York: Harper, 1961.

Madhubuti, Haki. "Sonia Sanchez: The Bringer of Memories." In *Black Women Writers (1950–1980): A Critical Evaluation,* edited by Mari Evans. Garden City, N.Y.: Anchor/Doubleday, 1984. 419–32.

———. "Lucille Clifton: Warm Water, Greased Legs, and Dangerous Poetry." In *Black Women Writers (1950–1980): A Critical Evaluation,* edited by Mari Evans. Garden City, N.Y.: Anchor/Doubleday, 1984. 150–60.

Maloff, Saul. "The Poet as Cult Goddess." *Commonweal* 103, no. 12 (1976): 371–74.

May, Elaine Tyler. *Homeward Bound: American Families in the Cold War Era.* New York: Basic Books, 1988.

McCann, Janet. "Sylvia Plath's Bee Poems." *South and West: An International Literary Magazine* 14, no. 4: 28–36.

McCluskey, Audrey T. "Tell the Good News: A View of the Works of Lucille Clifton." In *Black Women Writers,* edited by Mari Evans. Garden City, N.Y.: Anchor/Doubleday, 1984. 139–49.

McDowell, Margaret B. "Groundwork for a More Comprehensive Criticism of Nikki Giovanni." In *Studies in Black American Literature.* Vol. 2: *Belief vs. Theory in Black American Literary Criticism,* edited by Joe Weixlmann and Chester J. Fontenot. Greenwood, Fla.: Penkevill, 1986. 135–60.

Mellow, James R. *Charmed Circle: Gertrude Stein and Company.* New York: Praeger, 1974.

Messenter, Ann. *His and Hers: Essays in Restoration and Eighteenth-Century Literature.* Lexington: University Press of Kentucky, 1986.

Miller, Adam David. "Some Observations on a Black Aesthetic." In *The Black Aesthetic,* edited by Addison Gayle Jr. New York: Doubleday, 1972. 397–404.

Miller, Cris. "Terms and Golden Words: Alternatives of Control in Dickinson's Poetry." *ESQ* 28 (1982): 48–62.

Miller, Cristanne. *Emily Dickinson: A Poet's Grammar.* Cambridge: Harvard University Press, 1987.

―――. "The Humor of Excess." In *Comic Power in Emily Dickinson,* by Suzanne Juhasz, Cristanne Miller, and Martha Nell Smith. Austin: University of Texas Press, 1993. 103–36.

Moynihan, Daniel Patrick. *The Negro Family: The Case for National Action.* Washington, D.C.: Superintendent of Documents, US Government Printing Office, 1965.

Neal, Larry. "The Black Arts Movement." In *The Black Aesthetic,* edited by Addison Gayle Jr. New York: Doubleday, 1972. 272–90.

Neruda, Pablo. "Explaining a Few Things." In *Residence on Earth and Other Poems.* Translated by Angel Flores. 1946. Reprint, New York: Gordian Press, 1976.

Newman, Charles, ed. *The Art of Sylvia Plath: A Symposium.* Bloomington: Indiana University Press, 1970.

Nims, John Frederick. "The Poetry of Sylvia Plath: A Technical Analysis." In *Ariel Ascending: Writings About Sylvia Plath,* edited by Paul Alexander. New York: Harper, 1985. 46–60.

Oberg, Arthur K. "Sylvia Plath and the New Decadence." In *Sylvia Plath: The Woman and the Work,* edited by Edward Butscher. New York: Dodd, 1977. 177–85.

Ovid. *Metamorphoses.* Vols. 1 and 2. Translated by Frank Justice Miller. The Loeb Classical Library. Cambridge: Harvard University Press, 1916.

Ostriker, Alicia. *Stealing the Language: The Emergence of Women's Poetry in America.* Boston: Beacon, 1986.

Parker, Patricia. *Literary Fat Ladies: Rhetoric, Gender, Property.* New York: Methuen, 1987.

Parker-Smith, Bettye J. "Running Wild in Her Soul: The Poetry of Carolyn Rodgers." In *Black Women Writers,* edited by Mari Evans. Garden City, N.Y.: Anchor/Doubleday, 1984. 393–410.

Perkins, George, ed. *American Poetic Theory.* New York: Holt, Rinehart and Winston, 1972.

Perloff, Marjorie. "Angst and Animism in the Poetry of Sylvia Plath." In *Critical Essays on Sylvia Plath,* edited by Linda W. Wagner. Boston: Hall, 1984. 109–24.

―――. "Extremist Poetry: Some Versions of the Sylvia Plath Myth." *Journal of Modern Literature* 2, no. 4 (1972): 581–88.

―――. "On the Road to *Ariel*: The 'Transitional' Poems of Sylvia Plath." In *Sylvia Plath: The Woman and the Work,* edited by Edward Butscher. New York: Dodd, 1977. 125–42.

―――. "Poetry as Word-System: The Art of Gertrude Stein." In *The Poetics of Indeterminacy: Rimbaud to Cage.* Princeton: Princeton University Press, 1981. 67–108.

―――. "Sylvia Plath's Collected Poems: A Review Essay." *Resources for American Literary Studies* 11, no. 2 (1981): 304–13.

―――. "Sylvia Plath's 'Sivvy' Poems: A Portrait of the Poet as Daughter." In *Sylvia Plath: New Views on the Poetry,* edited by Gary Lane. Baltimore: Johns Hopkins University Press, 1979. 155–78.

―――. "The Two Ariels: The (Re)making of the Sylvia Plath Canon." *American Poetry Review* 13, no. 6 (1984): 10–18.

Plath, Sylvia. *Ariel.* Edited by Ted Hughes. New York: Harper, 1961.

———. *The Collected Poems.* Edited by Ted Hughes. New York: Harper, 1981.

———. *The Colossus and Other Poems.* 1957. Reprint, New York: Vintage, 1968.

———. *Crossing the Water: Transitional Poems.* Edited by Ted Hughes. New York: Harper, 1971.

———. *Johnny Panic and the Bible of Dreams, and Other Prose Writings.* Edited by Ted Hughes. New York: Harper, 1979.

———. *The Journals of Sylvia Plath.* Edited by Frances McCullough. New York: Dial, 1982.

———. *Letters Home: Correspondence 1950–1963.* Edited by Aurelia Schober Plath. New York: Harper, 1975.

———. *Plath Reads Plath.* Cambridge, Mass.: Credo Records, 1975.

———. *Sylvia Plath, Stings, Original Drafts of the Poems in Facsimile.* Reproduced for the Sylvia Plath Collection at Smith College. Northampton, Mass.: Smith College Library Rare Book Room, 1982.

Porter, David. *Dickinson: The Modern Idiom.* Cambridge: Harvard University Press, 1981.

Pound, Ezra. *The Cantos of Ezra Pound.* New York: New Directions, 1970.

Rich, Adrienne. "When We Dead Awaken: Writing as Re-Vision." In *On Lies, Secrets, and Silence: Selected Prose 1966–1978.* New York: Norton, 1979. 33–49.

Roche, Clarissa. "Sylvia Plath: Vignettes from England." In *Sylvia Plath: The Woman and the Work,* edited by Edward Butscher. New York: Dodd, 1977. 81–96.

Rodgers, Carolyn M. "Black Poetry—Where It's At." In *Homage to Hoyt Fuller,* edited by Dudley Randall. Detroit: Broadside Press, 1984. 144–55.

———. *How I Got Ovah: New and Selected Poems.* Garden City, N.Y.: Anchor/Doubleday, 1975.

———. *Songs of a Black Bird.* Chicago: Third World Press, 1969.

Ronell, Avital. *The Telephone Book: Technology—Schizophrenia—Electric Speech.* Lincoln: University of Nebraska Press, 1989.

Rose, Jacqueline. *The Haunting of Sylvia Plath.* Cambridge: Harvard University Press, 1992.

Ruddick, Lisa. "A Rosy Charm: Gertrude Stein and the Repressed Feminine." In *Critical Essays on Gertrude Stein,* edited by Michael J. Hoffman. Boston: Hall, 1986. 225–40.

Russ, Joanna. *How to Suppress Women's Writing.* Austin: University of Texas Press, 1983.

Sales, Estella M. "Contradictions in Black Life: Recognized and Reconciled in *How I Got Ovah.*" *CLA Journal* 25 (Sept. 1981): 74–81.

Sanchez, Sonia. *A Blues Book for Blue Black Magical Women.* Detroit: Broadside Press, 1974.

———. "Exploding Myths: An Interview with Sonia Sanchez." With Herbert Liebowitz. *Parnassus: Poetry in Review* 12–13 (1985): 357–68.

———. *Home Coming.* Detroit: Broadside Press, 1969.

———. *It's a New Day (poems for young brothas and sistuhs).* Detroit: Broadside Press, 1971.

———. *Love Poems.* New York: Third Press, 1973.

———. *Uh, Uh; But How Do It Free Us? The New Lafayette Theatre Presents Plays With Aesthetic Comments by 6 Black Playwrights,* edited by Ed Bullins. New York: Anchor/Doubleday, 1974. 165–215.

———. *We A BaddDDD People.* Detroit: Broadside Press, 1970.

Schwartz, Murray M., and Christopher Bollas. "The Absence at the Center: Sylvia Plath and Suicide." *Criticism* 18 (1976): 147–72.

Sewall, Richard B. *The Life of Emily Dickinson.* New York: Farrar, 1974.

Shange, Ntozake. *A Daughter's Geography.* New York: St. Martin's Press, 1983.

———. *for colored girls who have considered suicide/ when the rainbow is enuf.* 1977. Reprint, New York: Macmillan, 1989.

———. *Some Men.* n.p. 1981.

———. "Unrecovered Losses/Black Theater Traditions." *See No Evil: Prefaces, Essays & Accounts* 1976–1983. San Francisco: Momo's Press, 1984. 18–25.

Sigmund, Elizabeth. "Sylvia in Devon: 1962." In *Sylvia Plath: The Woman and the Work,* edited by Edward Butscher. New York: Dodd, 1977. 100–107

Silliman, Ron. *The New Sentence.* New York: Roof Books, 1989.

Simon, Linda. Appendix to *The Biography of Alice B. Toklas.* New York: Doubleday, 1977. 255–86.

Smith, Martha Nell. *Rowing in Eden: Rereading Emily Dickinson.* Austin: University of Texas Press, 1992.

Smith, Welton. "malcolm." In *Black Fire: An Anthology of Afro-American Writing,* edited by LeRoi Jones and Larry Neal. New York: William Morrow, 1968.

Sollers, Werner. *Amiri Baraka / LeRoi Jones: The Quest for a "Populist Modernism."* New York: Columbia University Press, 1978.

Staples, Robert. "The Myth of Black Macho: A Response to Angry Black Feminists." *Black Scholar* 10, nos. 6, 7 (Mar./Apr. 1979): 24–33.

Stein, Gertrude. *The Autobiography of Alice B. Toklas.* [1933.] In *Selected Writings of Gertrude Stein,* edited by Carl Van Vechten. New York: Random, 1962. 1–237

———. *Bee Time Vine and Other Pieces [1913–1927].* 1953. New York: Books for Libraries, 1969.

———. *Everybody's Autobiography.* 1937. New York: Vintage, 1973.

———. *Fernhurst, Q.E.D., and Other Early Writings.* New York: Liveright, 1971.

———. *Four in America.* New Haven: Yale University Press, 1947.

———. "Four Saints in Three Acts." In *Operas and Plays.* 1927. Reprint, Barrytown, N.Y.: Station Hill Press, 1987.

———. *Geography and Plays.* 1922. Reprint, New York: Something Else, 1968.

———. *Gertrude Stein's America,* edited by Gilbert A. Harrison. New York: Liveright, 1974.

———. "The Gradual Making of The Making of Americans." In *Lectures in America.* 1935. Reprint, Boston: Beacon, 1985. 135–61.

———. *How To Write.* 1931. Craftsbury Common, Vt.: Sherry Urie, 1977.

———. *Lectures in America.* 1935. Boston: Beacon, 1985.

———. *A Long Gay Book.* 1933. Reprint, New York: Something Else, 1972.

———. *Lucy Church Amiably.* 1930. New York: Something Else, 1969.

———. *The Making of Americans: Being the History of A Family's Progress.* 1925. Reprint, New York: Something Else, 1966.

———. "Patriarchal Poetry." In *Bee Time Vine and Other Pieces [1913–1927].* 1953. Reprint, New York: Books for Libraries, 1969. 254–94.

———. "Poetry and Grammar." In *Lectures in America.* 1935. Reprint, Boston: Beacon, 1985. 209–46.

———. "Portrait of Mabel Dodge at Villa Curonia." In *Portraits and Prayers.* 1934. Reprint, New York: Random, 1955. 98–102.

———. *Reflection on the Atomic Bomb.* Los Angeles: Black Sparrow, 1973.

———. "Sacred Emily." In *Geography and Plays.* 1922. Reprint, New York: Something Else, 1968. 178–88.

———. *Tender Buttons.* 1914. Reprint, New York: Haskell, 1970.

———. *Three Lives.* 1909. Reprint, New York: Random, 1936.

———. *Useful Knowledge.* 1928. Reprint, New York: American Alpine, 1972.

———. *What Are Masterpieces.* 1940. Reprint, New York: Pitman, 1970.

———. *Writings and Lectures 1911–1945.* Edited by Patricia Meyerowitz. London: Peter Owen, 1967.

Stewart, James T. "The Development of the Black Revolutionary Artist." In *Black Fire: An Anthology of Afro-American Writing,* edited by LeRoi Jones and Larry Neal. New York: Morrow, 1968. 3–10

Stilwell, Robert L. Review of *Ariel.* In *Critical Essays on Sylvia Plath,* edited by Linda W. Wagner. Boston: Hall, 1984. 44–45.

Stimpson, Catharine R. "The Mind, the Body, and Gertrude Stein." *Critical Inquiry* 3, no. 3 (1977): 489–506.

———. "The Somagrams of Gertrude Stein." In *Critical Essays on Gertrude Stein,* edited by Michael J. Hoffman. Boston: Hall, 1986. 183–96.

Tate, Claudia, ed. *Black Women Writers at Work.* New York: Continuum, 1984.

Uroff, Margaret Dickie. *Sylvia Plath and Ted Hughes.* Urbana: University of Illinois Press, 1979.

Van Dyne, Susan R. " 'More Terrible Than She Ever Was': The Manuscripts of Sylvia Plath's Bee Poems." In *Critical Essays on Sylvia Plath,* edited by Linda W. Wagner. Boston: Hall, 1984. 154–70.

———. *Revising Life: Sylvia Plath's Ariel Poems.* Chapel Hill: University of North Carolina Press, 1993.

Vendler, Helen. *The Breaking of Style: Hopkins, Heaney, Graham.* Cambridge: Harvard University Press, 1995.

Wagner, Linda W., ed. *Critical Essays on Sylvia Plath.* Boston: Hall, 1984.

Wagner-Martin, Linda. *Favored Strangers: Gertrude Stein and Her Family.* New Brunswick: Rutgers University Press, 1995.

Wagner-Martin, Linda W. *Sylvia Plath: A Biography.* New York: Simon, 1987.

Walker, Alice. *The Color Purple.* New York: Washington Square Press, 1982.

Walker, Cheryl. *The Nightingale's Burden: Women Poets and American Culture before 1900.* Bloomington: Indiana University Press, 1982.

Wallace, Michele. *Black Macho and the Myth of the Superwoman.* 1978. London: Verso, 1990.

Webster, Noah. *An American Dictionary of the English Language.* New York: n.p., 1844.

———. *An American Dictionary of the English Language.* Springfield, Mass.: n.p., 1855.

Weininger, Otto. *Sex and Character.* New York: Putnam's, 1906.

West, Paul. Review of *Crossing the Water.* In *Critical Essays on Sylvia Plath,* edited by Linda W. Wagner. Boston: Hall, 1984. 48–51.

Williams, William Carlos. *Autobiography of William Carlos Williams.* New York: New Directions, 1967.

Wilson, Edmund. *Axel's Castle: A Study in the Imaginative Literature of 1870–1930.* New York: Scribner's, 1931.

Wittke, Carl. *Tambo and Bones: A History of the American Minstrel Stage.* Durham, N.C.: Duke University Press, 1930.

Index

Black Power movement, 172, 190

Black Scholar gender debates, 252n

Blankley, Elyse, "Beyond the 'Talent of Knowing': Gertrude Stein and the New Woman," 237n, 238n

Brans, Jo, 243n

Bridgman, Richard, *Gertrude Stein in Pieces*, 86

Brinnin, John Malcolm, *The Third Rose: Gertrude Stein and Her World*, 76, 85–86, 235n

Brocade, 5, 55–57, 323n

Broe, Mary Lynn, *Protean Poetic: The Poetry of Sylvia Plath*, 164, 246n

Brontë, Charlotte, 4–6

Brooks, Gwendolyn, 215, 251n

Browning, Elizabeth Barrett, 34, 230n

Buckingham, Willis J., *Emily Dickinson's Reception in the 1890s: A Documentary History*, 232n

Burns, Robert, "A Red, Red Rose," 84

Cameron, Sharon, *Choosing Not Choosing: Dickinson's Fascicles*, 16, 227n, 230n

Chessman, Harriet Scott, *The Public Is Invited to the Dance: Representation, the Body, and Dialogue in Gertrude Stein*, 96, 237–38n

Cinderella, 152

Cixous, Hélène, 12

Cleaver, Eldridge, *Soul on Ice*, 179, 249n

Clifton, Lucille, 215–16; "A Simple Language," 251–52n; "We Are the Grapevine," 252n

Coleridge, Samuel Taylor, "Kubla Khan," 52

Confessionalism, 126

Continuous present, 90–91

Cortez, Jayne, 217–20

Crouch, Stanley, 217–18

Cullen, Countee, *Caroling Dusk: An Anthology of Verse by Negro Poets*, 168–69, 170, 177, 180, 181

Cushman, Stephen, *Fictions of Form in American Poetry*, 229n

Dante, 33

Daphne, 139, 140, 141, 144, 148

Davidson, Michael, "On Reading Stein," 237n

Decorum, 11–15, 24, 58, 182, 228n

DeKoven, Marianne, *A Different Language: Gertrude Stein's Experimental Language*, 91, 95, 237n

de Man, Paul, *Allegories of Reading*, 107–08, 239n

Derrida, Jacques, 12, 17

Dickinson, Austin, 26–27, 37, 39, 60

Dickinson, Emily, 4–6, 18, 25–74; Letters: #22, 26; #45, 19, 27; #65, 231n; #113, 37, 53; #238, 38; #261, 30, 57; #265, 29–30; #268, 35, 37; #271, 32–37, 230n; #368, 18; #444a, 38; #573a, 38; Poems: "[A still—Volcano—Life—]," 41; "[All overgrown by cunning moss]," 4–6, 227n; "[As if I asked a common Alms]," 29–30; "[Between the form of Life and Life]," 45–46; "[Further in Summer than the Birds]," 231n; "[Grief is a Mouse—]," 65–67, 71; "[I cannot dance upon my Toes]," 32, 36; "[I felt a Cleaving in my Mind—]," 69–70; "[I felt a Funeral, in my Brain]," 68–71; "[I found the words to every thought]," 61, 71; "[I reckon—when I count at all—]," 72–74; "[I rose—because He sank—]," 54; "[I would not paint—a picture—]," 39; "[It was given to me by the Gods—]," 44–47; "[It would never be Common—more—I said]," 19, 42–44, 46–58; "[O Sumptuous moment]," 45–46; "[On my volcano grows the Grass]," 232*n*; "[One need not be a Chamber—to be Haunted]," 64–65, 67; "[Safe in their Alabaster Chambers—]," 38; "[She dealt her pretty words like Blades—]," 54; "[Rearrange a 'Wife's' affection!]," 61–64, 233*n*; "[The thought beneath so slight a film—]," 54; "[There's a certain Slant of Light]," 45, 231*n*; "[They shut me up in Prose—]," 49, 233*n*; "[This was a Poet—It is That]," 39; "[To pile like Thunder to it's close]," 41; "['Twas like a Maelstrom, with a notch]," 54; "[You know that Portrait in the Moon]," 54; "[You see I cannot see—your lifetime—]," 54

Dickinson, Susan Gilbert, 38

Difference, 44–57, 95, 101, 103, 104–08, 231*n*, 239*n*

Elegy, 6, 182, 183, 184, 185, 186, 187, 189

Eliot, T. S., *The Waste Land*, 96, 117, 238*n*

Embroidery, 6, 10, 58

Emerson, Ralph Waldo, "The Poet," 50

Erkkila, Betsy, *Wicked Sisters: Women Poets, Literary History, and Discord*, 38, 60, 230*n*, 231*n*, 232*n*

Excess, 7, 9–10, 12–16, 18–22, 24, 27, 37, 39, 58–59, 77, 86, 87–88, 91, 92, 93, 95, 128–29, 137, 174–75, 181, 185, 202, 209, 223

Femininity, 26–27, 62, 119–20, 191–92, 194, 203, 208, 209, 213, 214, 217, 224

Fifer, Elizabeth, "Is Flesh Advisable: The Interior Theater of Gertrude Stein," 233*n*

Fire!! A Quarterly Devoted to the Younger Negro Artists, 170

Forché, Carolyn, 23

Fuller, Hoyt, "Towards a Black Aesthetic," 249*n*

Gates, Henry Louis, Jr., *Figures in Black: Words, Signs, and the "Racial" Self*, 172

Giddings, Paula, "Nikki Giovanni: Taking a Chance on Feeling," 250*n*

Gilbert, Sandra, "In Yeats's House: The Death and Resurrection of Sylvia Plath," 244*n*

Gilbert, Sandra and Susan Gubar, 2, 3; *The Madwoman in the Attic*, 2

Ginsberg, Allen, "America," 249*n*

Giovanni, Nikki, 194–200, 250–51*n*; "Black Poems, *Poseurs* and Power," 195–96, 197; "For Saundra," 198; "Love Poem (For Real)," 198; "My House," 250–51*n*; *Re:Creation*, 198–99; "Revolutionary Dreams," 198–99; "Seduction," 197–98; *Those Who Ride the Night Winds*, 226; "The True Import of the Present Dialogue: Black vs. Negro," 194–96, 198; "When I Die," 250*n*

Griffin, Susan, "Red Shoes," 7

Hamilton, Edith, *Mythology*, 3

Hamlet, 98

Harlem Renaissance, 167, 168–71

Harris, William J., "Sweet Soft Essence of Possibility: The Poetry of Nikki Giovanni," 250*n*

McDowell, Margaret B.,
"Groundwork for a More
Comprehensive Criticism of Nikki
Giovanni," 197, 250*n*
Madhubuti, Haki, 202, 216, 252*n*
Malcolm X, 168, 182–89, 192; *The
Autobiography of Malcolm X*,
250*n*
Marginalized writers, 2, 15, 18, 21,
23–24, 167, 175, 215, 226, 241*n*
Masculinity, 61, 179
May, Elaine Tyler, *Homeward
Bound: American Families in the
Cold War Era*, 120
Mellow, James R., *Charmed Circle:
Gertrude Stein and Company*, 80,
234*n*
Miller, Adam David, "Some
Observations on a Black
Aesthetic," 21, 171–72
Miller, Cris[tanne], *Comic Power
in Emily Dickinson*, 230*n*; *Emily
Dickinson: A Poet's Grammar*,
231*n*, 232–33*n*; "Terms and
Golden Words: Alternative of
Control in Dickinson's Poetry,"
51–53, 231*n*, 232*n*
Minstrel shows, 175–76
Moynihan, Daniel P., *The Negro
Family: The Case for National
Action*, 191

Nation of Islam, 190–91, 203, 206,
207, 208, 250*n*
Neal, Larry, "The Black Arts
Movement," 248*n*
Neruda, Pablo, "Explaining a Few
Things," 84
Nightingale, 1–6
Nims, John Frederick, "The Poetry
of Sylvia Plath: A Technical
Analysis," 128, 243*n*, 244*n*
Nonsense, 77, 78, 84, 179, 188

Oberg, Arthur K., "Sylvia Plath and
the New Decadence," 244*n*
Ostriker, Alicia, *Stealing the
Language: The Emergence of
Women's Poetry in America*, 237*n*
Ovid, 1–6, 139
Owen, Wendy, 134

Parker, Patricia, *Literary Fat Ladies:
Rhetoric, Gender, Property*, 17
Parker-Smith, Bettye J., 251*n*
Perkins, George, *American Poetic
Theory*, 229*n*
Perloff, Marjorie, "*Angst* and
Animism in the Poetry of Sylvia
Plath," 243*n*; "Extremist Poetry:
Some Versions of the Sylvia Plath
Myth," 244*n*; "On the Road to
Ariel: The 'Transitional' Poetry
of Sylvia Plath," 243*n*, 244*n*,
245*n*; "Poetry as Word System:
The Art of Gertrude Stein," 239*n*;
"Sylvia Plath's *Collected Poems*:
A Review Essay," 244*n*; "Sylvia
Plath's 'Sivvy' Poems: A Portrait
of the Poet as Daughter," 246*n*;
"The Two Ariels: The (Re)Making
of the Sylvia Plath Canon," 127,
244*n*, 245*n*, 247*n*
Philomela and Procne, 1–6, 24, 249*n*
Plath, Aurelia, 248*n*
Plath, Sylvia, 20, 118–65; *Ariel*,
21, 126, 127, 128, 131, 132, 134,
135, 136, 154, 162, 163, 244*n*;
"Ariel," 154; "The Arrival of the
Bee Box," 139, 145–49, 155, 161,
162; "The Bee Meeting," 135–45,
146, 147, 150, 153, 155, 160, 161,
162; "The Beekeeper's Daughter,"
146, 147, 163, 164; *The Bell Jar*,
134; *The Collected Poems*, 127,
165, 242*n*, 244*n*, 248*n*; *Colossus*,
20, 126, 127, 163; "Daddy," 153,
155, 242*n*; "Edge," 164–65; "The